The
Family

The Family

A Christian Perspective on the Contemporary Home

Jack O. Balswick and Judith K. Balswick

BAKER BOOK HOUSE
Grand Rapids, Michigan 49516

Copyright 1991 by
Baker Book House Company

Paperback edition, June 1991

Printed in the United States of America

Library of Congress Cataloging-in-Publication Data

Balswick, Jack O.
      The family : a Christian perspective on the contemporary home / Jack O.
Balswick and Judith K. Balswick.
            p. cm.
      Includes bibliographical references.
      ISBN 0-8010-0993-6
      1. Family—Religious life. 2. Family—United States.
      3. Marriage—Religious aspects—Christianity. 4. Parenting—Religious
aspects—Christianity. I. Balswick, Judith K. II. Title.
      BV4526.2.B357   1991
      261.8'3585—dc20   89-38124
                                                                                                              CIP

The Scripture references are taken from the King James Version (KJV); the Living Bible (LB),
copyright © 1971 by Tyndale House Publishers; the New Englsh Bible (NEB), copyright
1961, 1970, by Oxford University Press and Cambridge University Press; the New
International Version (NIV), copyright © 1973, 1978, 1984, by the International Bible Society
(used by permission of Zondervan Bible Publishers); and the Revised Standard Version
(RSV), copyright © 1946, 1952, 1971, 1973, by the Division of Christian Education of the
National Council of Churches in the United States of America.

A copy of *Strengthening Your Family Life,*
the study guide to this book,
can be obtained by sending a check for $5.00 to:
Jack Balswick,
Fuller Theological Seminary,
182 Oakland, Pasadena, CA 91182.

With Our Love and Appreciation

to

Agnes and **Arvid Nelson**

Frances and **Orville Balswick**

Contents

Part Four.   Sexuality: *Identity in Family Life*

Part Five.   Communication: *The Heart of Family Life*

Part Six.   The Social Dynamics of Family Life

Part Seven.   Family Life in Modern Society

Illustrations

Figures

Tables

Preface

The purpose of *The Family: A Christian Perspective on the Contemporary Home* is to present an integrated view of contemporary family life which is based upon social-science research, clinical insights, and biblical truths. We have attempted to utilize the best social-scientific knowledge about family life, while also striving to avoid a cumbersome style by keeping documentation to a minimum. The biblical perspective we have incorporated reflects broad theological truths woven throughout the Scriptures rather than specific proof texts. The overarching biblical themes of *covenant, grace, empowering,* and *intimacy* are the foundation of our theology of family relationships.

Our book is divided into seven parts. In Part One, "Theological and Social Perspectives on Family Life," we present a basic theology of relationships and theoretical perspectives on the family as a developing system. Part Two, "Marriage: The Foundation of Family Life," is devoted to the topics of mate selection and establishment of a strong Christian marriage. In Part Three, "Parenting: The Expansion of Family Life," we focus on the development and rearing of young children as well as address the stress and strain of parent/adolescent relationships. In Part Four, "Sexuality: Identity in Family Life," we consider the changing definitions of masculinity and femininity, the implications these changes have for family life, and various dimensions of our creation as sexual beings. Part Five, "Communication: The Heart of Family Life," describes the expression of love and intimacy as well as the expression of anger and conflict between family members. Part Six, "The Social Dynamics of Family Life," discusses some of the more problematic areas of family life: power, stress, divorce, single parenthood, remarriage, and reconstituted families. Part Seven, "Family Life in Modern Society," considers the effects which modern industrialized society has upon family life. Some suggestions are made as to how social structures can be changed to create a healthier family environment.

Rather than taking a piecemeal approach, devoting each chapter to a specific topic, we have attempted to make each chapter an integral part of the theme of the whole book. We have aspired to weave into the content of each chapter our theological basis for family relationships and our view of the family as a developing system. We thank Dawn McNeal Ward for allowing us to use in chapters 16 and 17 material which she and Jack originally presented at a seminar at Fuller Theological Seminary in November 1984. We are very grateful to Jon Good and Gretta Hassel for their help in editing. Georgia Kess, Sue Sheets, Bette Springer, Leslie Nation, and Audrey Jones are much appreciated for their clerical help. We also wish to acknowledge Ron Wheeler for drawing the cartoons and Ray Wiersma of Baker Book House for editorial supervision.

Since our contributions to the book are about equal, we agreed that our names should appear alphabetically. Jack is a professional sociologist who has over twenty years of teaching, research, and writing experience at the university and seminary level. A marriage and family therapist for twelve years, Judy has now been teaching at the university and seminary level for over six years. Both Jack and Judy have had postdoctoral seminary training in theology and biblical studies.

Although we have attempted to blend together an academic, clinical, and theological understanding of the family, our interest in family life is not merely academic. The core of our lives has been experienced in the context of family, and our joint calling is to minister to families.

We feel ourselves most fortunate to have both been reared and nurtured in loving Christian homes. Our parents modeled an unconditional love for us. They are today active senior citizens in whose homes we continue to find great strength, comfort, and security.

We have been married for over twenty-six years. We have a married daughter, Jacque, and an adopted Korean son, Joel, who is a college student. We have personally experienced the emotional joys and pain, ups and downs, stress and elation of family living. Thirteen years ago our beloved ten-year-old son Jeff died of bone cancer. Working through the pain of that loss has impacted us all. We are currently living in an extended-family arrangement with Jacque, our son-in-law Bill, and our two young grandsons, Curtis and Jacob. We have learned a lot and continue to learn as we grow through each stage of family life. Having preached on the fragility of the isolated nuclear family, we are deeply involved in learning about the advantages and stresses of living in a three-generation household. We trust that what we have learned will benefit our readers.

PART 1

Theological and Social Perspectives on Family Life

Introduction

We begin our study with fundamental theological and sociological perspectives on family life. In chapter 1 we present a theology of family relationships which is based on what the Bible says about God as parent in relationship to the children of Israel, and about Christ as groom in relationship to the church as bride. The emergent theology of family relationships stresses the elements of covenant, grace, empowering, and intimacy.

In chapter 2 we introduce two sociological perspectives. The systemic perspective, viewing the family as a unit of interrelated parts, concentrates on the relationships between family members. The developmental perspective focuses on the various stages of family life. By integrating these two sociological perspectives we will discover some of the basic marks of a strong, functional family.

A Theological Basis for Family Relationships

Recent Efforts

In the 1960s, leaders in the field of marriage and the family promoted a new emphasis, namely, basing theoretical models on research findings. Most of the Christian writings on marriage and the family had been based on scriptural interpretation rather than on scientific and empirical evidence. Also, those authors who wrote from a Christian perspective tended to support their positions with various Bible verses. Few established a more encompassing theology of the family.

Kenneth Gangel's four-article series published in the *Journal of Psychology and Theology* in 1977 was one attempt to do more. Gangel's strategy was to work "Toward a Biblical Theology of Marriage and the Family" by citing and briefly discussing biblical references relevant to an understanding of the purpose of marriage and family. This included the roles of the various family members, the function of the family as a social system, and the issues and problems of family life. Although his work is an invaluable source as a systematic examination of scriptural references relevant to the family, Gangel failed to set forth a theology of marriage and the family.

The relationship between God and the children of Israel has proven to be the most fruitful model for the development of a theology of the

19

family. Myron Chartier (1978) has suggested that if God's actions toward Israel are taken as a model, parenting of children will be characterized by loving, caring, responding, disciplining, giving, respecting, knowing, and forgiving.

The establishment of a covenant between God and the nation of Israel has become an important focus in developing a theology of the family. In his book *On Being Human*, Ray Anderson (1982) utilizes this concept of covenant to build a theological anthropology. Beginning with the theological truth that "humanity is determined as existence in covenant relation with God" (p. 37), Anderson applies the concept of covenant to human relationships, including those of husband/wife and parent/child. Anderson considers such covenantal relationships in the family as a "*secondary* order, made possible by the *primary* order of differentiation as male or female" (p. 52). God's plan in creating male and female in complementary relationship achieves the purpose of interdependence and cooperative interaction between people. This idea is referred to as "cohumanity."

Anderson and Dennis Guernsey (1985) develop the concept of covenant as a paradigm of the family in another book, *On Being Family.* Here the authors describe covenant as the "unilateral relation established by God with his people Israel, through specific actions by which he summoned individuals and finally an entire nation into a history of response" (p. 33). In applying the concept of covenant to the family, they stress the unconditional quality of covenant: "It is covenant love that provides the basis for family. For this reason, family means much more than consanguinity, where blood ties provide the only basis for belonging. Family is where you are loved unconditionally, and where you can count on that love even when you least deserve it" (p. 40).

Stuart McLean (1984), in a paper entitled "The Language of Covenant and a Theology of the Family," suggests ways that covenant can effectively be used as a metaphor for marriage and family relationships. Describing the relational components of covenant, he makes the following observations: (1) people are social and live in community; (2) the basic unit of family and of covenant is the dyad; (3) persons living in community will experience struggle and conflict as well as harmony; (4) persons living in covenant must be willing to forgive and be forgiven by each other; (5) persons living in covenant must accept their bondedness to each other; (6) persons living in covenant will accept law in the form of patterns and order in relationships; and (7) persons living in covenant will have a temporal awareness as they carry a memory of the past, live in the present, and anticipate the future (pp. 4–32).

We agree that the concept of covenant is the fundamental and essential element in developing a theology of the family. With this as the principal starting point, the purpose of this chapter is to develop a theology of family relationships. When focusing on family relationships we will deal with social and theological questions pertaining to the nature of family process rather than family structure.

Elements in a Theology of Family Relationships

We propose a theology of family relationships which involves four sequential, but nonlinear, stages: *covenant, grace, empowering,* and *intimacy.* We further suggest that family relationships will either be dynamic and maturing, or stagnant and dying. A model of this process of family relationships is presented in figure 1. The logical beginning point of any family relationship is a covenant commitment, which has unconditional love at its core. Out of the security provided by this covenant love develops grace. In this atmosphere of grace, family members have the freedom to empower each other. Empowering leads to the possibility of intimacy between family members. Intimacy then leads back to a deeper level of covenant commitment.

The sequential change in figure 1 is depicted by a spiraling inward in order to represent the potential for family relationships to grow into ever deeper levels of mutual commitment, grace, empowering, and intimacy.

FIGURE 1   **A Theological Basis of Family Relationships**

Degree of
Commitment

Initial Covenant

Degree of
Intimacy

Mature
Covenant

Degree of
Grace

Degree of
Empowering

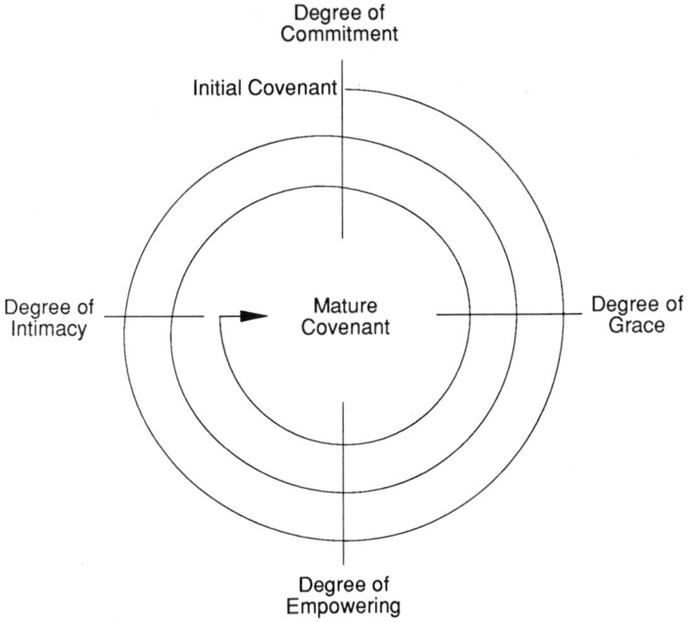

For example, the relationship between a parent and infant child begins as a unilateral (one-way) love commitment; as the parent lives out that commitment, the relationship may grow into a bilateral (mutual) love commitment. In order for growth to take place in a relationship there must be involvement by both persons. Growth in family relationships can be blocked or retarded at any point when one person in the relationship is unable or unwilling to reciprocate covenant love, grace, empowering, or intimacy. Thus, growth in a relationship can come to a standstill at any point in this cycle. Since relationships are dynamic and ever changing, we would argue that if a relationship does not spiral in to deeper levels of commitment, grace, empowering, and intimacy, then it will stagnate and fixate on contract rather than covenant, law rather than grace, possessive power rather than empowering, and distance rather than intimacy.

We are not proposing a tightening of family relationships which would exclude or ignore nonfamilial relationships. On the contrary, the depth of bonding in familial relationships equips family members to develop empowering relationships with those in the wider human community.

The four elements of growth in a family relationship are considered as separate sequential stages for analytic purposes only. In practice, covenant, grace, empowering, and intimacy often overlap in family life. Thus, the futility or awkwardness of pressing the suggested logical sequence into a strict linear model is evident. However, considering each separate dimension in depth will provide a better understanding of these four elements in family relationships.

These elements of family relationships are derived from an examination of biblical writings on how God enters into and sustains relationships with humanity. The Bible teaches that God desires all humankind to be in relationship with the Creator as well as in relationship with one another. We recognize, however, that although we are created in the image of God, we are fallen creatures who will fail in all aspects of relationship with God and others. There is a sense in which no person can ever make a covenant commitment in the way that God covenants with us. Nor will any of us be able to foster an atmosphere of grace in the same way God gives grace. Our empowering attempts will often resemble possessive power, and our attempts at intimacy will pale into insignificance when compared to God's knowing and caring. And yet we are hopeful, because God has been revealed perfectly in Jesus Christ. He is our model and enabler as we live out our lives and relationships according to God's purpose.

Covenant: To Love and Be Loved

Although the concept of covenant has a rich heritage in Christian theology, its biblical meaning has often been eroded by defining it in contractual terms (McLean 1984:2). The central point of covenant is that it is an unconditional commitment which is demonstrated supremely by God in the role of parent.

The first biblical mention of a covenant is found in Genesis 6:18, where God says to Noah, "I will establish my covenant with you, and you will enter the ark" (NIV). God goes on to tell Noah what he must do: "[Take] your sons and your wife and your sons' wives with you. You are to bring into the ark two of all living creatures, male and female, to keep them alive with you." We are told in Genesis 6:22 that "Noah did everything just as God commanded him." A little later God repeats this promise of covenant: "I now establish my covenant with you and with your descendants after you and with every living creature that was with you" (Gen. 9:9–10). God actually extends this covenant to include even non-human creatures.

The second biblical reference in which God makes a covenant is Genesis 15:18, where a covenant is extended to Abraham. This covenant is later amplified in Genesis 17:1–7:

> The LORD appeared to him and said, "I am God Almighty. Live always in my presence and be perfect, so that I may set my covenant between myself and you and multiply your descendants." Abram threw himself down on his face, and God spoke with him and said, "I make this covenant, and I make it with you: you shall be the father of a host of nations. . . . I will fulfil my covenant between myself and you and your descendants after you, generation after generation, an everlasting covenant, to be your God, yours and your descendants' after you. [NEB]

Abraham's role in the covenant is specified in Genesis 17:9: "God said to Abraham, 'For your part, you must keep my covenant, you and your descendants after you, generation by generation.' "

What can we learn from these two accounts of God's establishing a covenant with Noah and Abraham? First, we see that God was not offering either Noah or Abraham any choice in the matter. That is, God was by no means saying, "Now I am going to commit myself to you *if* this is your desire." Instead, the establishment of the covenant was based entirely on God's action. God's offer was in no way contractual; that is, it was not based upon either Noah's or Abraham's keeping his end of the bargain. God's commitment was there whether it was accepted or not.

Second, God did desire and even commanded a response from both Noah and Abraham. Did this make God's covenantal offer conditional? Was God free to retract the offer if it was not reciprocated? The answer is a resounding no! The covenant which God offered was to remain "an everlasting covenant" regardless of what Noah or Abraham did.

Third, while the covenant itself was not conditional, the potential benefits or blessings it provided were. Both Noah and Abraham were given an option by God in the covenantal offer. If they were to benefit from the offer, they had to agree to fulfil their end of the bargain. Although the continuation of God's love was not conditioned upon the nature of Noah's or Abraham's response, their receiving any of the blessings or the fulfilment of the covenant was conditional. Here there are the offer and the responsibility to react favorably in order to receive the blessing of the covenant.

Fourth, we notice in the passages cited that God extended the covenant to more than just these two individuals. The covenant included their families as well. God extended "an everlasting covenant" to Abraham which included "generation after generation." With Noah, God even extended the covenant to include "every living creature." There is, of course, no way that animals could respond to the covenant offer. Neither could Abraham anticipate obedience on the part of his descendants. This is further evidence of the unconditional nature of the covenant.

Again, the blessings of the covenant were to be conditional on the descendants' following God. Indeed, the biblical account of the relationship between God and the children of Israel can best be understood by pointing to the analogy of an unconditional parental commitment to a child. A reading of the Old Testament Scriptures reveals the cycle of Israel's turning away from the true God and getting into difficulty, God's reaching out and forgiving them, Israel's being reconciled into the intended parent/child relationship, and Israel's being blessed and renewed in their relationship to God. This cycle is the central message especially of the Book of Hosea.

The life of Jesus is the supreme expression of unconditional love. It is noteworthy that Jesus told the story of the prodigal son (Luke 15) in response to the Pharisees' and scribes' criticism of his welcoming and sitting with sinners. Just as the father in the story welcomed his wayward son home with open arms, Jesus was also demonstrating unconditional love to a people who had rejected his Father. The unconditional nature of God's love is perhaps most clearly expressed in 1 John 4:19: "We love because he first loved us" (NIV). Or again in 1 John 4:10, which reads, "This is love: not that we loved God, but that he loved us." God's love is unconditional!

Having discussed the unconditional quality of God's covenant commitments, we now turn to a related consideration—the issue of reciprocity. Whereas there is no question regarding the unconditional nature of covenant love, we believe that in a familial context the concept of covenant can be used to refer to both unilateral and bilateral relationships. Figure 2 depicts the alternative types of commitment found in family relationships.

Any covenantal relationship is based on an unconditional commitment.

FIGURE 2 **Types of Commitment in Family Relationships**

	Conditional	Unconditional
Unilateral	Modern Open Arrangement	Initial Covenant
Bilateral	Contract	Mature Covenant

However, covenantal relationships can be either unilateral (one-way) or bilateral (two-way). We have labeled a unilateral unconditional relationship as an initial covenant, and a bilateral unconditional relationship a mature covenant. All biblical references to the covenants which God initiated are examples of initial covenants. It would be erroneous to think of an unconditional unilateral relationship as partial, dependent, or even immature, because from the individual's perspective a personal covenant without restrictions is being offered. From a relational perspective, unilateral unconditional commitment entails the attractive possibility of someday becoming a two-way street. The desire of God in each initiated covenant was that the unconditional commitment would eventually be reciprocal and mutual.

When a child is born, the parents make an unconditional commitment of love to that child. The infant or young child is unable, at that time in life, to make such a commitment in return. However, as the child matures, it is possible and desirable that the relationship which began as an initial (unilateral) covenant will develop into a mature (bilateral) relationship. True reciprocity occurs when parents themselves age and become socially, emotionally, and physically more dependent on their adult children. Here, in a mature bilateral commitment, reciprocal and unconditional love is especially rewarding.

Taking a slightly different view, James Torrance (1975) describes a covenant as unilateral and a contract as bilateral. This may be a legitimate corrective to those who interpret the meaning of covenant exclusively in a bilateral context. We do not think this is helpful for understanding family relationships, however. In order for Torrance to be consistent, he must restrict the word *covenant* to the individual level and resort to the word *contract* when describing a relationship. We believe that it is more accurate to speak of marriage and mature parent/child relationships as being based on unconditional bilateral commitments.

As shown in figure 2, there are two types of conditional family relationships. An emerging type, which we call the modern open arrangement, is symptomatic of a society in which persons are hesitant to make commitments. A typical example is a person who begins a marriage with the unspoken understanding that as long as his or her needs are being met, all is well; but as soon as those needs are no longer met, the relationship will end. When both partners adopt this conditional stance, the marriage amounts to a contract, a quid pro quo arrangement. Both husband and wife consider they have fulfilled the marital contract if they get about as much as they give.

In reality, much of the daily routine in family life is carried out according to informal contractual agreements. Those who are advocates of relationships based on covenant do recognize the importance of the mutual satisfaction and fairness promoted in these contractual agreements, but they also emphasize that family relationships based on contract alone will forgo the extraordinary dimensions of covenant love.

Grace: To Forgive and Be Forgiven

We indicated previously that we have separated the four elements of our theology of family relationship for analytical purposes only. It is especially difficult to distinguish between covenant and grace. By its very nature, covenant *is* grace. From a human perspective the unconditional love of God makes no sense except as it is offered in grace. Grace is truly a relational word. One is called to share in a gracious relationship with God. Grace means unmerited favor.

Family relationships as designed by God are meant to be lived out in an atmosphere of grace and not law. Family life based upon contract leads to an atmosphere of law, while family life based upon covenant leads to an atmosphere of grace and forgiveness. A family based upon law is a discredit to Christianity. The meaning and joy of being a Christian would be deadened if we conceived of our relationship with God in terms of law and not grace. The same is true in family relationships. At both the individual and family level, law leads to legalism, whereas grace provides a freedom from legalism. In an atmosphere of grace family members act responsibly out of love and consideration for one another.

The incarnation is the supreme act of God's grace to humankind. Christ came in human form to reconcile the world to God. This act of divine love and forgiveness is the basis for human love and forgiveness. We can forgive others as we have been forgiven, and the love of God within makes it possible for us to love others in the same unconditional way.

One may ask if there is any place for law in family relationships. Are we to believe that when grace is present in the family there is no need for law at all? Our answer must be the same as that given by the apostle Paul when he writes that "Christ ends the law and brings righteousness for everyone who has faith" (Rom. 10:4 NEB). It is not the case that the law itself is bad, for it points the way to God. However, since no human being is perfect, we can never fulfil the law. Christ is the end of the law in the sense that he is its perfect fulfilment. That we are righteous is due to Christ's perfection and righteousness, and not to our having kept the law. Our salvation is not dependent upon our keeping the law, but upon our faith in Christ.

The same can be said concerning family relationships. Through Scripture we can know something of God's ideal for family relationships, but none of us can expect to perfectly measure up to that ideal. In a family based on law, perfection will be demanded of each other. Rules and regulations will be rigidly set up to govern relationships. This kind of pressure for flawlessness adds guilt to the failure that is inevitable in such a situation.

Although the covenant of grace rules out law as a basis for family relationships, family members living in grace will accept law in the form of patterns, order, and responsibility in relationships. In reality, much of our daily routine of family life must be performed according to agreed-upon rules, regularity, and order. McLean's insights (1984:24) are helpful here:

> In the covenantal root metaphor, law and covenant belong together. The dyadic relationship necessarily involves creating specific forms, rules, and laws to guide community and personal relationships. The need for law, pattern, and form is mandatory, but the particular shape of law needs to be understood as relative to the actualization of dialogical-dialectical relationships, the creation of whole persons-in-community. The issue becomes which forms, which laws, which patterns are appropriate to the maintenance of humanity?

The application of the concept of grace in family relationships is a challenge when we are working out family structures, roles, and rules. Grace means that order and regularity are present for the sake of each family member's needs and enhancement and not as a means of repressing and limiting them.

Empowering: To Serve and Be Served

The most common and conventional definition of power is the ability to influence another person. In such a definition the emphasis is placed upon the ability or potential to influence, and not the actual exercising of the ability. Most research on the use of power in the family has focused on a person's attempting to influence or control the behavior of another (Safilios-Rothschild 1970; Scanzoni 1979; McDonald 1980; Szinovacz 1987). An underlying assumption in such analyses is that when using power, the strong often decrease rather than increase the power of the persons they are trying to influence. They tend to use power in a way which assures the maintenance of their own more powerful position.

Empowering is a biblical model for a use of power which is completely contrary to the common use of power in the family or in society at large. Empowering can be defined as the attempt to establish power in another person. Empowering does not necessarily involve yielding to the wishes of another person or giving up one's own power to someone else. Rather, empowering is the active, intentional process of enabling another person to acquire power. The person who is empowered has gained power because of the encouraging behavior of the other.

Empowering is the process of helping another recognize strengths and potentials within, as well as encouraging and guiding the development of these qualities. It is the affirmation of another's ability to learn and grow and become all that he or she can be. It may require that the empowerer be willing to step back and allow the empowered to learn by doing and not by depending. The empowerer must respect the uniqueness of those being empowered and see strength in their individual ways to be competent. Empowering does not involve controlling or enforcing a certain way of doing and being. It is, rather, a reciprocal process in which empowering takes place between people in mutually enhancing ways.

If covenant is the love commitment and grace is the underlying atmosphere of acceptance, then empowering is the action of God in people's lives. It is seen supremely in the work of Jesus Christ. The celebrated message of Jesus was that he had come to empower—"I have come that they may have life, and have it to the full" (John 10:10 NIV). The apostle John puts it this way: "But to all who received him, who believed in his name, he gave power to become children of God; who were born, not of blood nor of the will of the flesh nor of the will of man, but of God" (John 1:12–13 RSV). Ray Anderson (1985b) insightfully exegetes this text by noting that power "of blood" is power in the natural order, and "the will of the flesh" refers to tradition, duty, honor, obedience, and all that is a part of conventional power. In this passage, then, it is clear that the power is given by God and not by either physical or conventional means.

The power given by Jesus is power of a personal order—power which is mediated to the powerless. To us in our sinful and powerless condition God gives the ability to become children of God. This is the supreme example of human empowering. Jesus redefined power by his teaching and by his relating to others as a servant. Jesus rejected the use of power to control others, and instead affirmed the use of power to serve others, to lift up the fallen, to forgive the guilty, to encourage responsibility and maturity in the weak, and to enable the unable.

In a very real sense, empowering is love in action. It is the mark of Jesus Christ which family members need to emulate the most. The practice of empowering in families could revolutionize our view of authority in Christian families. We believe that authority in marriage is currently a controversial issue largely because the secular view of power has been widely accepted. The secular view is that power is a commodity which has a limited supply. Power is in the hands of the person who possesses the most resources. But the good news for Christians is that "according to Scripture, especially the New Testament, the power of God is available to human beings in unlimited amounts!" (Bartchy 1984:13). This unlimited power is seen in such passages as Ephesians 4:13 and Galatians 5:22–23, which rehearses "the fruit of the Spirit" (love, joy, peace, patience, kindness, goodness, fidelity, gentleness, and self-control) available to all Christians. This very character of God is available in unlimited supply because God's resources are inexhaustible!

Empowering in relationships is born out of the covenant and grace offered in God and Christ. The Spirit of God indwells believers and enables them to enable others. As this spiritual growth goes on in family members, it is possible for them to serve and give to each other in unlimited ways, in extraordinary ways. Family members will use their areas of strength to build each other up. This is the essence of 1 Corinthians 8:1: "Knowledge puffs up, but love builds up" (NIV).

Traditional thinking about parent/child relationships is also based upon the false assumption that power is in limited supply. Thus, it is often feared that as children grow older and gain more power, parental power is automatically reduced. By contrast an empowering approach to parenting begins by reconsidering the nature of power and authority. In the biblical sense, parental authority is an ascribed power. The Greek word for authority, *exousia*, literally means "out of being." It refers to a type of influence which is not dependent upon any personal strength, achievement, or skill, but rather comes forth "out of the being" of a person. The Greek word for power, *dynamis*, is the word from which "dynamo" is derived. The authority of Jesus flowed from his personhood. It was dynamic.

Parents, too, have authority over their children which flows from their personhood as they earnestly and responsibly care for their children's physical, social, psychological, and spiritual development. The process of empowering children certainly does not mean giving up this position of authority, nor does it mean that parents will be depleted or drained of power as they parent. Rather, parents and children will both achieve a sense of personal power, self-esteem, and wholeness. Successful parenting has to do with children's gaining personal power and parents' retaining personal power throughout the process.

Unfortunately, our human nature often stands in the way of family members' empowering each other. In the frailness of our human insecurity we are tempted to keep others dependent upon us, and in so doing find a counterfeit security in having power over them. Attachment which is based upon dependency is not love but addiction. Covenant love draws people to a mature attachment, which is free from dependency. It is a love that is loyal and supportive even when differences or adversity threatens to endanger the relationship.

All parents have experienced the temptation to keep a child dependent, which is often rationalized as something done for the child's own good. Many times, however, the child is kept in a dependent position for the parents' own convenience. Empowering is the ultimate goal, where parents release the child to self-control. Of course, mistakes will be made, and failure will be an occasional consequence of trying out new wings. Parents have a hard time letting their children make mistakes (especially the same mistakes they themselves made when young), so this is a difficult transition for parents and children alike. It is important to remind parents that the key to their authority lies not in external control, but rather in internal control which their children can integrate into their own personhood. When this happens, it is a rewarding and mutually satisfying achievement.

On the community level as well, Christians are called to live according to social patterns which are extraordinary. Even though we are sinners, God provides us with the ability to follow the empowering principle in our relationships. He empowers us, by the Holy Spirit, to empower others. The biblical ideal for all our relationships, then, is that we be Christian realists in regard to our own sinfulness and proneness to fail, but Christian optimists in light of the grace and power available to live according to God's intended purposes.

Intimacy: To Know and Be Known

Human beings are unique among living creatures in their ability to communicate with each other through language, a capacity which makes it possible for humans to know each other intimately. Our Christian faith is distinct from Eastern religions in its teaching that God has broken into human history to be personally related to us. One of the major themes which run throughout the Bible is that God wants to know us and to be known by us. We are encouraged to share our deepest thoughts and feelings through prayer. We are told that the Holy Spirit dwells within us and that God understands the very groaning within us which cannot be uttered (Rom. 8:26–27).

Adam and Eve stood completely open and transparent before God. It was only after their disobedience that they tried to hide from God out of a feeling of nakedness and shame. In their perfect creatureliness, Adam and Eve had been naked before each other and had felt no shame (Gen. 2:25). The intimacy which Adam and Eve felt was an ability to be themselves without any pretense. They had no need to play deceptive games. Today, however, shame is born out of the fear of being known intimately; and when shame is present, family members put on masks and begin to play deceptive roles before each other. By contrast, as we examine how Genesis describes the nature of the prefall human family (which is the only social institution that belongs to the order of creation), we find an emphasis on intimacy—on the knowing of the other.

Members of a family that is based on covenant and lives in an atmosphere of grace and empowering will be able to so communicate and express themselves that they intimately know and are known by one another. A concerted effort will be made to listen, understand, and want what is best for the other. Not only will differences be accepted, but valuing and respecting uniqueness will be a way of confirming the other person.

This is what it means to be a servant, to empty oneself as Jesus did when he took the form of a servant. This is how one is to be submissive and loving in relationships. It is also true that to have any union or partnership or interdependence with another, one must always be willing to give up something of one's own needs and desires. When family members come to each other with this kind of attitude and perspective, they will find a common ground of joy, satisfaction, and mutual benefit.

The capacity for family members to communicate feelings freely and openly with each other is contingent upon trust and commitment. Then they are not afraid to share and be intimate with one another. John gives us insight into this in 1 John 4:16, 18: "God is love. . . . There is no fear in love. But perfect love drives out fear" (NIV). God expresses perfect love, and we can respond in love because God loved us first (1 John 4:19).

This brings us back to the unconditional covenant love which is the cornerstone for family communication and honest sharing without the threat of rejection. As family members offer their love unconditionally to each other, the security that is established will lead to deeper levels of intimacy.

The unconditional love modeled by Jesus gives a picture of the type of communicative intimacy desirable in family relationships. Recall how Jesus at the end of his earthly ministry asked Peter not once, but three times, "Do you love me?" (John 21). Peter had earlier denied Jesus three

COVENANT LOVE MEANS ACCEPTING THE DIFFERENCES
AND UNIQUENESS OF EACH FAMILY MEMBER.

times; Jesus was giving Peter the opportunity to assert what he had previously denied and to reaffirm his love to Christ three times. Perhaps the relationship between Jesus and Peter had not been the same since Peter's triple denial. Likewise, family relationships will become strained as we disappoint, fail, and even betray those whom we love the most.

Forgiving and being forgiven will be an important part of renewal. There will be a need to confess as well as to receive confession. This is a two-way street which can clear out the unfinished issues between family members. Being willing to admit mistakes and admit being offended by another puts a person in a position of vulnerability. In intimacy, however, one need not be ashamed to admit failure and ask for forgiveness and reconciliation. It is desirable that family members verbally communicate feelings of love and affection toward one another, as well as ask forgiveness of and forgive each other. This will bring the relationship to full maturity.

Examining biblical themes which have a bearing on the nature of family relationships, we have suggested that (1) commitment is to be based upon a mature (i.e., unconditional and bilateral) covenant; (2) family life is to be established and maintained within an atmosphere of grace which embraces acceptance and forgiveness; (3) the resources of family members are to be used to empower rather than to control one another; and (4) intimacy is based on a knowing that leads to caring, understanding, communication, and communion with others. These four elements of Christian family relationships are a continual process: intimacy can lead to deeper covenant love, commitment fortifies the atmosphere of freely offered grace, this climate of acceptance and forgiveness encourages serving and empowering others, and the resultant sense of esteem leads to the ability to be intimate without fear. The end product of this process is deep levels of communication and knowing.

Living in covenant love is a dynamic process. God has designed family relationships to grow to a maturity which is analogous to that of individual believers who attain the full measure of perfection found in Christ (Eph. 4:13). This maturing of relationships eventually enables family members to reach out to persons beyond the boundaries of the family.

2

The Family as a Developing System

Experience shows that it is possible to observe family life, or even to be a part of family life, and yet to be limited in understanding it because our vision is limited. In fact, active involvement in family life may be the very reason we fail to understand it from a wider perspective.

In this chapter we will introduce two theoretical perspectives which family clinicians and sociologists have found helpful in gaining a wide-angle view of family life. The first one is called family-systems theory because it views family life not merely as the sum total of the actions of all the individual members, but rather as the interactions of all family members operating as a unit of interrelated parts. It considers individuals in the context of their relationships. The other is family-development theory, which views the family as developing over time through natural life-cycle stages. In this chapter we will explain these two family perspectives, which will serve as a basis for focusing attention upon family life as a whole.

Family-Systems Theory

One of the major cultural themes in modern society is individualism. Individualism has caused us to focus on the individual's needs and perspective rather than on relationships and groups. When analyzing contemporary society, we see that the delicate balance between individual rights and family rights has been skewed in favor of individual rights. Currently, however, a revolution in the clinical profession is shifting the focus from the individual to the broader family system. Both family therapists and sociologists now view family life from a systems perspective.

What is a family-systems perspective? Basically it is a holistic approach which understands every part of family life in terms of the family as a whole. A system is by definition any identifiable whole which is composed of interrelated individual parts. To understand any system one must begin by identifying the boundary around that system. For example, in Western societies the boundary of the family system is drawn around a husband and wife and their children. In many other societies the boundary also includes relatives beyond the nuclear unit, because in these societies the extended family is the basic system.

The fundamental concepts of systems theory are illustrated in figure 3. Anything which is within the boundary is considered part of the system, and anything which falls outside of the boundary is identified as part of the environment. Input includes any message or stimulus which enters the system from the environment. Output includes any message or response from the system to the environment. Boundaries around a system can be relatively open or closed. In an open family system, boundaries are said to be permeable, allowing for significant input from and output to the environment. In a closed family system, boundaries serve as barriers which limit such interaction.

Once a boundary has been established, objects within the system are identified as units of the system. In the newly established family there are two units (individuals), the husband and the wife, each with identifiable positions and roles within the family. As children come into the family, the system becomes more complex, since each new member occupies a given position in the system and is assigned a role to play within it.

In addition, as new members enter the family, the system becomes more complex because of the creation of subsystems. In a family which includes children there are at least two subsystems: the parental subsystem composed of the mother and father, and the sibling subsystem composed of the children (or, in the case of an only child, the child subsystem). Each sibling can also be identified as an individual subsystem. In most systems, rules of hierarchy exist between the subsystems. In the family the major rule is that the parental subsystem has authority over the sibling subsystem.

Theoretically, it is possible to regard any integrated whole as a system, and then identify the smaller units within it as subsystems. A church could be identified as a system, with each family or group within it a subsystem. Figure 4 serves to illustrate the levels at which social systems

FIGURE 3 **Family-Systems Theory**

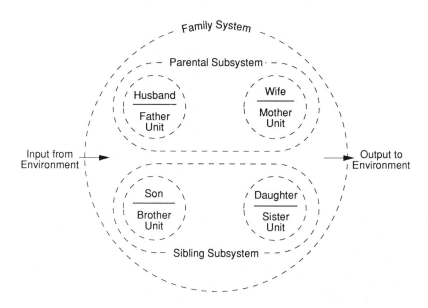

can be analyzed. Keep in mind that the environment and units are relative to the system which one is analyzing. For example, if one is studying the world social system, which includes all of the peoples of the world, the environment is all nonhuman phenomena, and the units are specific societies or cultures.

The popularity of systems theory is in large part a reflection of the inadequacies of cause-and-effect mechanistic models of social behavior. The difference between a process model like systems theory and a mechanistic model like behaviorism can best be seen in the various ways in which behavior can be controlled, balanced, or changed through a feedback process. There are four major levels of feedback operating within a system: simple feedback, cybernetic control, morphogenesis, and reorientation (Broderick and Smith 1979).

Simple feedback is identical with a cause-and-effect model. For example, in order to assist parents in toilet training a child, a behavior-modification therapist focuses on the behavior itself. Giving the child candy when the task is accomplished reinforces the behavior desired. On the other hand, withholding the reward (candy) conditions the child to relinquish the undesired behavior. Simple feedback is frequently used by family members as a stimulus for change. It is a simple exchange between the system and the environment.

Cybernetic control is somewhat more complex. Here an output from

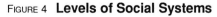

FIGURE 4 **Levels of Social Systems**

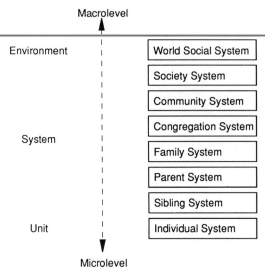

the system feeds back to a monitoring unit within the system, which sets in motion a systemic adjustment to the original output. Perhaps the best example of cybernetic control is the self-monitoring action of a thermostat. On a cold winter day we may set the thermostat at 70 degrees. When the room temperature gets below a certain point (say 68 degrees), the needle in the thermostat makes electrical contact and the heater is turned on. The heater will stay on until the needle rises to the point (say 72 degrees) where it loses electrical contact; then the heater turns off. This is cybernetic control because the heating system has a built-in mechanism to control itself.

Family life can be understood in much the same way. Families have rules or norms which define expected behavior for each family member. Each of these rules has a tolerance limit beyond which one cannot go without the family as a system taking some counteraction. In our thermostat analogy the tolerance limits were 68 and 72 degrees. The family will need some flexibility in setting its tolerance limits; for if they are set too rigidly, there will be a constant need to correct and normal family living will be impossible. For example, imagine what would happen to the heater if the tolerance limits were set at 69.999 and 70.001 degrees. The heater would be turning on and shutting off constantly, and all the energy would be exerted in that endeavor.

Consider a family which has a rigid rule that everyone must be home and be seated at the table at exactly 6 P.M. for the evening meal. Other members of the family may be willing to wait for about thirty seconds for Mary to get off the phone so they can begin. But they most certainly will not tolerate a five-minute delay. The system will draw upon its storehouse of memories and choose an action to correct the undesirable behavior. It may be that Mary's siblings will put pressure on her to hang up, or that her parents will warn her that she won't get anything to eat unless she hangs up immediately. In either case the system works as a whole to shape her behavior.

All families have rules which each member obeys for the good of the whole. Deviance from these rules is monitored by the system. Cybernetic control is that action which the system takes to maintain the rules or status quo. This is what is referred to as homeostasis in systems-theory language.

But families often go beyond cybernetic control, for they are continually redefining and changing their rules, regulations, and procedures. Expanding our illustration, let's suppose that the family is determined not to begin eating without Mary, and that none of their tried and proven techniques succeed in getting her off the phone. A system which functions only at a cybernetic level can do absolutely nothing. It must either resort to a past way of acting or do nothing. However, a system which operates on a morphogenetic level is capable of generating or creating new ways of responding to the situation. New responses are created whenever tested methods no longer work or the system is facing a situation for the first time.

One of the major advantages which functional family systems have over dysfunctional family systems is the ability to operate at this higher level. The family which is overly rigid is usually incapable of morphogenetic responses because it lacks flexibility. On the other hand, families that are chaotically structured with few rules or boundaries will have as much difficulty because they do not possess the cohesiveness to act in a united way.

The family is usually required to generate new response patterns whenever predictable changes in its life cycle as well as unexpected crises occur. For example, when a member of the family loses a job, gets sick, or dies, new response patterns are demanded. This is also true for the positive changes that occur, such as the birth or adoption of a child into the family, a wedding or anniversary celebration, or an unexpected inheritance of money. The family will be challenged to form new response patterns to these events as well.

The tendency in most families is to respond in old, familiar ways to new situations (homeostasis). It is likely that these old ways will be inadequate, and the family will become stuck in them rather than be stirred up to operate on the morphogenetic level. The functional family, however,

BOY, I'M SURE GLAD THAT OURS IS A FAMILY OF GRACE
WHICH FORGIVES ONE ANOTHER ON EVERY OCCASION!

has learned that flexibility and cohesiveness are needed in order to operate on the morphogenetic level.

The fourth and highest level is reorientation; here the family changes
its entire goal. In morphogenesis new ways of responding are generated,
whereas in reorientation the goals themselves are changed. Reorientation
involves a dramatic change in family life in which the entire system is
converted to new ways of thinking and behaving. For example, reorientation may occur when the family of an alcoholic comes to grips with
how every member is contributing to the problem, and they find treatment which impacts not only the alcoholic, but each and every one of
them. Another example is a radical change in a family's belief system,
such as a religious conversion which spreads to all members and results
in an entirely new pattern of family living.

It is true that this type of systemic change is fairly rare, and that in
most families morphogenesis or homeostasis is the more common response. However, reorientation will be prescribed when a family's existing patterns of behavior prove to be totally unworkable.

Family-Development Theory

Imagine that we had access to a time machine and could view the Smith family at different points in its development. Let us suppose that we could view Mr. and Mrs. Smith during their first month of marriage, the year their first child was born, the year their youngest child was born, the year their youngest child became a teenager, the last year that child lived at home, and the year their youngest grandchild was born. Altogether we would have six slices from the life of the Smith family. They would look very different at each of those different points. But there would also be certain elements of continuity: the basic organization of the family, the siblings' birth order (family constellation), family history and traditions, the presence of extended family, and so on. It should also be noted that each stage of family life has predictable times of tension, and certain stages require more family structure than do others.

The developmental perspective allows us to view the typical family's progression through various stages of life. The family is dynamic rather than static. Within each stage there are certain key developmental tasks which the family must accomplish in order to progress on to the next stage. Likewise, there are developmental tasks which must be performed by each individual family member at a particular age. To the extent that both the family as a unit and individual family members master their respective tasks, the family is prepared to move on to the next stage of development. To the extent that the developmental tasks are not mastered, the family will be ill prepared to move on.

Some developmental tasks are stage-specific; that is, they must be mastered at a specific stage and no other. Other tasks can begin to be mastered at one stage and will continue to be mastered at all subsequent stages. For example, in the first year of marriage it is necessary for a couple to master the task of establishing their own household. In contrast, interpersonal communication is a skill that will be worked on throughout the life cycle.

Table 1 lists the basic developmental stages, the major task associated with each stage, and the event which initiates it. It should be mentioned that all families are unique and that these stages are not so precisely laid out as the chart would indicate.

In general, a family can be said to have moved from one stage to the next when a major transition takes place. We begin our list with the premarital stage because of the importance of differentiation from one's family of origin (the family into which a person was born). This developmental task should be completed before marriage takes place. The process of differentiation actually begins in adolescence, but must be completed during the engagement period.

TABLE 1
Family Development

Stage	Major Task	Initiating Event
Premarital	Differentiating from family of origin	Engagement
Marital dyad	Adjusting to marital roles (establishing a household)	Marriage
Triad	Adjusting to new child	Birth/adoption of first child
Completed family	Adjusting to new family members	Birth of youngest child
Family with adolescents	Increasing flexibility in family system	Children's differentiating from the family
Launching	Accepting departure of family members	Children's choosing career and marriage partner
Postlaunching	Accepting years of aloneness and the aging process	Departure of last child from home

The most obvious and important transition in the life cycle is marriage. When two people marry, a new family begins in the form of a dyad. The major developmental task involves the husband's and wife's adjustment to each other in their new roles as married rather than single persons.

There is an incredible agenda to be accomplished during this stage: setting up a new household, dividing up household chores, creating a financial budget, establishing work and career roles, making sexual adjustments, developing friendships and planning social events, making decisions about church involvement and spiritual growth, and so on. This is an important time of establishing a sound foundation for future stages.

In view of the amount of energy and cooperation needed to accomplish the items on this agenda, it is vital that the newly formed couple obey the biblical mandate to "leave and cleave." If they are to make these many decisions, the couple must clearly define their united relationship. They will need encouragement and support from their respective families in this process, but if the families interfere, the foundation will be weakened.

The third family stage, the triad, begins with the birth or adoption of the first child. Research indicates that the optimal length of time to be married before the birth of the first child is two to five years. Most couples benefit from having at least two years together to adjust to being married and to have sufficient time to accomplish the tasks required of newlyweds. The early arrival of a child can prematurely shift the focus of attention from the tasks of the marriage relationship to those of the parent/child relationship.

When a child is born or adopted into a family, the existing system is changed to include the new member. New boundaries must be set up, new space must be provided, and new ways of relating are needed in order to accommodate the new member.

When children reach adolescence, increased pressure is put upon the family system to accommodate itself to increased demands for flexibility. This is the time when children begin to differentiate and separate from the family. It is also the time when parents approach midlife, which often involves stress of its own. Many difficulties arise when the stressful stages of adolescence and midlife occur simultaneously.

The launching stage begins when children reach marriageable age. The parents must be willing to allow their children to leave their family of origin. It is also crucial that parents accept their child's choice of mate and that person's family.

The postlaunching stage finds the family a dyad again. This can be a period of renewed closeness between husband and wife as they refocus their attention on each other and their independent and mutual meaning in life. On the other hand, if children were the major focus of what they had in common, this can be a period of great disillusionment and loneliness (the empty-nest syndrome). Such a couple may find that they have very little in common now that the children have left home. Given the expanded life expectancy in our society, the postlaunching stage accounts for nearly half of the length of the typical family system.

An Integration of Systems and Development Theory

Our strategy in this book is to use both the developmental and the systems perspective in discussing family life. The family is a developing system which needs to be open to the arrival of new members and their later departure. It must be able to tolerate and be responsive to the changing needs of its individual members; at the same time it must maintain a stability which is capable of providing a firm foundation for them. This is not an easy feat, especially with the demands that are made on the family system in our modern urban society. A multitude of extrafamilial systems (the work world, the educational system, the church groups, various clubs, and organizations) are all contending with the family for the time and devotion of family members. Only strong families will be able to survive the intrusiveness of our modern society.

To understand how to build strong families, we must begin with a definition of healthy family life. Table 2, which is based upon current

TABLE 2
The Characteristics of Strong and Weak Families

	Strong Families	Weak Families
Cohesion	Individuation Mutuality	Enmeshment Disengagement
Adaptability	Flexibility Stability	Rigidity Chaos
Communication	Clear perception Clear communication	Unclear perception Unclear communication
Role structure	Agreement on roles Clear generational boundaries	Conflict over roles Diffuse boundaries

clinical and sociological literature, presents a summary of various characteristics of strong and weak families. There are four major areas of analysis: cohesion, adaptability, communication, and role structure. In each area two characteristics mark the strong family.

Cohesion

Cohesion refers to the degree of closeness or oneness which exists in a family. In strong families the members are individuated, which means that each one possesses a healthy degree of separateness from the others. There is a feeling that "I am an individual and you are an individual; we are separate persons in this system. Though clearly distinct, we are still members of the same family."

When family members are too cohesive, they are described as enmeshed. In this case, family members lack a sense of separate identity or individuality, each being overly dependent upon the family for identity. An example of enmeshment is a whole family's being devastated by one member's problem. All the members become overly involved and make the problem their own. They lose perspective. In the process the problem worsens, and the chance of a solution lessens.

The opposite extreme is a very low level of cohesion, which can be described as disengagement. In the disengaged family the life of each member rarely touches the other members in any meaningful way. There is a lack of involvement, and they do not contribute to nor cooperate with each other. In times of personal crisis the disengaged family is likely to be indifferent and uninvolved. Here the system is not able to provide help or support for the hurting member. Each individual is too busy working out his or her own problems to notice what is happening with the others.

Strong families, by contrast, have a degree of mutuality and involvement which is supportive but not intrusive. This is lacking in both the enmeshed and disengaged families, which are actually the opposite ends of a continuum. In the middle of this continuum are strong families, which display an appropriate degree of cohesion.

For analytical purposes mutuality and individuation can be discussed separately, but in actuality they overlap in a condition which is referred to as differentiation. Disengagement, differentiation, and enmeshment are illustrated in figure 5. The bold lines in the figure represent the boundaries around the family, and the light lines indicate the boundaries around each individual family member. In the disengaged family (A) the lives of the individual members very rarely touch each other. Cohesion is so low that each person lives in psychological isolation from the others.

In the differentiated family (B) daily lives overlap, but each individual is also involved in activities outside the family. Each member has a separate life and identity and is therefore actively and meaningfully engaged with others. Although a vital part of each member's identity and support is found within the family, much is found beyond the family boundary as well.

In the enmeshed family (C) the lives of all are hopelessly entwined with each other. Each family member has little identity beyond the boundary of the family. Even within the family there is little space for a given member to be independent of the others. A member of an enmeshed family who tries to separate is likely to be labeled disloyal and to experience pressure from the others to remain enmeshed.

Needless to say, the amount of cohesion required to produce strong family life will vary from family to family, and from one life stage to another. For example, the degree of enmeshment will be higher in most families when young children are present and the emotional bonding between parent and infant or child is a primary concern. When children become teenagers and are working toward self-identity, it is appropriate that they separate and disengage emotionally in preparation for the independence necessary to leave home eventually. But even though the younger members become independent and establish their own lives, the functional family will have built a closeness, loyalty, and interconnectedness that will remain with them throughout life.

Adaptability

A second important criterion for judging family life is adaptability. Families that have an extremely high level of adaptability tend to be chaotic. They lack the needed structure and predictability which provide stability and security. At the opposite extreme, rigid families have a very low degree of adaptability and can be equally dysfunctional. These fam-

FIGURE 5 **Disengagement, Differentiation, and Enmeshment**

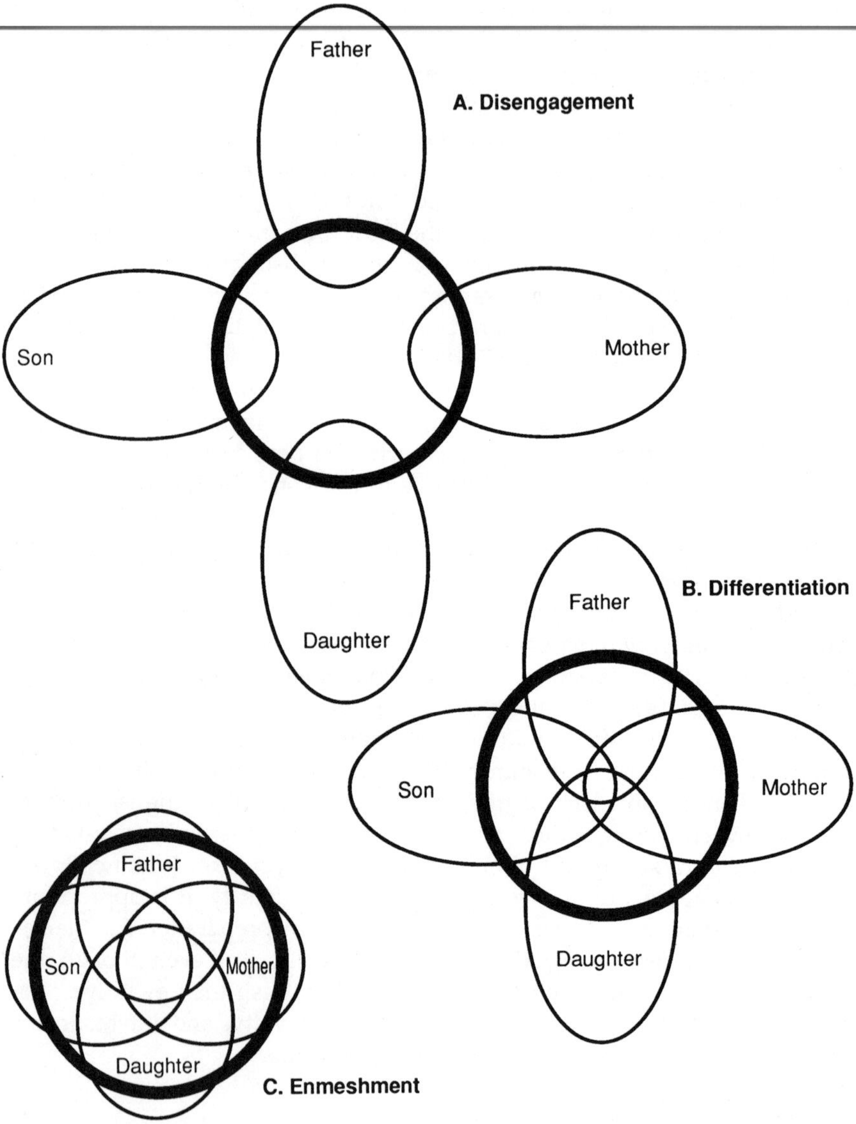

ilies have created such a tight, unbending structural system that they have no give or flexibility, a strength which is especially needed during periods of change and transition throughout the life cycle.

Strong family life will be characterized by an appropriate degree of adaptability. The two dimensions of flexibility and stability mark the orderly family. In strong family life there is a sense of orderliness which entails both flexibility and structure. The difference between families in this particular area can be observed in their dinner patterns. In the chaotic family, dinner is at no set time, and family members come and go from the dining table whenever it is convenient. In the rigid family it is understood that dinner is at 6 P.M. sharp and will not be altered. In the stable yet flexible family, dinner is scheduled for a certain time but can be changed as needed and agreed upon by the family as a whole.

David Olson, Douglas Sprenkle, and Candyce Russell (1979) have combined cohesion and adaptability and come up with what they call the circumplex model. The four families at the center of figure 6 are orderly differentiated families. The corners of the chart represent four types of dysfunctional families. The chaotic enmeshed family is extremely high in both cohesion and adaptability; the rigid enmeshed family is high in cohesion and low in adaptability; the rigid disengaged family is low in both cohesion and adaptability; and the chaotic disengaged family is low in cohesion and high in adaptability. It is important to note that a variety of family styles are functional and healthy. It is the families at the extremes which have serious problems.

Communication

There are probably more self-help books on family communication than on any other topic. Because communication contributes in such an important way to strong family life, this is probably as it should be. The dynamics of good communication boil down to clarity of perception and clarity of expression. Clarity of perception pertains especially to the receiver of communication. It involves good listening skills, the ability to pick up on the sender's intonations and body language, and willingness to ask for clarification when needed. In functional families, members have empathic skills, which include the ability to put oneself in the other's shoes and to understand what it feels like to be in that person's situation. This enables the communication to be on target and the receiver to make an appropriate response.

The more obvious dimension of good communication—clarity of expression—pertains to the sender. In strong families, members are able to communicate feelings, opinions, wishes, and desires in a forthright and unambiguous manner. In such families there will be a minimal amount of deceptive game-playing. Clarity in sending messages is often a result of agreement or congruency between the person's words and body language. Care in this area will go far to ensure effective communication.

FIGURE 6 **Circumplex Model of Family Systems**

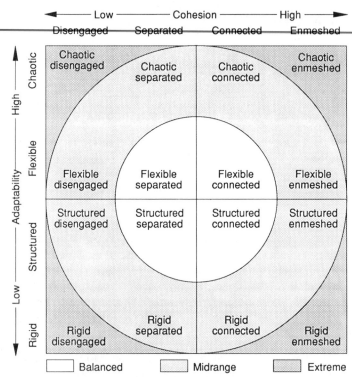

From David Olson, Douglas Sprenkle, and Candyce Russell, "Circumplex Model of Marital and Family Systems: Cohesion and Adaptability Dimensions, Family Types, and Clinical Applications." *Family Process* 18 (March 1979):17.

Role Structure

Shakespeare's suggestion that the world is a stage and we are merely actors and actresses provides dramatic insight into family relationships. Each family member has a role to play in the family. This role is usually defined by the family as a whole. In a family with at least two children, every member has at least two roles: the adults play the roles of spouse and parent, and the children play the roles of child and sibling. And, of course, each person has roles outside the family as well.

Conflict over roles is a common characteristic in dysfunctional families. When the role of one member is in conflict with the role of another member, there is contention. For example, husband and wife may both want to work outside the home and have the other spouse be responsible for the housekeeping and child care. Strong families in contrast are characterized by agreement on respective roles. The husband and wife agree on what their own role and the role of their spouse will be. It may be that, in the case just cited, they will decide together to share responsibility in the home so they can each work outside the home. Note that the issue here is not who plays a particular role, but whether there is mutual agreement about the roles.

A second dimension in regard to role structure has to do with the generational boundaries in the family. Strong families are characterized by clear boundaries around the parental subsystem and clear boundaries around the sibling subsystem. On the other hand, the boundaries are obviously diffuse when one sibling begins to play the role of parent to a brother or sister. Of course, when Mom and Dad are away for the evening, the oldest child may be put in charge. In healthy families this role is relinquished when the parents return home. But if the oldest child continues to take the parenting role when Mom and Dad are present, there is a blurring of generational boundaries.

Boundaries in functional families are clear but permeable. This means that family members have the freedom to take on different roles. For example, parents can become playful and childish at times, while children may sometimes act as nurturers to their parents. For a parent or child to occasionally break out of a fixed role is a sign of flexibility. A mother may playfully stand on the coffee table and perform for her children, or a child may comfort the parent who comes home discouraged and needs consideration and support. Though these are not their dominant roles, family members do have the freedom to take them on occasionally.

Although flexibility in roles and permeable boundaries are important, it is possible for generational boundaries to be too diffuse. It is confusing when one of the marriage partners assumes the role of parent or child to the other, or when a child becomes a parent to the other siblings or to the parents themselves. Such crossing of generational boundaries can lead to dysfunctional relationships when it is repeated and fixed into patterns. Another example is siblings who jump out of their age-appropriate roles and either regress to a younger sibling's rightful position or take over the position of an older brother or sister. Grandparents may attempt to parent grandchildren, thereby taking over the role that rightfully belongs to the parents. This may occur because the grandparents desire control or because someone has abdicated responsibility. But whatever the cause, the result will be confusion and problems for family members.

In the first part of this chapter we described the systemic and developmental approaches to understanding the family. By combining these two approaches we suggested what a strong developing system might look like. Our description of a strong family is based upon clinical and social-science findings on the type of family which is most functional in Western societies. Adding this description to the biblical basis for family relationships we presented in chapter 1, we have at this point two models for the family. This we believe is the necessary starting point for an integrated view of marriage and family relationships.

In the chapters that follow both social-science and biblical data will be presented. We will use the theological model of chapter 1 as a basis to integrate data from both sources. The task of integration, although vital, is delicate and difficult. Our Christian presuppositions include values and biases which will affect our understanding of the social-science literature concerning the family. Likewise, our social-science presuppositions will be present as we attempt to understand how Scripture applies to the contemporary family. We encourage the reader to join with us in the demanding task of integrating biblical and social-science knowledge about the family.

PART 2

Marriage:
The Foundation of Family Life

Introduction

F amily life comes after marriage, yet everyone has already experienced family life prior to marriage. When two people marry, they bring with them recollections and experiences from their families of origin. The comment that there are "six in the marriage bed" is a way of alerting young spouses that they each bring a set of parents with them into this new union.

Chapter 3 will focus on the coming together of two individuals and their respective families. The marriage ceremony proclaims to family, friends, and members of the community that a new union has been formed. The reception provides an opportunity for these groups of people to become introduced to one another so that new relationships may develop between them. The wedding day can be a stressful time for the new couple full of the emotions related to separation, endings, and beginnings. If the wedding is approved by both families, there will be accompanying support to help the couple establish a firm foundation for their union. If the new couple lacks support, on the other hand, they are likely to start out on shaky ground, and they will need to put forth a concerted and steadfast effort to achieve a stable marriage.

Chapter 4 will be devoted to the process of establishing a firm marriage. Family therapist Virginia Satir (1982:2) has referred to the marital partners as the architects of the family. They are also the foundation upon which the family will be established. The essential supports in a solid foundation include the strengths of the two families of origin, the character strengths which each spouse brings into the marriage, the strength of the relationship itself, and the strength that comes from friends and community. These sources of support are all crucial in establishing a well-functioning foundation. And in Christian homes, of course, the cornerstone is Christ.

Although the foundation is established early in marriage, it is important to recognize that the marital dyad is a dynamic and growing relationship. There is no such thing as a static marriage because, like any living organism, marriage is either in a state of growth or a state of decline. Chapter 5 will present the constituent elements of a marriage relationship that is based on and grows in accordance with biblical principles.

3

Mate Selection:
The Process of Finding the Ideal Partner

I n all societies there is a process whereby unmarried persons come to be married to a particular person of the opposite sex. This process is called mate selection. While the beginning phase of marriage is technically the first stage of family life, mate selection is a necessary preliminary.

Family life comprises the processes of two persons' joining together, reproducing children, nurturing them, and eventually separating from them. Mate selection is that point at which two young persons separate from their parents and unite to form their own new family. Understanding mate selection is, then, a very important starting point for understanding all other stages in the life cycle of the family.

Mate Selection in Traditional Cultures

In the United States selecting a mate is usually a very individual matter. Unmarried persons court and then choose for themselves whom they will marry. Contrary to popular opinion, this approach is actually a fairly recent development. In most societies throughout history, selecting a mate was a decision made solely by the parents, whose age and experience supposedly brought the wisdom to handle so important a matter.

In cross-cultural contexts the mate-selection process extends along a

55

continuum from parent-arranged marriage at one end to total free choice at the other. In societies which practice parental arrangement, mate selection is more a link between two extended families than a uniting of two individuals.

In societies where marriages are arranged by parents, there are two dominant approaches—the bride-price and the dowry systems. The bride-price system is the norm in subsistence economies, where the labor performed by women is greatly valued. In exchange for the bride, her family is given various goods by the groom's family. The dowry system is the norm in agricultural societies, where organized family units live on and work their own property. A dowry consists of goods which parents give to their unmarried daughter in order to make her an attractive commodity on the marriage market. In such a system, the wife brings the dowry with her into the new marriage.

The modernization process going on throughout the world today has challenged the tradition of parent-arranged marriages. Modernization has made it possible to influence the environment; developing countries usually embrace and make every effort to accelerate such technological advancements. This wholehearted acceptance of modernization has brought with it a strong emphasis on individualism. A by-product of individualism has been the gradual erosion of the extended family and parent-arranged marriages. In their place have emerged the nuclear family and romantic love as the basis for marriage.

Youth in traditional societies are increasingly exposed to a Western view of romantic love through the mass media. Many of these youth are very familiar with American and Western European movies, popular music, and magazines, all of which have a strong emphasis on romantic love. When youth in traditional societies begin to value the concept of romantic love, they do not immediately challenge the time-honored mate-selection procedure, but at an unconscious level new ideas begin to undermine the old ways. These new ideas come to be accepted in a sequential order: (1) two people should be romantically in love before they are married; (2) only the two persons directly involved can determine if romantic love is present in their relationship; and (3) romantic love is most effectively cultivated within a social environment where unmarried youth can become acquainted with persons of the opposite sex through dating.

In response to these new ideas parents may initially be willing to consider the opinion of their children and consult them about whether a selected mate meets approval. They may even be willing to allow a courtship time for the young persons to become acquainted and fall in love. However, young persons will gradually assert themselves more in regard to their eventual marriage partner and demand the acquaintance of a number of persons of the opposite sex. This changes the entire process.

In addition, the Western notion that compatibility of personality should be a factor in mate selection will eventually be adopted. Thus, unmarried youth will want the freedom to become acquainted with members of the opposite sex for the purpose of detecting both the presence of love and personal compatibility.

It is at this stage that dating enters in. This is often a major point of contention between parents and children, for control of the mate-selection process is passing from the hands of the parents to the hands of the unmarried youth. When two unmarried youth believe that they are in love and want to marry each other, the parental arrangement will be only a formality. In time, perhaps over several generations, even the formality of parent-arranged marriages will most likely cease to exist (Balswick 1975).

Mate Selection in Modern Society

Having considered mate selection in a traditional context, we will now move on to the way in which the process takes place in Western societies

MOM, DAD, THIS IS THE WONDERFUL, SUPERORDINARY, STUPENDOUS GUY I'VE BEEN TELLING YOU ABOUT.

today. Largely because of the acceptance of romantic love, mate selection in Western societies has become the prerogative of the two people directly involved.

The Role of Romantic Love

It is difficult to understand how the mate-selection process works in Western societies without understanding the role of romantic love. The concept of romantic love had its beginnings in European societies during the eleventh century, when "courtly love" became fashionable among the privileged class. Courtly love usually involved a romantic relationship between a married aristocratic lady and an unmarried knight or troubadour. As portrayed in Western literature, stereotypical courtly love involved either a knight going forth into battle, motivated by the love of his lady, or a troubadour serenading a young lady standing on her balcony on a moonlit night. According to this early version of romantic love, true love could last only if it was free of both sex and marriage.

The concept of courtly love served to introduce the element of affection into male/female relationships. This was uncommon in most marriages of the day, which were primarily economic arrangements. By the sixteenth century, courtly love had changed to include sexual involvement between the lady of nobility and her paramour. The emerging middle class of European society during the sixteenth and seventeenth centuries came to value romantic love, but it also valued faithfulness in marriage. This dilemma was solved when the love object changed from a married woman to a single woman. For a period of time during the seventeenth and eighteenth centuries, parent-arranged marriage and romantic love existed side by side. But when Western societies moved into the twentieth century, asking parents for their daughter's hand in marriage had become somewhat of a formality.

During the first half of the twentieth century, the irrational head-over-heels concept of romantic love reached its zenith. Confusion over the exact meaning of romantic love made it difficult for persons to know if true romantic love was present in their relationship. Psychiatrist Erich Fromm recognized this fact when he wrote *The Art of Loving* (1956). Fromm observed that most people see love primarily in terms of being loved rather than in terms of loving. He then argued that we need to learn how to love in the same way we learn how to play a musical instrument. Love is an art to be practiced, requiring discipline, concentration, patience, and supreme concern. When people start working at love, their relationship will be characterized by giving, caring, responsibility, respect, and knowledge.

During the 1950s the mate-selection process in Western societies moved to a new stage called rational-romantic love. This type of love incorporates rational consideration of compatibility with one's true love. Although few people would marry someone they do not love, it is also now true that few people will marry only on the basis of love. Rational-romantic love is especially common among persons who are college-educated and marry after their education is completed. Marriage today is as much a rational decision as it is a head-over-heels response to one's partner.

Roger Sternberg (1986) has attempted to sort out the complexity of what our society calls romantic love. He believes that love includes three dimensions: commitment, the cognitive component; intimacy, the friendship factor and emotional component; and passion, the motivational component. These three dimensions of love are quite similar to the three types of love known from ancient Greek culture, *agapē, philia,* and *erōs.* C. S. Lewis has written eloquently about these loves in his book *The Four Loves* (1960a). The self-giving *agapē* corresponds to commitment; *philia,* brotherly friendship, corresponds to intimacy; and *erōs,* physical desire for one's beloved, corresponds to passion.

Utilizing these dimensions, figure 7 depicts four types of love relationships. Complete love (A) embraces an equal portion of all three loves: commitment/*agapē,* intimacy/*philia,* and passion/*erōs.* In Western societies passion is likely to dominate at the beginning of courtship; there follow a surge in intimacy and, lastly, commitment. While all three dimensions of love are important for a Christian marriage, courtship which begins with commitment to the other person establishes an environment in which intimacy and passion can grow to full maturity after the marriage has been consummated. The ideal relationship will exhibit equal amounts of commitment, intimacy, and passion before two people marry.

In self-giving love (B) commitment is dominant. The resolution of a couple to be faithful and self-giving in their love is in many societies the most desired prerequisite for marriage. Commitment is a critical component in parent-arranged marriages. It is noteworthy that these marriages end in divorce far less frequently than do those based on romantic love. However, this statistic does not imply that parent-arranged marriages are more likely than love-based marriages to achieve the Christian ideal. For while there may be a potential for intimacy and passion to develop, the familial structure in traditional societies may actually hinder such development. Furthermore, the commitment which keeps these marriages together may be less a self-giving commitment to one's spouse than it is a commitment to the extended family and community, which in many cases severely condemn divorce.

In friendship love (C) intimacy is dominant. Although few relationships move into marriage on the basis of friendship alone, it is an essential factor in a good marital relationship. Many people describe their spouse as their best friend, an indication of the importance of being an

FIGURE 7 **Four Types of Love Relationships**

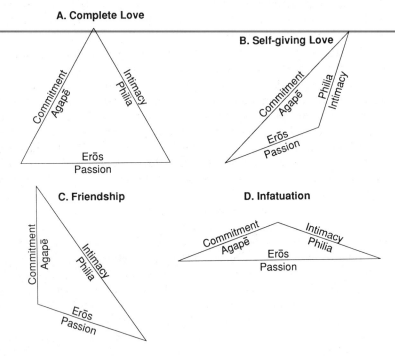

emotional companion to one's mate. Others complain that the friendship is so strong they find it difficult to feel passionate with their partner. This can lead to dissatisfaction in the marriage.

In infatuation (D) passion is dominant. Some relationships get off to a passionate start: two people connect on the basis of immediate attraction and sexual response. This may lead to an impulsive marriage. Such relationships do not ordinarily have the emotional core and stability of commitment to sustain the marriage. But since passion by itself usually cannot carry a relationship over time, infatuation often burns itself out before a decision to marry.

Theories of Mate Selection

In view of the flexibility and complexity of the modern courtship system, family researchers have been challenged to explain the mate-selection process. One of the most studied aspects of present-day mate selection is the degree to which people choose mates who are similar to or different from themselves. If we believe the two clichés, "like marries like" and "opposites attract," there may be ways in which husband and wife are both similar to and different from each other.

The theory that like marries like. Studies have shown that endogamous factors or similar social backgrounds are key components in mate selection. These factors include race, ethnicity, religion, education, occupation, and geographical proximity. It should be noted that some of these factors directly relate to the opportunity to get to know another person. Close contact in the workplace, for example, affords the opportunity to view someone as a potential marriage partner. For this reason it is fairly common for persons in the same occupation to marry. It has also been shown that homogamous factors or similar personal characteristics and interests are of importance. Included here are religious and political beliefs, moral values, hobbies, intelligence, height, weight, and physical appearance. Another important finding is that most people seem to marry partners with a similar amount of ego strength. A person with low self-esteem tends to marry a person with low self-esteem, and a person with high self-esteem will marry another person with high self-esteem.

The theory that opposites attract. Evidence that opposites attract is not as clear-cut as is the evidence that like marries like. Studies do suggest, however, that when opposites attract, personality factors are usually involved. There is a tendency for dominant persons to marry submissive persons, and for nurturing persons to marry persons who need nurturing. It appears that there is an unconscious desire to complete a perceived personal deficiency by choosing someone who can make up for what is lacking.

Filter theory. Alan Kerckhoff and Keith Davis (1962) have suggested that endogamy, homogamy, and complementary needs are three different filters through which a potential mate must pass (see figure 8). The first and broadest filter in the mate-selection process is endogamy, as most persons date and establish relationships with individuals from similar backgrounds. The second filter is homogamy, which is narrower and more selective. Only those persons who have similar interests and characteristics pass through this filter. Casual dating serves as a means for individuals to find out which other persons have compatible interests and characteristics. The last filter, complementary needs, is the narrowest. Whereas a number of potential mates may pass through the endogamous and homogamous filters, only a few will have the exact personality traits to meet one's most pressing needs.

Stimulus-value-role theory. The stimulus-value-role theory of mate selection is similar to the filter theory, except that it conceives of mate selection as an open market in which individuals try to find the best mate they can, given what they have to offer. At the stimulus stage, factors such as physical attractiveness, social competence, and status serve to draw persons to each other on the basis of "equity of the weighted amalgam of stimulus attributes" (Murstein 1980:785). In other words, the more

FIGURE 8 **A Filter Theory of Mate Selection**

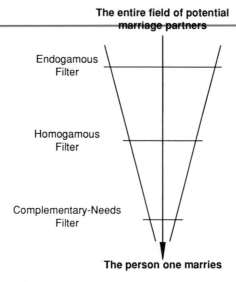

equal the mixture of these different stimulus factors, the greater the likelihood that two people will be initially attracted to each other. Some individuals will then move on to the value stage, where they assess the compatibility of their standards and beliefs. A few relationships will move on to the role stage, where each person will assess whether his or her expectations of a mate can be fulfilled by the potential partner. A relationship which passes through all three stages has the possibility of culminating in marriage. Some couples, however, launch into marriage after their relationship has passed only through stage one or two. When this happens, there is a greater possibility that divorce will occur.

Dyadic-formation theory. One of the most elaborate of the mate-selection theories was constructed by Robert Lewis (1972). His dyadic-formation theory conceives of a dating relationship as developing through six stages of increasing seriousness: (1) perception of similarities in each other's background, values, interests, and personality; (2) establishment of rapport as evidenced by ease of communication, positive evaluations of each other, satisfaction with the relationship, and validation of self by the other; (3) openness through mutual self-disclosure; (4) anticipation of the role each would play as a marriage partner; (5) adjustment of these roles to fit each other's needs; and (6) dyadic crystallization as evidenced by progressive involvement together, the establishment of boundaries around the relationship, commitment to each other, and emerging identity as a couple.

The wheel and clock-spring theories. Ira Reiss (1960) proposed the wheel theory of love in his explanation of mate selection in Western society. According to this theory, heterosexual love is a primary relationship which our society has singled out for special attention. The typical relationship between a man and a woman moves through four phases: (1) rapport—coming to feel comfortable with each other; (2) self-revelation—being open and sharing oneself with the other; (3) mutual dependency—the realization that one needs the other person as a confidant or a listener; and (4) intimacy-need fulfilment—the awareness that one's needs for sympathetic understanding are being met by the other person.

Dolores Borland (1975) expanded on the wheel theory by describing heterosexual love as a process of cycling through the four phases of courtship at increasingly deeper and deeper levels. This process, by which a couple comes to know each other's real self, she likened to tightening a clock spring. Borland warned that a love relationship will fail to grow if one of the partners is unable to move on to a deeper level of rapport, self-revelation, mutual dependency, and intimacy-need fulfilment.

A Christian Perspective

Taken together, the various sociological theories of mate selection comport very well with the theological model of family relationships which we presented in chapter 1. This will become clear as we describe what mate selection would be like if it developed according to the principles suggested in our theological model.

At the beginning of any courtship there is a minimal degree of commitment between the partners. With an increased degree of commitment comes an increased sense of trust and security. And as mutual commitment increases, grace can be expected to grow proportionately. Grace is experienced as acceptance and appreciation by the partner. The presence of grace promotes a feeling of security because differences are respected, and because there is an atmosphere of forgiveness whenever failure occurs. The partners are valued and accepted for who they are and not for what they might be or do for the other.

Out of grace emerges a mutual empowering process. In the early stages of courtship, the couple may operate on a quid pro quo basis, with each attempting to have personal needs met through the relationship. Where there is a minimal degree of commitment and acceptance, people are likely to think more in terms of what they can get from a relationship rather than what they can contribute to it. Certain courting relationships may, in fact, be based on mutual addiction. In addictive relationships the partners are so dependent on each other to have their needs met that neither the relationship nor the individuals can grow. These are often possessive relationships which entail turmoil, jealousy, and chaos. What persons in addictive relationships need most is empowering; what they do *not* need is the type of enabling that perpetuates the addiction.

~~The empowering model is hopeful in that it shows that love can be~~ elevated above self-centered exchange. A depth of commitment and grace can imbue each partner with a genuine desire to empower by both giving to and receiving from the other. This involves being interested in the growth of the other person and finding ways to encourage the partner to reach his greatest potential, to be all that she can be! It will, of course, take a servanthood attitude for such empowering to take place.

We live in a society which encourages people to think that they can have instant gratification. This mentality carries over into the dating relationship, where people look for instant intimacy. Much of the behavior in singles' bars centers around the search for the instant intimacy of the one-night stand which is free of long-term commitment.

In our theological model, however, intimacy entails knowing, understanding, and caring for the other person; it is not simply a physical or sexual encounter. Accordingly, intimacy must develop as a result of (not as a condition for) commitment, grace, and empowering. Building on the foundation of these other aspects of our model, persons who are courting can allow themselves to be more open and vulnerable by letting themselves be known. They can take off their masks and resist the temptation to put on pretenses or to be superficial. They can share at a deep level because their desire is to find out all they can about one another. As C. S. Lewis (1960a) expresses it, the partner is more interested in the beloved than in the mere pleasure of a sexual encounter. Intimacy of this nature leads to deeper levels of commitment, grace, and empowering.

Discerning God's Will

Marriage is an important, sacred event in most societies. Marriage is pivotal because it is necessary to the psychological well-being of most individuals, the social well-being of family life, the economic well-being of communities, and the biological survival of society itself. One of the advantages of parent-arranged marriage is that it protects young people from the pressure, confusion, and agony of having to make such a major decision. The obvious disadvantage is that they are excluded from this critical process which will have enormous impact on the rest of their lives. This leads us to the question of how Christians should decide to marry.

To answer this question we must begin by considering how one comes to discern God's will in the matter of choosing a mate. It should be noted that there are examples from Scripture where God reveals his will to an individual directly, to an individual on behalf of another, and to a group of people. There is, then, no particular style (parental arrangement or free individual choice) which can be deemed best.

Three guidelines will prove helpful as one seeks God's direction in this matter. First, one should seek God's will directly through prayer, Bible study, and meditation. Second, one should seek wisdom from parents, other family members, and friends. Trusted people who know the strengths and needs of a couple can provide a very helpful perspective. Premarital counseling, where the couple can examine their personalities and clarify expectations with an objective professional or pastor, will also prove beneficial. Third, the couple should seek wisdom from other Christians with whom they are in close fellowship. The body of Christ can provide a communal input and affirmation or disaffirmation.

Figure 9 depicts four possible approaches to mate selection. God's will can best be discerned through the biblically balanced approach (A). Here input from three sources—the individuals directly concerned, family and close friends, and the Christian community—will operate as a check against an incorrect decision. When decisions are made without input from all three sources, there is a greater probability of error. Given the power of passion and today's emphasis on intimacy in romantic relationships, the

FIGURE 9 **Approaches to Mate Selection**

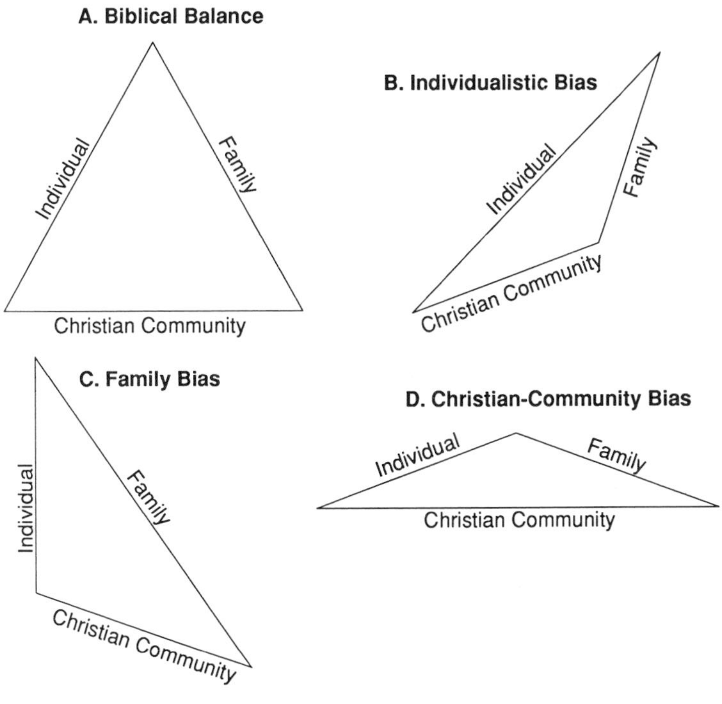

individualistic bias (B) is the most likely to have fatal consequences. Family bias (C) is typical of parental arrangements. When parents are discerning Christians, this may prove to be an acceptable system; but still there is no check on potential bias on the part of the parents. Christian-community bias (D) is probably the most difficult to detect and deal with, since it is generally felt that a corporate body will be less prone to bias. However, an obvious danger in this approach is that a particular leader or leaders of the community may wield undue clout. Such leaders are human and capable of making decisions for less than spiritually pure motives. Particularly troubling is the fact that there are some communities in which submission to the leader in such matters as marriage is regarded as a form of discipleship, and refusal to do as instructed is regarded as sin (Sparks 1977).

Even if one concedes the wisdom of our model, there is always the possibility that these three sources will disagree among themselves. Consequently, the individuals, family, and Christian community should work together to bring about a congruous decision. Such a decision will enhance the probability of a lasting commitment.

4

Establishing a Strong Marriage:
First Steps

The major preparation which people bring to marriage is their unique experience of having grown up in their particular family of origin. Accordingly, in most cultures marriage involves more than a uniting of two individuals; in reality, it is also a uniting of two extended families. The meshing of these two families is very important to the establishment of a strong marital unit. We begin, therefore, with a consideration of family background.

Resolving Issues Related to the Family of Origin

Parents as Role Models

Parents are powerful role models to their children. They teach their children through verbal communication, but their nonverbal behavior is probably even more influential. Children learn important lessons about marriage by observing how their parents communicate with one another—how they express their feelings of love, affection, and anger. Everything that parents do in their role as marriage partners will have profound influence upon their children's behaviors and attitudes as marriage partners.

No matter how good the parents' marital relationship, there are always a few things that an adult child vows to do differently. Fulfilling this vow, however, takes a very concerted and conscious effort. Since modeled behavior is such a strong conditioner, most people are not aware of how often they simply imitate their parents' actions.

Research indicates that regardless of whether we agree with the way our parents handled their marriage or parenting responsibilities, when a similar situation arises in our own family, our spontaneous reaction will be to behave exactly as our parents did. The young wife who witnessed her mother's temper whenever her father was running late for an occasion is determined that she will give her own husband the benefit of the doubt rather than lash out in anger. However, when a similar situation arises, she may scold her husband before he has a chance to explain his tardiness. The husband who may think that his father was less than considerate in not calling home when he knew he was going to be detained, nevertheless himself forgets to call his wife.

Young marrieds must make an effort to recognize and correct any faulty behavior they have picked up from their parents. It is imperative to avoid the fatalistic attitude which denies responsibility for one's own behavior by saying, "My parents have been such a strong influence on my behavior that there is nothing I can do about it!" To make excuses of this nature is tempting. A husband may say, "My wife wants me to be more open in communicating my feelings to her; she just doesn't realize that we didn't do that in my family." A wife may counter, "I can't help worrying about you when you go on a trip; my mother always worried about my father." These defeatist attitudes will not facilitate needed change.

Equally defeating is to naively believe that one's family of origin does not have any effect on one's own marital life. This leads to a denial of behavioral patterns which have similar negative outcomes in one's own marriage. Without personal awareness of these patterns, change is unlikely to occur.

Support

Research indicates that social, emotional, and financial support from parents and other relatives is a very important factor in helping a newly married couple establish a solid marriage. In an ideal situation, children have the freedom to move some distance from home for schooling or employment, and their parents remain available to them for emotional and financial support. This involves both appropriate differentiation and support. Less helpful parents will make geographical closeness a condition of continued emotional and financial support.

There is an important difference between supportive financial help and financial arrangements with undue conditions attached. Some parents are threatened by their children's independence and want to keep control. The demands which they make can undermine the newly established unit, forcing the couple to concentrate on meeting the expectations of the family of origin rather than on building up the newly formed marital dyad. The young couple that continually needs parental financial (or emotional) help has failed to accomplish the important task of establishing autonomy. This includes the ability to manage financially and to become functionally independent of parents. The manner in which supportive arrangements are made, and the accompanying attitude and expectations of both parents and married children, will determine whether such help will have positive or negative effects.

The principle of empowering can be applied here. Parents can empower their children by offering the kind of financial support and encouragement which will lead to independence and mutual respect rather than a sense of indebtedness or obligation. This is in stark contrast to parents who use money as a way to keep their married children dependent and emotionally controlled. In general, the more both sets of parents utilize the empowering process, the greater the likelihood that the couple will establish a strong marital foundation.

Differentiation

A person's identity is formed in the family of origin. In fact, until puberty it is hard to think of ourselves apart from our family. It is there we pick up the majority of our attitudes, beliefs, and values. Our self-concept is shaped by what we believe our parents think of us.

At puberty, however, differentiation begins to take place. This is the process by which teenagers establish an identity that is separate from their family. Differentiated individuals are both connected to their family and at the same time sufficiently separated socially and psychologically. It takes a great deal of emotional, intellectual, and spiritual energy to accomplish this extremely important task of sorting out and determining one's own values and beliefs rather than indiscriminately taking on the values and beliefs of one's parents. We will describe the process of adolescent differentiation in greater detail later (pp. 144–45). At this point it is sufficient to say that persons are not ready for marriage until they have clearly differentiated themselves from their parents.

There are two types of undifferentiated individuals: those who are enmeshed in their family of origin and those who are disengaged from it. Enmeshed persons are so tightly wound up with their family that there is no healthy separateness. Disengaged persons are so distanced from their family that there is no healthy connectedness.

Differentiation for the marital couple is described in Genesis 2:24: "Therefore shall a man leave his father and his mother, and shall cleave unto his wife: and they shall be one flesh" (KJV). There can be no leaving

HOW AM I EVER GOING TO DEVELOP A DIFFERENTIATED
SELF-STRUCTURE IN A FAMILY AS ENMESHED AS THIS?

of mother and father if there is a continued cleaving to them. Enmeshed persons are so overly connected with their parents that they are incapable of separating to create a new marital dyad. On the other hand, it is just as impossible to leave mother and father if there has never been a sufficient connectedness with them. Disengaged families produce children who will not know how to establish connectedness in their marriage, never having experienced the important dimension of being close and connected in their family of origin.

The concepts of enmeshment and disengagement are illustrated in the parable of the prodigal son (Luke 15:11–32). The prodigal son disengaged himself from his family. He wanted his full inheritance immediately and decided to sever all connections with his family. He cut off all social, emotional, and psychological ties by moving to a far country. On the surface this may appear to be a sign of independence and differentiation, but it proved to be premature.

One might think, on the other hand, that the son who stayed at home enjoyed a healthy, differentiated relationship with his family. But, as the story unfolds, he also appears to be undifferentiated. His reaction to his father's acceptance of his lost brother is indicative of enmeshment. A differentiated son would have established enough distance from his family that he, too, would have rejoiced to have his brother back. Instead, his jealous and angry reaction suggests that he was threatened by the belief that his father had only so much love to give, and that giving love to the younger brother meant that the father would have none left for him. He was not sufficiently separated from his family of origin, and his dependency led to possessiveness and jealousy.

Empowering would convey to both brothers in this parable that they are each unique and of equal worth, even in their differentness. There would be an assurance that love is abundant and that the father has more than enough love for both. The security that comes from such empowering can help produce differentiation: the feeling that one belongs and is connected as well as separate and independent.

The way God parented the children of Israel afforded them the possibility of achieving differentiation. God offered a covenantal love. When the children of Israel went their own way (disengaged), he held them accountable and responsible for their actions. On the other hand, God continually offered grace in the form of reconciliation and restoration. This balance of both offering emotional support and allowing independent action enhances differentiation and interdependence in relationships.

We have seen that a very important factor in establishing a solid foundation in marriage is for both partners to be differentiated from their families of origin. There can be no cleaving without leaving. When two individuals are differentiated and secure in their own identities, they can give themselves to one another and become one flesh as God intended. This means that they have a close and stable relationship with their parents and a loyalty to the system in which they were raised, but now they combine their family backgrounds into a new and distinct system.

Adaptability

People have a need for order. Scripture teaches that living in human community should be done with a sense of order. Healthy family life also needs a sense of order, yet there is a wide variation in how much order exists in contemporary families. Some families have an excessive amount of order; others have almost no order at all. For example, children's bedtimes may be observed so precisely in some families that if the youngsters are not in bed with the lights out at the prescribed minute, punishment is sure to follow. On the other hand, other families have such little regard for order that bedtimes are not even prescribed, let alone enforced. These two extremes are respective examples of very low and very high degrees of adaptability. Degree of adaptability is an important dimension which marriage partners bring with them from their family of origin (see pp. 45–47).

In general, candidates for healthy marriages come from homes which have a certain degree of flexibility (i.e., they are neither overly rigid nor chaotic). Marriages which have a capacity for adaptability wear well over time because they are more open to changes. This is especially important because change is inevitable over the various stages of married life.

But what happens when a person from a rigid home marries a person from a chaotic home? Both partners will attempt to implement their own family style, and they will be in for an interesting time to say the least! Couples who come from similar backgrounds will have an easier time. All couples will need to work out a compromise on such matters as the manner of celebrating particular holidays, resolving conflicts, and implementing various rituals such as prayer before meals. They will need to agree and establish their own set of rules and roles and rituals. In the process they will decide how adaptable they will be as a couple and eventually as a family.

The Process of Becoming One

Anytime two persons come together in a relationship as intense and demanding as marriage, one of four types of interaction is set in motion: competition, conflict, accommodation, or assimilation. Although some marriages are characterized by competition or conflict, these are not the most conducive qualities for establishing a firm marital foundation.

Assimilation is a process in which two separate entities become one, while accommodation is an agreement by two separate entities to be different. The biblical concept of one flesh might appear to be assimilation. However, the Bible also describes the relationship of the believer with Christ as becoming one with him. Does this mean that we lose our identity and personhood when we become Christians? Of course not! In fact, this is the difference between the various Eastern religions and Christianity. Salvation, according to the Eastern religions, is to acknowledge the self as an illusion and then to recognize a oneness with the eternal force in the universe. In Christianity, however, salvation is relational. It comes when the person or self is rightly related to God, the Creator and provider of eternal life.

Assimilation in marriage, where the personhood of one spouse is given up, is not Christian. Christian marriage is more like accommodation, where two separate people maintain their distinct personhood but agree to come together in a unity and oneness of commitment, meaning, and service. It is noteworthy that the key verses in Ephesians 5 which speak about the marriage relationship are introduced by the directive, "Be subject to one another" (v. 21 RSV). In Christian marriage each partner is subject to the other: each is to love and be loved, to forgive and be forgiven, to serve and be served, and to know and be known. A marriage in which one partner, the husband or the wife, is asked to give up his or her personhood for the sake of the other denies God's expression in and through a unique member of the creation. The relationship is remarkably more fulfilling when both persons are expressed equally through their union. This allows others the opportunity to know two distinct persons as well as the couple who have become one flesh.

A marital oneness or union before God does not mean there will be no conflict or differences between the spouses. Quite the contrary. Conflict is to be expected when two distinct and unique individuals express themselves equally. Marriage without conflict often signifies that one partner has given up personhood; there is agreement, but only at that partner's expense. Being subject to one's spouse does not mean giving in for the sake of avoiding conflict or maintaining harmony. In fact, giving in for the sake of avoiding conflict may be a way of letting a spouse down. Commitment involves a willingness to confront a partner in love as well as a willingness to listen when a spouse expresses a difference of opinion or is confrontational. Commitment assures a love that cares enough to listen, to understand, and to find ways to work out the conflicts.

Learning New Roles

There is a real sense in which marriage is a stage on which spouses play a multitude of roles. It is helpful to think of marriage as a role to be anticipated, learned, and played. Among the terms sociologists use to explain the process of adjusting to marriage are role taking, role playing, role conflict, and role making.

Role Taking

Before two people marry, they have each formulated in their minds a role for themselves and a role for the person they are to marry. This subjective anticipation of new roles before ever entering them is known as role taking. A rat running a maze is limited to learning by trial and error. It must randomly follow each corridor in search of food until it either reaches a dead end or finds the reward. Humans use their rich vocabulary and elaborate thinking ability to run a maze in their mind. In fact, before two people decide to get married, they both probably run through an elaborate symbolic maze by imagining what it would be like to be married to the other person for the rest of their lives. We constantly engage in role taking in anticipation of the new roles we will eventually assume.

An important ingredient in the achievement of marital adjustment is the ability to take on the role of another person. This requires empathy—

the ability to view the world from someone else's perspective and to stand in that person's shoes. Research shows that persons who have role-taking ability score high on marital-adjustment tests. It is extremely important that partners be able to see things from the point of view of their spouse. This is what understanding the other is all about.

Role Playing

After marriage, spouses engage in role playing. Role playing is the process of actually assuming the role of spouse and acting the part which has only been imagined up to this point. The first part of role playing can be called "playing at a role." Spouses play at a role to the extent that they are self-consciously unsure of themselves in their new situation.

Some very embarrassing experiences can occur when a person is merely playing at a role. A young woman straight out of graduate school will begin her college-teaching career with some insecurity and uncertainty. She will be careful to have all the right props in place. She has a new briefcase, is appropriately and professionally dressed, puts a friendly smile on her face, and walks into the classroom in a distinguished manner. She may have everything carefully planned as she is about to play at a new role. She mentally goes through the list once again: (1) Introduce self; (2) Explain the course requirements; (3) Pass out three-by-five index cards while asking the students for background information; (4) Don't forget to smile and be friendly. In the middle of the drama, she drops the entire stack of index cards out of nervousness and finds herself in an even more precarious situation. This new faculty member is still playing at a role that she is not quite sure of; it is not quite believable to either her or the class at this point.

We can engage in role taking hundreds of times. However, when we actually assume the role, we find it to be somewhat different from what we imagined. A newly married couple will experience awkwardness in playing at their new roles as spouses. It is amusing when they are caught off guard after being asked to introduce themselves to a group. Even though they are acutely aware of the fact that they are newlyweds, they are not yet accustomed to their new role as married persons. It takes time to become comfortable with the role so that it feels natural.

Role Conflict

Persons who begin marriage by playing at a role will in time become comfortable with it and start to spontaneously engage in playing the role of marital partner. Meanwhile, however, because of the expectations formed during the period of role taking, the early stages of marriage often bring role conflict. Both persons enter marriage with their own definition of what they think their role and their spouse's role should be. This can lead to confusion and difficulty.

There is a lot of emotion and expectation invested in one's new role as husband or wife—and consequently a great deal of potential conflict as well. A husband and wife may disagree in their definition of the husband's role. He may enter marriage thinking that husbands do not help with dishes, while the wife may consider this to be part of the husband's role. Similarly, a wife may view her role as including responsibility for the budget, but the husband may see this as part of his role. Such difference in perception and expectations brings forth role conflict.

Role conflict arises naturally out of differences in expectations and not necessarily because of immaturity or unpreparedness for marriage on the part of the husband or wife. Role conflict will need to be worked out through good communication and conflict-resolution skills. Marriage partners who can find ways to resolve these conflicts and agree together on how to work them out will have a solid base of operation. Those who are not able to achieve solutions are likely to struggle with these same conflicts throughout their married life.

Marital roles, unlike dramatic roles, are dynamic and ever changing. Role definitions which are appropriate in the beginning stages of marriage may be outmoded two or three years later. In the daily acts of being husband and wife, new ways of playing out roles are constantly attempted. Role taking does not stop when a couple gets married, but it continues throughout the life cycle.

A couple may have decided early in the marriage that one spouse would stay home with the children when they are young. But when that spouse begins to imagine what a full-time job outside of the home would be like (role taking), there may be role conflict. If some new course is decided upon, the couple must carefully consider how each of their roles will change. They will need to decide on such matters as housekeeping, cooking, and child care. Indeed, whenever changes occur in their relationship and life circumstances, married couples need to be aware of how their roles will be affected.

The most troublesome adjustments in marriages are those which are not clearly worked out ahead of time. The couple that makes impulsive decisions will undoubtedly experience conflict. In such situations each spouse may have unspoken expectations of which the other is unaware. Assuming that one's mate can read one's mind may lead to breakdown in the relationship. A typical example is the wife who assumes that her husband's agreement that she be employed outside the home means that he will help out in the home. When he fails to do so, she finds herself under an extra heavy load and understandably feels anger and resentment. Many women who imagine they are getting into an egalitarian marriage have learned afterward that they are expected to fill the superwoman role of doing it all.

Role Making

While the role of marriage partner is objectively defined by one's spouse, family, church, community, and society at large, it is subjectively defined by the person experiencing and performing it. There is rarely a one-to-one correlation between how a role is generally defined and how a person who is actually in that role defines it. Because each individual person is unique, role playing is always role making.

Each person plays the role of husband or wife according to one's own distinctive taste and style. Marriages in which either partner has a highly rigid definition of what the other's role should be will most likely encounter trouble. In healthy marriages each spouse is willing to let the other create and develop a uniquely personal role in accordance with God's intended purpose for that individual. This will enhance the quality of the individual and the unity in the relationship.

Let us give an example from our own marriage. During our early years together we occasionally argued over issues which we now believe were the result of overly rigid definitions of marital roles. The most conspicuous example was Jack's complaining that Judy was too much like her mother. Judy's mother happens to be a very spontaneous and expressive person who would freely wave to her grandchildren from the choir loft during church service. Such behavior would invariably embarrass Jack. Judy tended to express herself in very spontaneous ways as well. For example, when she would meet a friend in a public place, she would wave delightedly and yell out a greeting which would embarrass Jack, who was more reserved in public. He would then reprimand Judy for her behavior, since it caused him discomfort. He now looks back on his own behavior with equal embarrassment, as he recognizes that the rigidity of his role expectation for Judy resulted in his putting down and dampening her free spirit. When Judy confronted him and he took an honest look at himself, he understood what role rigidity can do. This realization led to an acceptance and appreciation of Judy as a unique person and became a significant stepping stone to growth in the relationship.

Adjustment in Marriage Roles

There are any number of reasons for adjustment in marriage: need for personal satisfaction, pressure from society, a change in responsibilities or lifestyle, or advancing age. Whatever the reason, both partners must agree about each other's role. Moreover, since both are continually changing in their roles, there is constant need for flexibility.

On occasion a marriage is adjusted at the expense of one of the partners, whose needs are not met. One spouse may give in to the demands of the other and in so doing deny his or her own personal needs. This is not in accord with what we believe adjustment entails for a Christian marriage. There must be satisfaction with the other's marital role *and* with one's own role as well. Each partner must derive fulfilment and pleasure from the marriage relationship. Out of their commitment to each other, the relationship, and the institution of marriage before their Creator, the healthy couple will be flexible and open to changes in both roles.

5

Christian Marriage:
A Model for Modern Society

While the previous chapter dealt with some of the social and psychological issues involved in marriage, this chapter will apply our theological basis for family relationships, as given in chapter 1, to marriage in modern society. It is a common mistake for Christians to attempt to defend a cultural version of marriage as the biblical ideal. This is a trap they can fall into by reading the customs of their own culture into biblical passages or by regarding the biblical accounts of specific historical marriages as normative instead of descriptive. Records of marriages during biblical times do not necessarily reflect God's intention for today.

One variety of the mistake made by Christians is to assume that what our society regards as traditional marriage is biblical. Another mistake is to uncritically endorse secular humanistic ideals and embrace modern open marriage. Somewhere between these two extremes is what we believe to be the biblical model. Table 3 summarizes the major characteristics of traditional marriage, modern marriage, and biblical marriage, comparing them in terms of the four aspects of our theological model: covenant (commitment), grace (adaptability), empowering (authority), and intimacy (communication). Close examination will show that the traditional and modern relationships fall short of the ideal.

Commitment

"Marriage is a commitment!" This rather common statement is often misunderstood. Is it really true, as is generally believed, that marriages are less stable today because people are not as committed as they were in the past? The answer is both yes and no. The emphasis in the past was on commitment to marriage as an institution. There was a feeling that a couple should stay married for life because marriage is a sacred institution. There was also more of a collective emphasis in the past, a loyalty to the group (family or community) rather than to the individual. Over the years this collective emphasis has given way to an individ-

TABLE 3

Traditional, Biblical, and Modern Marriages

Traditional	Biblical	Modern
Commitment		
Commitment (to the institution)	**Covenant** (between partners)	Contract (Self-fulfilment)
Coercive	Cohesive	Disengaged
Dutiful sex (male pleasure)	Affectionate sex (mutual pleasure)	Self-centered sex (personal pleasure)
Adaptability		
Law	**Grace**	Anarchy
Predetermined (segregated roles)	Creative (interchangeable roles)	Undetermined (undifferentiated roles)
Rigid/Stilted	Adaptable/Flexible	Chaotic
Authority		
Ascribed Power	**Empowering**	Possessive Power
Authoritarianism (male headship)	Mutual submissiveness (interdependence)	Absence of authority (no submissiveness)
Male-centered	Relationship-centered	Self-centered
Communication		
Inexpressiveness	**Intimacy**	Pseudointimacy
Pronouncement (legislation)	Discussion (negotiation)	Demand (stalemate)
Nonassertive/ Aggressive	Assertive	Aggressive

ualistic emphasis. The focus has shifted to the individual's right to personal happiness. This means that commitment to marriage as an institution is rejected if it interferes with the individual's rights to happiness and self-fulfilment.

Divorce was rare under the traditional system because of an intrinsic commitment to marriage as an institution. Divorce was unthinkable because it violated a strongly held belief that breaking down the institution was morally wrong. The youth counterculture movement of the 1960s challenged these traditional ideas and asserted that commitment to the institution was an invalid reason to remain in a marriage. It was argued that too many people were committed to institutional norms rather than to self-fulfilment. The self-fulfilment movement continued in the 1970s in the form of various sensitivity and encounter groups, and eventually an attitude of narcissism became firmly implanted in our culture.

Accordingly, in the early 1970s a dramatic rise in the divorce rate began, which was to last for nearly ten years. Social scientists now believe that one of the major reasons for this phenomenon was that persons who were unhappy increasingly turned to divorce as a way to remove themselves from their past and to find happiness. Since they believed that they had a right to personal happiness, this value took precedence over commitment to the sanctity of marriage as an institution.

In the modern open marriage, continued commitment is contingent on self-fulfilment. Indeed, one of the main criteria which sociologists now use to measure marital success is happiness. A marriage is considered successful if the partners describe themselves as happy. In many contemporary marriages, however, it seems as though the baby has been thrown out with the bathwater. Realizing that there is something missing in the concept of commitment to marriage as an institution, many people have thrown out the whole concept of commitment in favor of individual happiness. This is a tragedy because commitment is the cornerstone of the marriage relationship. The problem in the past was too narrow a definition of marriage, whereas the contemporary secular pronouncement is too narrow a definition of self-fulfilment.

The solution must include the biblical perspective that God created humans in the context of relationship. Genesis 2 recounts that God created the man and immediately saw that it was not good for the man to be alone, so he created the woman. The man recognized her as equal and complementary, bone of his bones and flesh of his flesh; they became one flesh, and were naked and not ashamed (vv. 23–25). This is a picture of interdependency.

Marriage is not only a commitment to the institution, but is also a commitment to the relationship. The relationship is vital in and of itself, and it needs to be nourished in order to grow. The commitment of Yahweh

to Israel as depicted in the Book of Hosea provides a beautiful example of a commitment that endures, renews, forgives, and restores.

Marriages are strong if both partners are committed to the institution, to the relationship, and to each other as persons. Commitment only to the institution results in legalism; commitment only to the relationship results in idealism; commitment only to the other person results in humanism. A commitment to all three (person, institution, and relationship) results in balance. Such an approach takes into account the importance of caring for the needs of the individual, the relationship, and the social system.

A balanced commitment will be reflected in the view toward sexuality. In traditional marriage, sex is viewed as a right to pleasure for the male and as a duty to be endured by the female. In open marriage, sex tends to be self-centered, with the emphasis placed upon the individual's right to personal pleasure. Sex manuals have become technique-oriented, focusing on those techniques which can bring the greatest sexual pleasure to oneself, and incidentally to one's spouse. There is much to be said for the idea that married persons are to be fulfilled sexually, but when this becomes the dominant emphasis, the relationship suffers and thus the real meaning of sexuality is lost.

The biblical response emphasizes affectionate sex in marriage. Scripture advocates mutual pleasure and mutual benefit. This involves a mutual decision to give and receive in love. First Corinthians 7:3-4 clearly states that our bodies are for one another as the ultimate expression of ourselves to each other.

The security that stems from a commitment to the marriage relationship provides an atmosphere of freedom and willingness to learn together through the sexual expression of love. By mutually accepting each other a couple can discover ways to mesh together as sexual persons in the security of a committed marriage. The biblical ideal, then, is much more than one person's deriving sexual pleasure, or one spouse's submitting to the other out of commitment to the institution of marriage. It is learning to knit together intimately at all levels: body, mind, and soul. The scriptural concept of one flesh entails a mutual commitment before God to be faithful to one's mate, the relationship, and the institution.

Adaptability

In traditional marriage the roles are segregated. While the husband usually assumes the role of working outside of the home, the wife assumes the role of homemaking and caring for the children. Most persons who argue for separation in marital roles are not aware of how recent a phenomenon this is. Until the Industrial Revolution 90 percent of all families lived on farms, and even as late as one hundred years ago two-thirds of all families in the United States lived on farms. That the marital roles there were far from segregated will be no surprise to anyone who has ever lived on a farm. Whereas some kinds of work were designated as the man's or the woman's province, both husbands and wives did manual labor on the farm, and both shared the responsibility of parenting their children.

Segregation in marital roles developed only with the emergence of the urban family, where home life and work life are divided. In this type of family the husband works outside of the home, leaving child care to the wife. One would be hard pressed to argue, on the basis of either history or biblical evidence, that woman's place is in the home and man's place is in the business world outside the home.

When the advocates of open marriage react against the segregation in the traditional system, they tend to prescribe that marital roles be undifferentiated, that is to say, that there be no agreement designating which marriage partner will assume a given responsibility. In an open marriage the various tasks to be done are worked out according to a system of social exchange. This system is based on the simple assumption that all relationships involve costs and rewards. That which one gives to a relationship is experienced as a cost, and that which one receives is experienced as a reward. Marriages thrive when the rewards outweigh the costs for each partner. As long as one gets more than or as much as one gives, there is no reason to abandon the relationship. The concept of social exchange can be stated as a formula: Rewards − Costs = Profit.

Let's imagine that a couple in an open marriage is trying to decide who will cook the evening meal. The conversation may begin with the husband's suggesting that his wife cook, pointing out that he has had a hard day at the office and he also cooked the previous night. The wife may respond that she has had an equally hard day at work and that she cooked dinner three out of the last four evenings. The husband may then suggest that he will cook if she will clean up, wash the dishes, and take out the garbage. The point here is that unless partners possess good bargaining and negotiating skills, disaster looms where roles are not clearly differentiated.

We suggest that roles be differentiated, but not segregated. In segregation certain tasks are considered female and others male, with no room for interchange. Those who argue this position will have to depend on cultural evidences rather than on the Bible for support. Role differentiation, on the other hand, means that husbands and wives agree to serve one another by taking on assigned tasks which contribute to the maintenance of the household. These tasks will be reviewed periodically so that they may be reassigned or exchanged at appropriate times.

Although there are no Bible verses which specifically deal with marital roles, Scripture does teach that everything ought to be done with a sense of order and harmony, consideration and love. Assigning tasks on the basis of a person's interests, skills, or availability is a loving way to work out marital roles. It also respects differences and recognizes the unique talents of each spouse to contribute in special ways to the marital relationship.

Of the various tasks to be performed, parenting is without question one of the most crucial. In the traditional family which has emerged in our urban technological society, most parenting is done by the mother. This occurs to the detriment and neglect of fathering, which is the weakest aspect of child rearing in our society today.

In open marriages, parenting roles and responsibilities may be shirked as each parent pursues personal happiness and fulfilment. Now we would certainly not deny that day care for children is an important responsibility of our society to parents who must be in the work force, especially single parents. Good child-care facilities are crucial for these children in light of the obvious economic hardship such a family bears. However, some parents choose to escape the difficult role of parenting by making use of child-care facilities so they can fulfil their own personal goals. They fail to make parenting a high priority in their lives.

In a balanced marriage both the mother and father are actively involved in the parenting process. There is no biblical evidence which would lead one to believe that a mother's involvement with children is more important than a father's involvement. Rather, Scripture refers to the responsibility of both parents, as in Ephesians 6:3–4: "Children, obey your parents, for it is right that you should. 'Honour your father and mother.' . . . You fathers, again, must not goad your children to resentment, but give them the instruction, and the correction, which belong to a Christian upbringing" (NEB). Dual parenting seems especially critical today since breakdown in the family system is often related to the lack of effective fathering.

In the traditional marriage, roles are stilted and rigidly defined. There is very little flexibility as to how they may be performed. In the open marriage, expectations are so loose that marital roles can be described as truly chaotic. Without any set procedures to bring stability to these roles, the marriage relationship will be very confusing. The balanced marriage will have flexible and interchangeable roles as each occasion calls forth what is needed.

Since change can be expected throughout a marriage relationship and the cycles of family life, it is vital that marriages be flexible and adaptable. Married life and family life are at their best when they are neither predetermined nor undetermined, but when they have structured security. This structured security allows spouses and family members to experience the extraordinary process of each working for the good of the whole. Family members can be served and be empowered to serve others as they cooperate together in working out marital and family roles.

Authority

Authority in marriage is currently a controversial issue among Christians. Until very recent times, authority in marriage has exclusively meant male headship. Christians and non-Christians alike have adhered to the idea that the husband is to be the head of the home, whereas the wife is expected to submit to her husband. Now, however, there are both an emphasis on mutual submission and a focus on the servanthood role of the husband, who is directed to love, serve, and submit to his wife just as Christ gave his life for the church.

Modern opposition to the traditional marriage and the current cultural emphasis on individualism have contributed to the weakening of authority and hierarchy in marriage. Open marriage stresses democracy, freedom, and the right to self-fulfilment, all of which work against traditional patterns.

Once again the system of social exchange comes into play. The idea is that two persons are likely to stay in a marriage relationship if they are receiving from the marriage at least as much as they are giving. It's the quid pro quo notion of getting something for something—"if you scratch my back, I'll scratch yours." Partners are satisfied as long as everything comes out equal and neither partner perceives that there is a better alternative outside the marriage relationship. In such a marriage the authority or decision-making power belongs to the spouse who has more to offer in terms of money, sex, love, nurture, protection, security, or whatever else the partner may value.

Under a system of social exchange, negotiation is the way to deal with conflict and make decisions. Each partner, from a rather self-centered perspective, tries to maximize the returns on his or her investments in the marriage. Accordingly, research shows that in this system wives who work outside the home have greater power in the marriage relationship than do wives who do not. The money earned can be converted into power, thus elevating the authority of the wife in the marriage.

It should be noted that the system of social exchange is built on an assumption about human beings which is consistent with Christian thought, namely, that people are basically self-centered by nature. In reality, social exchange is a fairly good model to describe how many modern marriages operate. We would, however, question the assumption that self-centeredness should be held up as the ideal. The Christian world-view, by contrast, entails self-giving love and going the extra mile.

Authority in Christian marriage involves dual submission to the lordship of Jesus Christ and to one another. Another view is that the wife should submit to the husband, who in turn is to submit to God. This chain-of-command view, popular in many conservative Christian circles, often fails to focus on the New Testament teaching of mutual loving, serving, and forgiving.

Ephesians 5:21, "Be subject to one another out of reverence for Christ"

(NEB), is crucial in this connection. It sets the foundation for the verses that follow. Husbands are told, "Love your wives, as Christ also loved the church and gave himself up for it" (v. 25). From this it is clear that headship, if that is the view one espouses, is to be understood not in the hierarchical sense of the husband's lording it over his wife, but rather in the sense of taking the role of a suffering servant. Christ's example as a compassionate servant who gave his life for his bride, the church, is the model of how the husband is to act as head. Wives, too, are called to this same self-giving, suffering-servant role. Mutual submissiveness, then, is the overriding message of Ephesians 5.

Communication

In the traditional marriage there is little need for verbal communication. What communication there is tends to take the form of pronouncements, a talking at one's spouse rather than a talking with one's spouse. The husband as head of the marriage legislates without consulting his wife. When conflicts or delicate matters arise, they are often dealt with by side-stepping the issue. The reason verbal communication is de-emphasized is that meeting socioemotional and companionship needs is not considered to be a major part of marriage. Marriage is regarded more as an institutional arrangement which provides for economic needs and social status.

Communication in the modern open marriage can be characterized as a series of declarations and demands which each spouse makes of the other. When conflicts arise, confrontation is the way to get one's needs and disappointments out on the table. The motto is, "Openly express what you feel you need from your mate." While such openness can be refreshing when compared to the traditional pattern, a combative posture and insistence on satisfying personal needs will obviously obstruct a sensitive caring for the other. Making aggressive demands, such as "I want my needs met regardless of how you are affected," results in counterdemands which ultimately lead to stalemate.

In a balanced marriage, the partners will communicate by expressing themselves in a caring and concerned manner. When one talks, the other will listen. They will want what is best for their partner. Differences will be dealt with by respecting the other's needs and desires. There will be an effort to understand each other's point of view and to respond with empathy. There will be an attitude of submission and a willingness to consider giving up one's own needs and desires for the sake of the other and the relationship. Both spouses will work together to seek solutions through mutual acceptance, commitment, forgiveness, and servanthood.

When we asked our friends Gene and Virginia the secret of their fifty-year marriage, Gene teased, "You have to be willing to give up!" We laughed a little about the way his answer could be interpreted, but after thinking about what he had said it seemed rather profound. This is, indeed, what it takes to be a servant: a willingness to give up one's own needs for the sake of the relationship. Philippians 2 describes Christ as emptying himself and taking on the form of a servant. This is how one becomes submissive and loving in relationships. It takes an attitude of giving up and letting go. To do so is very difficult, but true love requires allowing one's mate to affirm self-identity. True love does not cling to one's own agenda for one's spouse. Rather, it requires a giving up of control and one's own desires and expectations for the partner. This is what a commitment to one's spouse as a person is all about.

It is true that to have any union, partnership, or interdependence, we must be able to give up something of our own needs and desires. If both partners come to marriage with this kind of attitude and perspective, they will find a common ground of joy and satisfaction. They will benefit both as individuals and in their marriage relationship as well.

PART 3

Parenting:
The Expansion of Family Life

Introduction

I n this section we move beyond the marriage relationship to parent/child relationships. It is a universal truth that an enormous amount of change occurs when a child comes into the family. For some couples the change from the dyad to the triad is smooth, whereas for others the transition to parenthood is a difficult and trying time. While the marriage is the foundation of family life, children are the building blocks through which the family structure grows. Like any sound structure, the family must have well-planned, carefully organized blueprints if it is to survive the twists and turns of life. The following chapters will present some of the blueprints for living with children.

Chapter 6 introduces a model of Christian parenting which encourages and emphasizes the development of children into mature, healthy, functional adults. We will look at the pros and cons of some common parenting styles and then offer a biblical model which we believe incorporates the best of these styles. We will propose that as children mature, parents must also mature in order for mutual empowering to occur.

In chapter 7 we look at the life of the child from the perspective of several developmental theories. We will evaluate how these theories comport with the Christian view of human personhood and will then utilize them in discussing some important aspects of parenting young children. A primary concern in this discussion will be the matter of empowering.

Finally, in chapter 8 we examine the stresses and strains of adolescence and midlife. Included in this discussion is our theory of the origin of the adolescent stage in American society. Whenever adolescence and midlife, both of which are often accompanied by crisis, strike a family simultaneously (a not infrequent occurrence), there may be far-reaching negative effects.

6

The Goal of Parenting:
Empowering Children to Maturity

We live in a technique-oriented society. On any topic from growing flowers to creating scrumptious gourmet dishes to raising children we can find a hundred and one how-to formulas which promise that the right technique will produce beautiful flowers, succulent meals, and perfect children. This may work for flowers and gourmet dishes, but children and parenting are more complex than that. In fact, in most societies parents simply expect their children to grow up to be normal, healthy adults—no special techniques are deemed necessary. In our society, though, we are conditioned to believe just the opposite—we presume that we will fail as parents and therefore need the experts to tell us how to be successful. Parents are sometimes reduced to a state of fear that they may do something that will have a lasting harmful effect on their children. As a result of this insecurity they have increasingly turned to the experts for advice on how to raise children. We have, in fact, developed a cult of the expert as parents keep keen eyes and ears concentrated on the "Phil Donahue Show," "Dear Abby," or James Dobson's "Focus on the Family" for the latest pearls of wisdom on parenting. Living as we do in a very child-oriented society, we are extremely sensitive and concerned about our parenting role. We are personally involved with our children's success or failure because we perceive it as a reflection on ourselves as parents.

As contributors to the growing body of expert opinion, we would hasten to add that we have no quarrel with listening to expert opinion, but rather with the dogmatism of some of the advice given. Parents begin to feel their own judgments are not to be trusted. We advocate informing parents about child development and parenting methods, but also encourage them to critically analyze the information and compare it with biblical principles. Effective parenting will also take into account the particular needs of the family and incorporate or discard ideas accordingly.

The Christian life is described in various New Testament passages as growth from spiritual infancy to maturity. The new believer starts as an infant and eventually grows up in Christ. One moves from a state of dependency, in which others model, teach, and disciple, to a mature walk with God. As this growth occurs, the believer also begins to assume discipling responsibility for others. While it is true that the believer is always dependent on God and the Holy Spirit in that growth process (sanctification), there is also a natural progression in maturity which leads the believer to be used by God to serve and minister to others.

In the human developmental process there is a similar progression from dependency and infancy toward maturity and adulthood. Maturity is often defined as self-sufficiency and independence from one's parents. Most developmental theorists, however, hold that maturity involves more than independence; it also entails the capacity to contribute in a positive and constructive way to the good of others.

The notion of empowering is described in the New Testament as a building up of one another in the Christian faith. It involves loving and serving others and helping them mature spiritually. This description is consistent with the social-science literature regarding the type of parenting which helps children mature. The parenting model we will present in this chapter stresses the interaction of the parent/child relationship. Each parent and child is developing and maturing throughout the entire process. We believe that our model, which places an emphasis on empowering children to maturity, is a needed alternative to other Christian models which emphasize control and power. Our model is based on engendering hope and growth in parents and children as they journey together toward maturity.

Speaking for a moment from our personal experience as parents rather than as experts, we would suggest that parents concentrate less on the technique of good parenting and more on the process of being a parent. Good parenting is a matter of interacting with our children day in and day out. It is these day-to-day experiences which build our relationship with them. The best advice that we can give to parents is to throw away their how-to-parent books and simply become real persons to their children. Even though these materials offer useful guidelines which contribute to an understanding of the child-rearing process, it is also true that parents can function more freely and openly in their role if they are simply willing to be more genuine with their children.

Parenting Styles

Now that we have dispelled the notion that there is one correct way to develop perfect children, let us investigate what the social-science literature says about various parenting styles and their effects upon children. Parents and other primary caretakers have a significant impact on their children's emotional, social, cognitive, and spiritual development. While some parenting styles encourage growth and are empowering, many others hinder or block growth either by fostering dependency or by expecting self-reliance prematurely.

Early research into parent/child relationships distinguished between permissive and restrictive parenting. Proponents of permissive parenting, while not denying the need for discipline, stressed that a child's greatest need is for warmth and security. The restrictive school of thought, while not rejecting parental affection, emphasized that a child's greatest need is for discipline, responsibility, and self-control (Miller and Swanson 1958).

More-recent studies have taken the same approach, but use the terms *control* and *support* instead of restrictive and permissive parenting. In their review of the literature between 1960 and 1974 Boyd Rollins and Darwin Thomas (1979) identify 235 studies on the influence of these two factors. Support is defined as making the child feel comfortable in the presence of the parent and giving the child a sense of being accepted and approved as a person. Control is defined as directing the child to behave in a manner desirable to the parents (Rollins and Thomas 1979:321). Examples of control include giving guidelines and setting limits.

In one of the most comprehensive investigations into the effects of parental support and parental control upon children, Diana Baumrind (1967, 1978) identified three types of parents—authoritative, authoritarian, and permissive. She found that a combination of high levels of control and support, a style which she called "authoritative," is most conducive to developing competency in children. She suggested that an authoritarian style (low support and high control) produces children who have a respect for authority, but show little independence and only moderate social competence. Permissive parenting (high support and low control) tends to produce children who lack both social competence and interdependence.

Another body of research has focused upon the socioemotional and instrumental aspects of parenting. Research on small groups has found that there are two basic types of leadership (Slater 1961). Instrumental leadership is task-oriented, focusing on the things that need to be accomplished in the group. Such leadership organizes activities, sets goals, and generally keeps the group focused on accomplishing those goals. Socioemotional leadership, on the other hand, is person-oriented, concentrating on maintaining a healthy relationship between group members. Research indicates that both types of leadership skills are necessary if small groups are to function. Interestingly enough, it has also been discovered that the two types of skills are rarely found in the same individual.

The studies on instrumental and socioemotional leadership in small groups apply to the family as well. Instrumental parenting aims at inculcating beliefs, values, and attitudes. It involves teaching children what they must know and how they must behave to be in good standing within the family. Socioemotional parenting attends to the emotional nature of the relationship between parents and children. Whereas instrumental parenting focuses on tasks and content, socioemotional parenting focuses on the affective bonding between parent and child (Zelditch 1955; Crano and Aronoff 1978).

Having briefly defined parental support and control, as well as instrumental and socioemotional aspects of parenting, we are ready to combine these two areas of concern in order to discuss alternative styles of parenting and their effects upon children. Our strategy will be to consider various instrumental styles and then several socioemotional approaches.

Instrumental Parenting

Figure 10 represents the four styles of instrumental parenting. Two dimensions are involved: action and content. Parenting styles can be classified as either high or low in action. That is, some parents actually engage in and thus demonstrate the type of behavior they want their children to adopt; other parents make no such effort. Likewise, parenting styles can be either high or low in content. Some parents verbally communicate through a rich elaboration of rules, norms, values, beliefs, and ideology; others simply do not bother to teach their children.

Neglecting. Parenting which is low in both action and content we call the neglecting style. Proper behavior is neither displayed nor taught. Because no direction is given either verbally or otherwise by the parents, the children are on their own to latch on to any social norm or form of behavior. The parent who is neglectful in instrumental parenting is also likely to be neglectful in socioemotional parenting. This style leaves much to be desired, since the children lack good supportive care and must learn by trial and error to fend for themselves.

Teaching. Parenting which is low in action and high in content we call the teaching style. The parent in effect says to the child, "Do as I say, but don't look to my behavior as a model." Children in such a situation feel

FIGURE 10 **Styles of Instrumental Parenting**

Action

	High	Low
High	Discipling	Teaching
Low	Modeling	Neglecting

Content

that they are being preached at. Though this style may be effective in bringing about the desired behavior in the children, it may also breed disrespect for the parents, whose words do not match their lives. As children mature, they become increasingly sensitive to any form of contradictory behavior in their parents. The typical teenager is quick to point out such inconsistency.

In spite of its shortcomings, teaching is better than the neglecting style. The teaching style does become a problem for children, however, when there is incongruence between the parents' teaching and behavior. It may be that the parents do not intentionally cause this confusion, for they truly believe in and desire to live up to the standards they enunciate, but fail to do so.

Modeling. Parenting which is high in action and low in content we call the modeling style. It also is only partially effective in that a child must rely entirely upon the behavior of parents in order to gain a system of values, norms, and beliefs. Modeling does have some advantage over the teaching style, however. While the teaching style lacks behavior to back it up, the modeling style offers the behavior (but with little or no explanation of the values behind it). The old adage that what children learn is caught rather than taught applies here, and parents will find that modeling is an effective way to inculcate values and desired behavior in their children. Recent research has verified the effectiveness of modeling.

Discipling. Parenting which is high in action and content we call discipling. This style is complete in that parents teach their children by word and by deed. It is curious, however, that while the concept of discipling is popular in the contemporary church, it is rarely used to refer to parental training.

Unfortunately, the terms *discipline* and *punishment* are often confused in our society. The question at issue is whether parents should physically punish (by spanking or other means) their children. Physical punishment is defended by some Christians on the basis of verses like Proverbs 13:24, "He who spares the rod hates his son" (NIV). However, it is important to consider how the rod was used in the pastoral culture of Old Testament times. It was an instrument to guide ignorant sheep, not a means of beating them into submission. Note how the verse concludes: ". . . but he who loves him [his son] is careful to discipline him." The term *discipline* is related to the word *disciple,* which refers to one who accepts certain ideas or values, and leads or guides others to accept them as well. Discipling, then, is a system of giving positive guidance to children.

Socioemotional Parenting

Figure 11 represents the four styles of socioemotional parenting. Here again there are two dimensions, support and control, each of which can be classified as high or low. The four styles depicted should be thought of as hypothetical rather than precisely representative of the way any one person engages in parenting.

Neglectful parenting. The easiest style to criticize is neglectful parenting because of its obvious shortcomings. Where there are low levels of support and control, very little bonding develops between parents and children. There are many homes, particularly those where economic factors play a devastating role, where children are indeed neglected. This parenting style can also be found in homes where our modern individualistic society leaves little time to meet the demands of caring for and providing sufficient structure for the children. The latchkey child may be a victim of this system. Single parents have little choice and agonize over the fact that there is not adequate time for providing support and exercising control since so many other demands are made on them.

There are those who advocate this very free lifestyle for children. They see no need to teach morals; rather, children should experiment and come to their own conclusions about personal values. This philosophy emphasizes the child's right of freedom to discover one's own beliefs and lifestyle, and suggests that character is built by allowing children to make their own way in the world.

This low-control, low-support style of parenting is characteristic of disengaged families in which each member's life rarely touches the others

FIGURE 11 **Styles of Socioemotional Parenting**

Support

	High	Low
Control High	Authoritative	Authoritarian
Control Low	Permissive	Neglectful

in any meaningful way. It is also characteristic of many urban families in which both parents work outside the home or in which there is only one parent. The tentativeness which many people show in making a commitment to another person may be a result of being reared in a neglectful home.

Christopher Lasch (1977) believes that a home without an authority figure is fertile ground for the authoritarian leader, group, or cult that preys on neglected young people. Indeed, some of the recent literature suggests that most recruits to the authoritarian cults come from neglectful homes. These individuals hunger for a strong and strict leader to follow and obey without question. Such people are most susceptible to the dictates of an authoritarian figure, because they have never experienced a bonding with any authority figure. Such persons lack a developed superego (internalized societal rules) to serve as a guide and rule for their behavior. Lacking a value base, they often yield themselves to an authoritarian cult leader who in essence becomes their superego. Needless to say, there is no biblical support for the neglectful home.

Authoritarian parenting. When support is low and control high, we have what is called authoritarian parenting. A partial bonding between parents and children takes place in such homes. The children are likely to be respectful and obedient to their parents. What is missing, because of a lack in the bonding process, is a sense of warmth, openness, and intimacy between parents and children.

In a variation of the authoritarian style, the father is cast in the role of the instrumental leader who expects obedience from his children and teaches them what they need to know, while the mother assumes a socioemotional role. Thus there is high emotional support in the home, but only on the part of one parent—the one who is not seen as the ultimate authority figure.

This pattern is found in many Far Eastern cultures. In Korea it is believed that a warm, intimate relationship between parent and child automatically forfeits the child's respect for and the authority of the parent. For this reason Korean fathers do not get too emotionally close to their children. This parenting style was also prevalent among European immigrant families of the nineteenth century. In addition, it is common in most patriarchal agrarian societies. While it seems unproductive to dichotomize the parenting roles, this may be the most widespread style of our day, a result of the industrialized society. Dad was taken out of the home and assigned most of the instrumental tasks, while Mom was left at home and assigned the relational ones.

Permissive parenting. Where control is low and support high, we have permissive parenting. It is based upon the assumption that a newborn is like a rosebud, needing only tender love and support in order to blossom slowly into a beautiful flower. Present-day permissive parenting is traced back to the ideals of the counterculture movement of the 1960s, which can in turn be traced back to the Bohemian morality of a century earlier (B. Berger 1967). The thinking here is that every child has special potentialities at birth which are destroyed by societal rules and standards. Therefore, children need to be allowed to find their own purpose through free expression. During the 1960s this philosophy came to be expressed in the phrase, "Do your own thing."

Noticeably absent from the permissive style is any idea that children tend to be quite self-centered and need parental guidance in learning values and interpersonal skills. Consequently, children raised in permissive homes tend to lack a sense of social responsibility; they also fail to develop interdependence.

Authoritative parenting. Authoritative parents combine the best qualities found in the authoritarian and permissive styles. Authoritative parents

attempt to direct the child in a rational, issue-oriented manner; encourage verbal give and take, explain the reasons behind demands and discipline but also use power when necessary; expect the child to conform to adult requirements but also to be independent and self-directing; recognize the rights of both adults and children; set standards and enforce them firmly.

These parents [do] not regard themselves as infallible but also [do] not base decisions primarily on the child's desires. [Maccoby 1980:376]

It has been well documented that socially competent children are products of homes in which the parenting style is authoritative. Social competence results when parents attend to their children's self-esteem, academic achievement, cognitive development, creativity, moral behavior, and instrumental abilities. Children thrive in such an environment of high support and high control.

Note, however, that parental control can take different forms. It has been found that certain kinds of control are more effective and produce better results than do others (Rollins and Thomas 1979; Peterson and Rollins 1987). For example, a coercive approach forcing children to act against their will usually results in low levels of social competence. Withdrawing one's love in order to obtain compliance tends to be almost as ineffective. Inductive control—giving explanations, using reasoning, and encouraging a child's voluntary compliance by avoiding direct conflict of wills—proves to be the most effective. Coupling this type of control with strong emotional support will produce competent children.

A Biblical Model of Parenting

Having summarized the social-science literature on the effects of various parenting styles, we will now present a biblical model, with the goal of eventually integrating these various materials into a model of Christian parenting.

An all-too-common method of presenting a biblical model of parenting consists of picking out verses from Scripture and then arranging them as one would arrange flowers. Such bouquets of Bible verses are designed to support the particular point of view held by the arranger (this method has yielded biblical models of parenting to support virtually every conceivable position along the restrictive-permissive continuum). Such a method, when devoid of exegetical analysis, results in an abuse of scriptural data and yields rather shallow and simplistic models of parenting.

We believe that a biblical model of parenting can be derived from the scriptural depiction of God as parent. Myron Chartier (1978) has marshaled the biblical evidence to show that God displays parental love in seven ways. (1) God cares for people. Although this is preeminently demonstrated in the incarnation, death, and resurrection of Christ, numerous other biblical passages stress the caring nature of God (Luke 15:11–32; 1 Pet. 5:7). (2) God is responsive to human needs. This can be seen in the covenant that was established after the flood (Gen. 9:8–17), in the rescue of Israel from Egypt, and in the free offer of mercy and restoration

(John 3:16; Titus 3:3–7). (3) God bestows the richest gifts on us—the only begotten Son and the Holy Spirit as Comforter. (4) God shows respect for, values, and cherishes us; there is no attempt to dominate, and we are given the freedom to be ourselves. (5) God knows us, for Jesus came in human likeness (John 1:14; Phil. 2:5–8; Heb. 2:17–18; 4:15); this is a knowledge which penetrates to the core of our existence (Ps. 44:21; John 2:25). (6) God forgives (Matt. 26:28; John 3:16–17; Eph. 1:7). (7) God disciplines us (Prov. 3:11–12; Heb. 12:5–8; Rev. 3:19). The discipline of Israel can be seen as an attempt to create a faithful and obedient people.

Taken as a whole the biblical emphasis is clearly on the love and grace which God so freely gives. However, this unconditional love is not free of expectations and demands. God's love includes disciplinary action for our good. His love as parent bears a striking similarity to the parenting style advocated in the social-science literature: a high degree of support and of inductive (rather than coercive) control.

The actions of God as parent clearly point to a model in which parental love (support) and discipline (control) intertwine to help children develop toward maturity. This model comports well with the theological basis for family relationships which we introduced in chapter 1—covenant, grace, empowering, and intimacy. Parent/child relationships begin when the parents make an initial covenant (a one-way unconditional commitment) of love with their child. Although the infant cannot return this commitment, it is desirable that as the child matures, the initial covenant grow into a mature covenant (a two-way unconditional commitment). This maturing of the parent/child relationship is possible because the covenant commitment establishes an environment of grace and forgiveness in which parents can empower their children and reach new levels of intimacy with them. Intimacy is defined here as a mutual knowing and caring in which there is no embarrassment or shame.

In an ideal situation, the four elements of the parent/child relationship are in a continual process of maturing: intimacy leads to deeper covenant love, which enhances the atmosphere of grace, which strengthens the empowering process, which leads to deepened intimacy, and so on. This cycle is relational and requires reciprocity. The foundation consists of a faithful commitment and accepting environment where children and parents can be vulnerable and open with one another. This allows the empowering process to flourish, as parents and children serve and give to one another.

Empowering is obviously the central element in our biblical model of parenting. Exactly what is involved here? We know, of course, that differences in status and resources place parents in a position of power over their children, and that power is defined in the conventional social-science literature as the ability to influence others (Safilios-Rothschild

1970; Scanzoni 1979; McDonald 1980; Szinovacz 1987). Good parenting is the wise exercising of that position and ability. Empowering is the process of instilling confidence, of strengthening and building children up to become more powerful and competent. The most effective empowerers are those individuals who have themselves been empowered by the unconditional love of God and the Holy Spirit.

Jesus came to empower others to have abundant life. His model for human relationships shows that empowering entails serving others. Witness his radical reply to the disciples who wanted to sit in powerful positions with him in glory: "Whoever wants to become great among you must be your servant, and whoever wants to be first must be slave of all. For even the Son of Man did not come to be served, but to serve, and to give his life as a ransom for many" (Mark 10:43–45 NIV). Jesus redefined power by his teaching and by his action in relating to others as a servant. He rejected the use of power to control others, and affirmed instead the use of power to serve others, to lift up the fallen, to forgive the guilty, to encourage responsibility and maturity in the weak, and to enable the unable.

The capacity to be a servant to others requires a high level of maturity and unconditional love. It demands that a person achieve a maturity that goes beyond self-sufficiency to interdependency. Abundant life is more than a narcissistic euphoria in which all of one's personal needs and desires are met. It involves having a meaning beyond oneself. The admonitions in the New Testament to submit to one another, to love, forgive, serve, and value all of God's people, are actually a call to mature living.

Jesus' relationship to his disciples should be understood in terms of empowering. He even provided for a continuation of the process after his departure: "But your Advocate, the Holy Spirit whom the Father will send in my name, will teach you everything, and will call to mind all that I have told you" (John 14:26 NEB). He wanted them to have the capacity and confidence to carry on the message. They had been prepared by his teaching ministry to be independent and by his example to be servants.

Parents who are empowerers will help their children become competent and capable persons who will in turn empower others. Empowering parents will be actively and intentionally engaged in various pursuits—teaching, guiding, caring, modeling—which will equip their children to become confident individuals able to relate to others. Parents who empower will help their children recognize the strengths and potentials within and find ways to enhance these qualities. Parental empowering is the affirmation of the child's ability to learn, grow, and become all that one is meant to be as part of God's image and creative plan.

Empowering, from a biblical perspective, does not entail the child's gaining power at the expense of the parent. The view that the supply of

AND JUST WHY DO YOU FEEL I'M KEEPING
YOU FROM GROWING UP?

power is limited is purely secular. When empowering the children of Israel, God did not give up power, but rather offered it in unlimited supply. Jesus' authority (*exousia*) flowed from his personhood; it was in no way diminished when he empowered his disciples. Similarly, the authority of parents, which flows from their personhood, is not diminished when they exercise the responsibility to nurture their children to maturity. The process of empowering them does not mean relinquishing parental authority, nor are parents depleted or drained of power when they empower their children. Rather, when empowering takes place, authority and ascribed power are retained as children develop, grow, and achieve a sense of personal power, self-esteem, and wholeness. Successful parenting will result in the children's gaining as much personal power as the parents themselves have. In the Christian context, children who have been empowered love God and their neighbors as themselves. They are capable of going beyond themselves to reach out to others.

Christian Parenting: Empowering to Maturity

Figure 12 is a visual representation of the process by which Christian parenting empowers children to reach maturity. The bell-shaped line is the empowering curve, which represents the levels of parental control and socioemotional support. Note that these levels vary with the different styles of parenting (telling, teaching, participating, delegating). At the extreme left very little empowering is being done. Here we find parents who perpetuate dependency in their children. At the extreme right the children have reached the goal of empowerment, the opposite of dependence.

The first parenting style is *telling*, which is characterized by one-way communication—parents tell their children what to do. This parenting style is needed when children are young and unable to do things on their

FIGURE 12 **Christian Parenting: Empowering to Maturity**

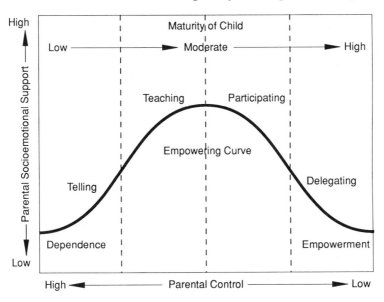

Adapted from Paul Hersey and Kenneth Blanchard, *Management of Organizational Behavior*, 4th ed. (Englewood Cliffs, N.J.: Prentice-Hall, 1988), p. 287.

own. During their early years children need the clear directions and close supervision which telling provides. Exercising a high level of control, the parents clearly define the tasks to be performed, telling their children what is to be done, as well as where, when, and how. Socioemotional support is minimal, but is offered as a reward for compliance. (It needs to be stressed that in this connection low socioemotional support has reference only to the tasks which the parents are trying to get the child to master. At this stage they will of course need to give much unconditional socioemotional support. In fact, young children probably need more unconditional [non-task-related] socioemotional support from their parents than will be required at any subsequent stage of development.)

The second parental style, *teaching,* is best for children who are low to moderate in maturity. As children move into latency, they may be willing to take responsibility for specific tasks or functions, but not always know how to do them. Teaching involves moderately high levels of both control and socioemotional support. Teaching differs from telling in that communication can be two-way. Children at this age ask many questions and are able to learn through dialogue and discussion; in time they can be encouraged to attempt to find their own answers. Most of the communication, however, is still done by the parents, who must decide when to reduce the amount of direct instruction and increase the level of task-related socioemotional support.

At the third stage, *participating,* parents become player-coaches who directly engage in activities with their children. Instruction is still taking place, but proper behavior is modeled in addition to being taught. This parenting style is particularly good for children who are moderately to highly mature, the level of a typical preteenager. Although preteenagers may have the ability to do certain tasks and carry out fairly important responsibilities, they typically lack the confidence to do so. Participating parents encourage their children to begin doing things in their own ways; in that process the amount of parental control is reduced. Participating parents encourage their children to be their own persons, allowing them to learn through trial and error and offering support and consolation when needed.

The *delegating* style is for highly mature children who are both able and willing to take responsibility and perform tasks on their own. In delegating responsibility, parents do not need to exercise a high level of control or give a substantial amount of socioemotional support. While a continued high level of socioemotional support may on the surface appear to be desirable, an overabundance of it could be interpreted as a sign of lack of confidence in the child.

Parents whose children mature to the point where the delegating style is in order are often simultaneously empowered by them. Parenthetically, we might observe that willingness to learn from and be empowered by one's children is a sign of parental maturity. Reciprocal giving and receiving is an indication of a mature relationship. Parents who can let go and give increasing amounts of freedom to their children at appropriate stages are showing respect for and belief in them. This is an empowering experience for the child, especially if the letting go is done with a genuine blessing and not with reluctance and conditional love. With the added measure of freedom the teenager will often make independent choices and express opinions different from those held by the parents. This is the beginning of an adult relationship of mutual respect that empowers children to become their own persons. Through reciprocal giving and serving, parents and children become close friends as well at this point. When parents allow themselves to be served and empowered by their own children, intimacy deepens. This kind of reciprocity is good preparation for the relationships which the children will eventually experience as adults.

The four parenting styles—telling, teaching, participating, and delegating—develop along a continuum reflecting the child's increasing maturity. There is also a sense in which the parents must be able to grow with their maturing children. Parents who cannot change their styles to meet the progressing needs of their children will retard the growth of all involved. Maturation of the parental style is an essential factor in the mutual empowering process. Parents must have both the insight and skill to employ the parenting style most appropriate to each situation.

As suggested earlier, the combination of high parental support and high inductive control produces the most competent children. The empowering curve in our model does not contradict this view, but it does present a refinement. It suggests that with increased maturity children will need less support and control. We are not suggesting that parents need to hold back their unconditional support as their children mature, but only that the children will be decreasingly dependent upon their parents' support. God's ideal is that children mature to the point where they and their parents empower each other.

It should be noted here that this ideal is most efficiently achieved if both parents bring their respective strengths to the empowering process, that is, if they complement each other. There are two types of complementarity. First, parents complement each other over time; this is longitudinal complementarity. One parent may be better at dealing with infants or young children, while the skills of the other emerge once the children have developed a greater cognitive ability. Second, parents complement each other on a day-to-day basis throughout their parenting years; this is situational complementarity. Here the situation determines which parental skills are most needed. Thus, while one parent may be more capable of helping a child with homework, the other may be more able to provide encouragement when the child is lacking in self-esteem. The virtue of complementary parenting is that one parent does not have to attempt to meet all of the child's needs.

Social-science literature suggests that the combination of high parental support and high inductive control produces the most competent children. While this is true, the majority of studies have failed to take into account the developing maturity of children. The empowering curve in our model suggests that with increased maturity children will need less support and control. The conclusion of Rollins and Thomas (1979) that coercion has an adverse effect on the development of social competence in children supports the type of empowering we have suggested. Parenting which empowers children to maturity is conceptually similar to the New Testament depiction of discipling. Jesus gathered and trained disciples, enabling them in turn to "go and make disciples of all nations" (Matt. 28:19 NIV). Parenting follows a similar course. The ultimate reward for parents and children occurs when those who have been empowered in turn empower others!

7

Child Development

It has been said that every society except ours expects its children to grow up into normal adults. Part of the reason for the insecurity of many American parents is a fear that they may be doing something which is contrary to expert opinion. There are two types of experts on child rearing. One is the scientific investigator who systematically studies child development. The other is the popularizer of this knowledge who offers advice on how to be the perfect parent who raises the perfect child.

As we mentioned in the previous chapter, we believe that parents need to resist bowing uncritically before expert opinion as well as the idea that a simple formula will guarantee parenting success. It is more important to develop a parenting philosophy which is gathered from many different sources. For example, it is important to take into account such items as cultural heritage, personal strengths and limitations (both one's own and those of one's children), knowledge derived from firsthand experience and common sense, social-science data, and the biblical perspective. Confidence in one's ability as a parent comes from integrating these elements with the findings of the child-development experts. Parents who wait with bated breath for the next gem of wisdom to be uttered by the how-to-parent authorities are setting themselves up for disillusionment when their offspring do not automatically develop into the ideal children they were promised. Child rearing is a much more complex process than most people recognize.

This chapter will summarize the evidence currently available in the area of child development. We intend to describe some of the major theories as objectively as possible. An integration of this material with our theological basis for family relationships will follow.

Theories of Child Development

Theories of child development consist of systematically organized knowledge which has been accumulated through empirical observation of children. A good theory is like a pair of glasses in that it allows one to focus more sharply upon that which is being observed. The reason it is important to pay attention to what all of the major child-development theories have to say is that in the process of focusing upon the fundamental ideas of one theory, it is possible to ignore other significant factors.

To illustrate this, let us suppose that representatives of the major theories of child development are viewing a child playing in the family living room. Although the observers will be exposed to the same behavior, they will not see it through the same set of eyeglasses. Each observer will perceive the child's activity in accordance with a set of predetermined assumptions about human behavior. For example, the cognitive-development theorist will be especially aware of the particular stage to which the child has developed; the Freudian theorist will look for unconscious motivations in overt behavior; the symbolic interactionist will concentrate on the child's self-concept; and the proponent of the social learning theory will pay special attention to what the child has learned from observing others. Although it is not a conscious process, all of our theorists actually engage in selective perception, viewing the child's actions in accordance with their own general conceptualization of human behavior.

Table 4 compares the major theories of child development: psychoanalytic, social learning, symbolic interaction, and cognitive development. (Moral development and faith development are extensions of the cognitive-development theory.) The concept of development implies growth toward an end point and not merely change in behavior. It should be noted that social learning theory is not, in the strictest sense of the term, a developmental theory in that it does not speak of specific stages of qualitative change. As we present the major theories, we urge the reader to try to identify how each one defines development.

Psychoanalytic Theory

Sigmund Freud, the father of psychoanalysis, presented a theory of child development which concentrates on the interplay between biological instincts and parental influence. A key to understanding Freud's theory is to recognize the importance he placed upon the unconscious and the

TABLE 4
Major Theories of Child Development

	Psychoanalytic	Social Learning	Symbolic Interaction	Cognitive Development		
				Piaget	Kohlberg (Moral)	Fowler (Faith)
(0–1½) Infancy	Oral	(No stages given)	Preparatory	Sensorimotor		Undifferentiated
(1½–3) Toddler Stage	Anal		Play	Preoperational	Punishment and obedience	Intuitive-projective
(4–6) Early Childhood	Genital		Game			
(7–12) Childhood				Concrete operations	Self-interested exchanges	Mythic-literal
(13–21) Adolescence				Formal operations	Maintenance of good interpersonal relationships	Synthetic-conventional
					Maintenance of law and order	Individuative
(21–) Adulthood					Social contract and individual rights	Reflective
					Universal ethical principles	Conjunctive
						Universalizing

irrational aspects of human motivation. His fundamental theory of the mind has been referred to as the iceberg theory because it holds that the major part of the mind lies below the surface; only the tip rises to the level of consciousness.

Freud (1949) depicted the personality in three parts: the id, ego, and superego. The id is the source of energy present already at the birth of a child, whereas the ego and superego develop as the child is socialized. There is a high degree of conflict in the mind, with the id and the superego battling each other for control of the ego. The id is amoral, impulsive, ruled by the unconscious and irrational, and demands immediate gratification. The superego, which consists of internalized parental and societal restrictions, is moralistic and seeks to deny the irrational impulses of the id. The superego operates as a moral police officer as it attempts to contain the id and control the ego. When the superego gets its way, it rewards the ego by building up self-esteem; but it punishes the ego with a guilty conscience when it does not get its way.

Freud believed that the first six years of life are vitally important for developing the three parts of the mind and determining how they will interrelate to form personality. During the first six years of life a child moves through three developmental stages, in each of which a different part of the body serves as the locus of gratification.

First comes the oral stage—in the first twelve to eighteen months pain and pleasure are centered in the oral zone. Pleasure is experienced when the infant receives food from a loving mother or sucks on a thumb or some other object, while pain is experienced when the infant is deprived of such oral gratification. Children who are weaned too abruptly or are inadequately nurtured during the oral stage may grow up to be oral-type personalities: greedy materialists, thumb suckers, smokers, pencil biters, excessive babblers, and so on. Each of these individuals has discovered a substitute form of oral gratification.

Toilet training begins the anal stage, at which time control over excretion becomes an important issue between children and parents. Overly rigid toilet-training methods which involve unrealistically high expectations can contribute to the child's developing an anal-type personality—meticulous, punctual, tied down by petty self-restraints. Or the child may react by becoming the very opposite—messy, disorderly, and lacking in self-control.

After toilet training, children enter the genital stage, at which time attraction to the parent of the opposite sex and bonding with the parent of the same sex are major concerns. Freud explained that boys desire an exclusive relationship with their mother independent of their father (the Oedipus complex), while girls desire an exclusive relationship with their father independent of their mother (the Electra complex). In a healthy family, the love between the mother and father will be unwavering, and the child will eventually conclude that the parent of the same sex cannot be defeated in the competition for the exclusive affection of the parent of the opposite sex. The psychological solution is for the child to seek to be like (identify with) the parent of the same sex and suppress the attraction for the parent of the opposite sex. In a dysfunctional home, the weak bond between the mother and father may result in failure to identify with the parent of the same sex.

In traditional psychoanalytic theory, the genital stage is the period in which sexual identity is formed. Adult problems that can be tied to unsuccessful resolution of this stage include preoccupation with proving one's masculinity or femininity, confusion in sexual identity, hesitancy to marry, and sexual dysfunctions.

Between the ages of six and thirteen, children go through the latency stage; during this period they strongly identify with other members of their sex. This is the age of the girls against the boys. If healthy conditions have prevailed during the first six years of life, gender identity and self-esteem will firmly develop during the latency stage. But if childhood conditions were less than ideal, there may well be difficulty in relating to others, increasing self-doubt, and lack of self-esteem. By puberty the basic personality has been formed; change thereafter will be minimal.

Social Learning Theory

Social learning theory is an offspring of classical conditioning, which is well illustrated by Ivan Pavlov's celebrated stimulus-response experiment. By ringing a bell just before giving food, Pavlov in time conditioned a dog to salivate upon merely hearing the bell. This simple experiment contains the major elements of classical conditioning: the food is the unconditioned stimulus; salivation at the sight of the food is the unconditioned response; the bell is the conditioned stimulus; and salivation at hearing the bell is the conditioned response.

During the past half century, behaviorism has been shaped by the creative research and writing of B. F. Skinner. Skinner (1953) developed what is known as operant conditioning, which is a modification of classical conditioning. Rather than using a stimulus to bring about a desired response, Skinner's model emphasizes reinforcement, that is, a system of rewards for desired behavior and punishment for unacceptable actions. The basic principle here is that behavior is shaped and maintained by its consequences. Operant conditioning has proven useful in bringing about changes in behavior.

A most useful model has been social learning theory. This theory, developed by Albert Bandura (1977), emphasizes learning by observation rather than through direct reinforcement. Children learn how to behave

FIGURE 13 **Reciprocal Determinism in Social Learning Theory**

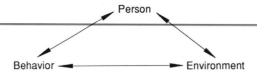

Adapted from Albert Bandura, *Social Learning Theory* (Englewood Cliffs, N.J.: Prentice-Hall, 1977), p. 204.

by observing the consequences of the behavior of other persons. For example, learning not to hit other children on the playground comes primarily by observing that children who do hit others experience some negative consequences, such as getting hurt themselves or being reprimanded.

Social learning theory also emphasizes that children learn from the modeling of people who are important in their lives. Parents are role models, influencing their children in both positive and negative ways by their actions. Comparison of direct learning (reinforcement) and indirect learning (observation and imitation of modeled behavior) reveals that the latter is more effective. Resourceful parents will model the behaviors they would like their children to implement.

In social learning theory the stimulus of change is not found exclusively in the environment, as in classical learning theory. The idea that learning comes through the child's observation and interpretation of behavior implies a self-consciousness and self-determination within the child. Change, then, can be activated both by environmental stimuli and by the child. This slant has taken learning theory a long way from its initial ideas.

On the other hand, social learning theory does not take us away from a deterministic model of human behavior. Bandura introduces the concept of reciprocal determinism, which holds that behavior, the person (i.e., one's cognitive makeup), and the environment reciprocally influence each other (see figure 13). Thus children both change their environment and at the same time are being changed by it. This idea reflects the recent psychological trend away from a hard determinism to a softer social determinism, which perceives humans as acting upon, as well as reacting to, their external environment.

Symbolic-Interaction Theory

The symbolic-interaction theory is more sociological in nature than the other major child-development theories. This school stresses that child development can take place only in a context of interaction with other humans. It has been documented that in instances of extreme neglect children fail to develop either speech or social awareness. Some symbolic-interaction theorists go as far as to suggest that infants are not born human, but become human through social interaction. As the name of the theory implies, it is the symbolic interaction with one's caretakers which enables the infant to become human in a social sense.

Of all living creatures, human beings are unique because of the vast amount of culture (learned and shared) which they possess. The accumulation of culture is possible because humans have elaborate language systems. The more elaborate the language system, the greater the potential richness of a culture. The infant is born without language, without culture, and without a sense of self or of others. All of these develop as the caretakers communicate with the infant.

The father of symbolic interaction, George Herbert Mead, explains that child development takes place in three stages (1934). First comes the preparatory stage. During this period the infant is being prepared to use language.

Communication can be thought of as occurring on two different levels. Most communication between animals involves gestures. A gesture can be defined as any part of a social act that is a sign for something else. Thus, a beaver slapping its tail on the water, a rooster crowing, or a dog barking can all be thought of as communication by means of a gesture. On the human level, gestures have meaning, but the meaning is not precise enough to build an elaborate language system.

A language system can develop only when oral gestures become significant symbols. A significant symbol is a gesture which has the same meaning for the creature giving it as for the creature receiving it. Notice the difference in emotional reaction when "juicy steak" is changed to "juicy snake." The words *steak* and *snake* are significant symbols because of the precise meaning (and resultant feeling) they carry from one person to another.

Parents begin to communicate with their children through gestures— a smile, a soft pat on the hand, a warning glance, or wave of the finger. Words accompany the gesture, and thus children learn the meaning of a word in the context of specific situations. In time they come to view the word from the parents' perspective and in this way learn its general meaning. For instance, once the word *no* is understood in relation to a behavior which has never been forbidden before, the child has learned its general meaning.

Children develop a self-concept in much the same way; they see themselves from their parents' point of view. And not only do children see themselves as they think their parents see them, but in defining themselves they make use of their parents' very words. If parents tell their three-year-old Sally that she is good and smart, little Sally will view herself as good and smart. If Greg's parents continually tell him that he is bad as well as stupid, he is likely to view himself as bad and stupid. Children develop their self-concept by internalizing their parents' attitudes toward them.

When children are able to communicate through significant symbols, they have entered the second stage of development, the play stage. The play stage begins between the ages of one and two and continues for several years. During this period children begin to play (imagine themselves in) the roles of a number of other persons. They play at being Mommy, Daddy, big sister, or doctor. Putting themselves in the place of each of these individuals, they assume or take on that person's attitude toward them as well. For example, a three- or four-year-old child may move from one dining-room chair to the next and take on the personality of the individual whose chair is presently being occupied. While sitting in Daddy's chair, little Kathy turns toward the chair she usually occupies and asks in a deep voice, "Did you have fun today, Kathy?" She actually takes on what she believes her father's attitudes toward her are. Having tired of this, Kathy proceeds to the chair where her older sister sits and says, "You are a crybaby!" In each instance Kathy is adding to her self-concept by taking on what she imagines the other person's attitude toward her is.

During the play stage, children are limited to taking on the role of only one person at a time. In the process they come to view themselves as they think others view them. Increasingly, there is a sharpening of the child's sense of self as distinguishable and separate from others.

At age four or five, children reach the game stage, at which time they are able to take on the roles of a number of others simultaneously. Before reaching this stage it is impossible for children to play certain games because they are unable to take on the role of more than one person at a time. Note the futility in trying to play hide-and-seek with a three-year-old, for instance. To play hide-and-seek one must be able to take on the perspective of both the hider and the seeker. To play a game like baseball is even more complex, for one must be able to take on the perspective of each team member at the same time.

During the game stage, children develop an idea of how they appear to others in general. Thus, when a ballplayer strikes out with the bases loaded, she imagines the team's collective attitude toward her. As a child listens to the applause after he has recited a poem at the school program, he gains a general impression of the audience's evaluation of his performance. The cumulative effect of relationships with other individuals and groups is that children continue to take on new and changing attitudes toward themselves.

All of life can be thought of as the process of moving out of certain groups and into others. We acquire a general view of ourselves from each group to which we belong (and even from groups which we desire to join). Personal identity is found in the groups which we use to define ourselves. Some aspects of our identity are firm and stable, such as male or female. This particular aspect, which is anchored in gender categories, calls forth gender-appropriate behavior already in the first year of life. Other aspects are formed when children encounter new experiences. For example, on the first day at school, they begin to identify themselves as students. Through time individual identities are both reinforced and altered. In the end, human personality is the sum total of self-concepts which an individual has experienced and developed through a variety of relationships.

For our purposes the most important idea in symbolic-interaction theory is that our self-concept reflects what we believe others think of us, and we behave accordingly. Our lives, then, take on the character of a self-fulfilling prophecy. This contention of symbolic-interaction theory is supported elsewhere in child-development literature. For example, it has been found that children who fail in school have from an early age had low opinions of their learning abilities, whereas children who excel have developed positive views of themselves as learners.

This point leads us to the labeling theory, an offspring of symbolic interaction. It has been discovered that juvenile delinquents are likely to have been told as children that they were no good, worthless, and destructive. Having been so labeled, they proceeded to behave in accordance with the brands which had been placed on them.

Cognitive-Development Theory

The cognitive-development theory incorporates many of the ideas of symbolic interaction, especially its emphasis on the relationship between self-concept and behavior. Developed by Swiss psychologist Jean Piaget, the cognitive theory has become extremely influential in the United States (Flavell 1963, 1985).

Piaget started with the assumption that children, far from being passive objects in the conditioning process, actively construct their own reality; they turn their life experiences into action. Piaget observed that babies are born with sucking, looking, and grasping reflexes. Making contact with an object, an infant instinctively sucks, looks at, or grasps it. As children develop mobility, they will also bang or drop the object. Thus, a baby of six months who is given a block will experiment by in turn looking at it, grasping it, sucking it, banging it, and dropping it. The child is actually playing the role of a little scientist, experimenting and discovering the scheme into which the block fits. Once the scheme is discovered, the child will consistently act toward the object in the same way. As an example, a ball cannot be sucked or banged, but once it is dropped to the floor, the child discovers that it is bounceable. Give a child a ball, and the parent will inevitably be involved in playing a new game of dropping and retrieving the ball.

With the acquisition of language comes a wide variety of new possibilities. Since parents are usually eager to be verbally recognized by their children, among the first words learned are "Mommy" and "Daddy." Once they are learned, each new person who enters the child's world becomes either "Mommy" or "Daddy." At this point parents begin the task of teaching their child the distinctions between Mommy and other females and between Daddy and other males. With time, the child learns to discriminate and refers to a stranger not as "Mommy" or "Daddy," but rather as "man" or "woman" (or "boy" or "girl").

In analyzing this process, Piaget utilized the terms *assimilation, accommodation,* and *equilibration.* Assimilation is taking information in and construing it in terms of one's established way of thinking. Whatever is perceived is made to fit into existing schemes. The more refined a scheme, the less likely it is that new pieces of information will be misplaced. If, on the other hand, a child's color scheme is so undeveloped as to include only red and yellow, the child will be constrained to place a green object into one of those two categories. Similarly, an atheist who denies the possibility of divine healing will be forced to interpret any improvement in someone's physical health naturalistically.

Obviously, if the only thing children could do with new experiences were to assimilate them into existing categories, no new scheme would ever emerge. But many things simply do not fit into existing schemes, forcing the formation of new schemes. This is the process of accommodation—altering the existing cognitive structures to allow for new external stimuli. The atheist who witnesses one miraculous healing after another may be thereby enticed to come up with a new scheme which allows for divine healing.

Children continually engage in assimilation and accommodation. The balance between the two is called equilibration. Persons with mature cognitive structures will engage in both assimilation and accommodation. People with immature cognitive structures will fail to engage in one or the other and thus not achieve equilibration or cognitive balance.

The following story will illustrate our point. A man who thought he was dead went to several doctors, all of whom tried to assure him that he was still alive. He continued to disbelieve it. Then he encountered a doctor who asked him if dead men could bleed. When the man replied, "Of course not!" the doctor proceeded to prick the man's finger to draw blood. When the man saw the blood, he exclaimed, "Well, what do you know; dead men bleed after all!" Now while his thinking was certainly logical, it was faulty. This tends to be the way children think. They have not yet developed to the point where they can refine their cognitive schemes so as to accommodate data which simply do not fit.

According to Piaget, cognitive development in a child takes place in four major stages (see table 5). The first is the sensorimotor stage, which covers the period from birth until about two years of age. During this stage, children are developing basic motor skills and learning to adapt their behavior to the external environment. The child learns to classify objects by acting upon them. Experimentation teaches whether they can be sucked, dropped, or banged. The child also begins to grasp the concept of object permanence, that is, to realize that objects which are out of sight have not ceased to exist.

Children also begin to coordinate the different parts of the body during the sensorimotor stage. For example, when trying to reach for an object, they will stand on their tiptoes and stretch their arms as high as they can.

TABLE 5

Piaget's Major Stages of Cognitive Development

	Approximate Age	Major Tasks
1. Sensorimotor	0–2	• Classification of objects by acting upon them
		• Realization that out-of-sight objects still exist (object permanence)
		• Coordination of different parts of the body
		• Intentional goal-directed behavior
2. Preoperational	2–7	• Language acquisition and development of thought
		• Movement from egocentric thought toward decentering
3. Concrete Operations	7–11	• Comprehension of the principle of invariance
		• Comprehension of reversibility (conservation of quantity)
		• Classification of objects by various criteria
4. Formal Operations	12+	• Acquisition of scientific method (deductive reasoning)
		• Concern for basic values and truth
		• Understanding of logical relations between classes
		• Formal logic

Toward the end of the sensorimotor stage, children intentionally engage in goal-directed behavior. In order to reach a cookie on a table, children will push a chair up to the table, climb on the chair, and then pull the cookie dish toward them, all in an orderly sequence.

While mastery of certain motor skills is primary during the sensorimotor stage, mastery of linguistic tasks is primary during the preoperational stage. Children learn the names of objects, begin to place words together into meaningful sentences, and at the same time construct a view of reality. All of this is possible only because of language acquisition.

There is a sense in which the preoperational stage is not a stage at all, but rather a transitional period. Technically, a developmental stage is characterized by a new level of equilibrium and stability. But because the acquisition of language skills is so complex a task, the thinking and behavior of a child in the preoperational stage are characterized by unsettledness, fears, and confusion. That is the precise reason we speak of it as a *pre*operational stage.

Parents should not be surprised that their child's thinking at this age is sometimes quite puzzling to adults. When the child fails to come up with what the parents think are simple, logical conclusions, they may underestimate the child's abilities. For example, the child may conclude that fire fighters, since they always appear at the scene, set fires, or that police initiate trouble. Parents must be mindful that the child is still in the *pre*operational stage and needs help in logically explaining the events he or she experiences.

In the beginning of the preoperational stage, children are quite egocentric, thinking that everybody else experiences the world as they do. If they are happy, they project happiness onto everyone else; when they are sad, then everyone else must be sad. Children who stand on one side of an object cannot understand why someone who is on the opposite side does not see what they are seeing. An important part of this stage is decentering, which is the process of moving beyond egocentric thought.

When children are about seven years of age, they reach the stage of concrete operations. This is the time when thought processes become more stable and consistent. For example, when children at the preoperational stage are shown two different-shaped glasses containing equal amounts of water, they will say that there is more water in the tall, narrow glass. Children at the concrete-operations stage realize that regardless of the shape of the container, the volume of water remains the same when poured from one glass to the other. They have come to understand the principle of invariance: certain matters of time, space, and weight are in some sense unchangeable. A related concept which children come to understand during the concrete-operations stage is reversibility. Younger children cannot conceive of the fact that the water, when poured back into the original glass, still has its original volume. But children at the concrete-operations stage understand that the water's volume does not change, no matter the shape or size of the container it is poured into.

At this stage children are avid collectors of just about anything: baseball cards, matchbooks, coins, dolls. They will proceed to classify and arrange their priceless objects on the basis of color, size, shape, and every other aspect imaginable. This is a reflection of an expanded reasoning ability.

In the last stage of development, the formal-operations stage, children understand causality and perform scientific experiments. By the use of deductive reasoning, hypotheses are formulated, experiments are carried out, and conclusions are reached on the basis of the evidence. There is also an increased concern for basic values and truths.

Moral-Development Theory

Building upon Piaget's assumption that children reason differently at different stages of development, Lawrence Kohlberg (1963) suggests that moral development can be understood in an analogous way. Kohlberg's concern is exclusively with the form of a person's moral reasoning, not with the content. He accepts the assumptions that the sequence of moral development is invariant for all persons, that no one ever reverts to an earlier stage, and that no one ever skips a stage.

Kohlberg's theory has been criticized by Carol Gilligan (1982) as having a built-in male bias in that it bases the making of moral decisions upon a concern with rights and justice. She argues that females, rather than stressing rights and justice, emphasize one's responsibility in the context of personal relationships.

From a Christian point of view, we also question the completeness of a moral-development theory which fails to take content into consideration. We do agree with Kohlberg's assertion that children advance in moral reasoning through a process that corresponds to cognitive development. This needs to be taken into account when teaching children how to reason about moral issues. But, more than that, it is essential to teach values, norms, and rules which are based on biblical truths.

Faith-Development Theory

James Fowler (1981) has also utilized cognitive-development theory in his model of faith development. Fowler speaks of a "faithing process." He argues that faith is always relational in the sense that there is always someone or something to trust in or be loyal to. For our purposes, it is important to note that Fowler squarely relates the capacity to have faith to the bonding process between parent and child:

In the interaction of parent and child not only does a bond of mutual trust and loyalty begin to develop, but already the child, albeit on a very basic level, senses the strange new environment as one that is either dependable and provident, or arbitrary and neglectful. This covenanting pattern of faith as relational becomes clearer as we reflect on what the parent or parents bring with them to the care and nurture of the child. They bring *their* way of seeing and being in the world. They bring *their* trusts and loyalties. They bring *their* fidelities—and infidelities—to other persons and to the causes, institutions and transcending centers of value and power that constitute their lives' meanings. Long before the child can sort out clearly the values and beliefs of the parents, he or she senses a structure of meaning and begins to form nascent images . . . of the centers of value and power that animate the parents' faith. As love, attachment, and dependence bind the new one into the family, he or she begins to form a disposition of shared trust and loyalty to (or through) the family's faith ethos. [1981:16–17]

The specific stages of faith development which Fowler posits are less significant for us than is his suggestion that ability to enter into the faithing process is dependent on one's relationship with the primary caretakers during childhood. Children who are deprived of trusting and caring relationships, who have not bonded with their parents, may be hindered from developing a mature faith and trusting relationship with God. The ability to experience God as a loving and trustworthy Father is related to having had a loving and trusting relationship with human parents or caretakers.

A Critique of Child-Development Theories in the Light of Biblical Teachings

Although it is beyond the scope of this chapter to present a complete synthesis of the child-development theories discussed, it will be helpful to briefly critique them on the basis of how well they comport with biblical teachings on being human. We shall build our critique around three biblical doctrines: (1) humans are in a state of constant internal tension: though created in God's image, they have fallen into sin; (2) they are active agents who have the capacity to make choices; and (3) humans are created for community.

Internal Tension

All of the theories seem to share a naturalistic perspective in that they view human behavior as part of the natural order. One of the basic assumptions of naturalism is that the principles which govern the human species are no different from those that govern other species. None of the theories adequately takes into account the biblical view that human beings are distinct from all other living creatures in that humans have the image of God within, even though it is a broken image. The biblical view also holds that the human condition is marked by internal tension. As Paul states in Romans 7:21–24: "So I find this law at work: When I want to do good, evil is right there with me. For in my inner being I delight in God's law; but I see another law at work in the members of my body, waging war against the law of my mind and making me a prisoner of the law of sin at work within my members. What a wretched man I am! Who will rescue me from this body of death?" (NIV).

Perhaps psychoanalytic theory comes the closest to the view that human beings are trapped in a state of internal tension between good and evil. Freud believed that a child is born with both constructive (eros) and destructive (thanatos) instincts. This tension, which arises when the child develops a superego, corresponds with the biblical view which sees internal tension as a natural human condition.

Symbolic interaction looks on the self as being caught in a state of internal conflict between the impulsiveness of the I and the conformist orientation of the Me. However, this tension is explained as the result of inconsistent internalization of the external norms of behavior. The I, which is the core part of the self, was internalized in the distant past. The Me, the more exterior part of the self, was internalized more recently. In the individual's subjective experience, the I is what one really wants to do, and the Me is what one thinks others want one to do.

The Capacity to Make Choices

The Bible presents the view that we are choice-making creatures who are responsible for our behavior. On the other hand, there is probably in all of the child-development theories a built-in bias which explains behavior on the basis of environmental conditioning. The theories do differ significantly, however, in the degree to which they conceptualize humans as choice-making creatures. Whether we are mechanistic or active organisms is still debated in the social-science literature.

Classic learning theory assumes that children are born as clean slates upon which social conditioning imprints the cultural script. In this mechanistic view people operate on much the same principles as do machines. Thus the behaviorist John B. Watson boasted, "Give me the baby and my world to bring it up in and I'll make it crawl and walk; I'll make it climb and use its hands in constructing buildings of stone or wood; I'll make it a thief, a gunman, or a dope fiend. The possibility of shaping in any direction is almost endless" (quoted in Matson 1966:30). Although there is great variation in contemporary psychoanalytic theory, Freud's original goal to establish a scientific psychology led him as well to a mechanistic model of human behavior.

Social learning theory, in contrast, leans toward the conviction that children are active organisms who continually act upon and construct their own environments. And likewise the cognitive-development and symbolic-interaction theories, both of which are based upon the assumption that children act upon, as well as react to, their environment.

As a whole, the professional wisdom on cognitive development has moved closer to what we believe is the biblical view of free will. It would be incorrect, however, to interpret contemporary theories on child development as emphasizing free will to the exclusion of determinism. Rather, the prevailing understanding is that some children are freer than others because they have been given more options. In some homes children have limited access to reading materials and, consequently, little opportunity to educate themselves about their world and the choices available to them. Other children live in environments which offer more options. The contemporary theories maintain that children are unable to take any action apart from the options which are presented by their environment. While we can use the wisdom of child-development theories to understand human freedom, we must not allow this knowledge to deter us from accepting the scriptural view of free will.

Creation for Community

Whereas child-development theories have only recently leaned toward the view that children are active organisms, they have been in continuous agreement that human input is necessary if children are to take on human characteristics. Human behavior begets human behavior. Deprived of human social environment, there is very little in the biological structure of children which would induce them to embrace norms, values, or attitudes. On the other hand, when children are a part of a human social environment, they take on the attitudes and behaviors of that community.

We learn from Genesis 2:18 that human beings were created by God to live in community: "The LORD God said, 'It is not good for the man to be alone. I will make a helper suitable for him' " (NIV). The need to live in community is a common theme woven throughout the Old and New Testament Scriptures. The reader will recall that in chapter 1 we detailed the major relational themes in Scripture. Humans require an empowering community of grace which is based upon covenant commitment. This foundation leads to an intimacy within which they can experience the secure emotional bonding they crave.

Children need to be nurtured within an intimate family community. The unilateral covenant which parents make with their children can eventually mature and lead to a bilateral covenant. We have argued that this is the biblical ideal. The child-development literature offers two additional suggestions. First, developing the capacity to enter into covenantal relationships is contingent upon the child's experiencing unconditional parental love. Research on infants and young children who receive little attentive care confirms this. Sociologist Ira Reiss declares, "The evidence in this area . . . indicates that some sort of emotionally nurturing relationship in the first few years of life between the child and some other individual is vital in the child's development" (1980:36).

Second, the child-development theories suggest that human development is contingent upon achieving language skills, self-identity, and bonding capacity, in that order. This is to say that the emotional nurturing which Reiss asserts is imperative can culminate in bonding ability only if the child is in the process of acquiring language skills and self-identity. Children, of course, need both emotional and cognitive interaction with their parents, a point which we made in the previous chapter.

Parenting Young Children

The major theories of child development provide a basis for discussing important dimensions of parenting young children. In this section we will address the matter of how parents can best facilitate the social, psychological, and spiritual growth of their children. In keeping with our theological basis for family relationships, we believe that parents need to provide unilateral unconditional love. This is the most indispensable component in the empowering process. The fundamental qualities of loving, accepting, knowing, and communicating with our children will kindle in them the capacity for mature bilateral commitments.

The question of how to empower children comes down to a twofold concern: (1) how to build self-esteem and (2) how to discipline. These concepts have already been touched upon in our theoretical discussion of support and control (chap. 6); here we will present some practical suggestions. Rudolf Dreikurs and Vicki Soltz have done a good job of presenting these dimensions of parenting in their book *Children: The Challenge* (1964). Their approach, like our theology of relationships, proposes that children can best be empowered in an environment of love, acceptance, communication, forgiveness, service, and discipline.

Unconditional Love and Self-Esteem

Children need to be valued for who they are and what they contribute to their family and society. Parents who have high self-esteem and who model a mutual consideration and cooperation in their marital relationship will establish a climate where self-esteem is nourished and developed in their children.

Unconditional love should be shown not only in the parents' commitment to be responsible and faithful in their child-rearing tasks, but also in verbal and behavioral demonstrations of affection for their children. The children will then begin to recognize that they are loved not only for what they do, but for who they are. This gives them a sense of security and increases the incentive to be cooperative and helpful family members.

Acceptance of Differences Inherent in the Family Constellation

The order in which siblings are born is referred to as the family constellation. Each position in the family is important, and every child always needs to feel secure in his or her place. There are particular characteristics that accompany each position. For example, the oldest child is usually an achiever since parents tend to give first children special attention, push them to succeed, and expect them to take responsibility early. Middle children often try to compete with the older sibling(s), but sense they cannot catch up. Therefore, they often seek to achieve in areas untried by the older sibling(s). Sometimes middle children feel squeezed or lost. The youngest children are often catered to by the rest of the family, and tend to be more laid-back and relaxed. The terms *babied* and *spoiled* are usually affectionate labels, but there can also be resentment toward the youngest children. An only child is similar to a first child, but tends to be more adult in attitudes and actions. Children who come from large families tend to separate themselves into smaller sibling-groups.

Every position in the family has certain advantages and disadvantages. The only girl in a family of boys or the only boy in a family of girls has special privileges and problems. Siblings who are more than five years apart tend to feel separated into different subsystems. And of course there is also great variability in how each unique family reacts to each individual child.

It is important that every position be respected and that age-appropriate behavior be expected of every child. Parents who exert too much pressure or expect too much will burden a child unnecessarily; on the other hand, parents with low expectations or little faith in a child's abilities are guilty of insufficient stimulation or even neglect. Neither of these extreme approaches empowers the child.

Older siblings need assurance that their position in the family is special and secure. Knowing that younger children are not more loved or more valued will encourage them to be cooperative and helpful with their younger siblings rather than jealous or competitive. If middle children are noticed and perceive that they are cherished as unique, special, and capable, they will not feel the need to try to outdo the older children. If the youngest children are given adequate attention and encouraged to see themselves as qualified to accomplish appropriate tasks, they will be able to contribute to the family system without feeling invalidated, over-indulged, or coddled. Parents give their children a very strong message by believing in them and their ability to contribute to the well-being of others.

Communication

Parents use verbal and nonverbal communication to show that they respect and value their children. Critical to effective communication is the ability to be genuine rather than pretending to be something one is not or faking what one does not really feel. Most children can sense an inauthentic remark because the verbal claim is incongruent with the body language. It behooves parents to be honest and congruent. Expressing one's feelings honestly will give children clear and direct messages to which they can accurately respond.

When there is a discrepancy between the verbal and nonverbal messages, a child will be confused and frustrated. This is sometimes called the double bind: the child cannot respond to both messages at the same time without being contradictory. Therefore, the child responds in a dysfunctional and disturbed way. The major problem here is that neither parent nor child openly talks about the confusion, and they go about life as if this were normal communication, a situation which only further obscures the truth. Such distorted communication disrupts family functioning.

Communication will be enhanced if parents use encouraging statements like, "Mike, you did a fine job of cleaning out the sink," or "Barb, I know it's difficult for you to do those math problems, but you're getting better at it." These messages are very different from negative appraisals which tend to become self-fulfilling prophecies; for example, "What's wrong with you; don't you know any better?" Such remarks lead to discouragement and uncooperative attitudes.

The most important element of communication is listening. When we are listened to, we feel validated and cared for. Our children also need to be heard and understood. Considering their ideas and caring about their feelings are ways in which parents can show they accept their children. Taking the time to know them and how they think and feel produces intimacy. This is the very essence of how children gain the kind of confidence which culminates in self-esteem and good decision-making.

Here is a specific illustration to point out the supreme importance of listening. When eight-year-old Juan comes home because he has been hurt by his friend Reed, it is important for him to process his feelings with a parent who will listen and try to understand what he feels. This is not a time for the parent to question, scold, or insinuate that Juan was at fault, nor should the parent march to Reed's house to solve the dispute.

Listening is especially helpful because it gives Juan a chance to express and deal with his feelings in the company of someone who truly cares about him. This provides a perspective which most likely will enable him to decide for himself how to handle the situation. Knowing that parents accept, understand, and support them gives children an assurance that they are being attended to and believed. Given such assurance, they will be empowered to act appropriately.

Forgiveness

Forgiveness is a two-way process. Parents are not perfect and will need forgiving when they make mistakes. Children are not perfect, and they will need forgiveness for the mistakes they make as well. If family members were to say to each other every day, "I forgive you; do you forgive me?" they would experience a state of grace and acceptance that is rooted in unconditional loving.

Love You Forever, a wonderful children's book by Robert Munsch (1986), illustrates this kind of love. The boy in this story makes many mistakes throughout his growing years, infancy through adolescence. However, he is assured each night by his mother that he is loved unconditionally: "I'll love you forever; I'll like you for always!" This guarantee of always being accepted, no matter what he has done, gives him the confidence and incentive to love others in the same unconditional way. Such is the love we experience as God's children and ought to extend to others.

Serving

Empowering helps children sense that their contribution to the family is valuable. The perspective that each family member serves and supports the others imparts a feeling of worth and esteem to children and adults alike. When children are expected and encouraged to participate in the functioning of the family, both emotionally and physically, they sense that the family is more than a group of separate individuals. They begin to see themselves as part of a larger system which is greater than all of the individual members put together.

When children sense that they are an integral part of the family and that their input is esteemed, they will be glad to cooperate and serve. Their contribution will be not only instrumental (doing chores), but emotional (uplifting the family mood). They will help create family morale, identity, and unity.

Discipline

The Bible uses words like "love" and "honor" to describe the ideal parent/child relationship. Various Old and New Testament passages also discuss the importance of guidance and correction and promise that good training will pay off in that children will not depart from it. They will learn from sound discipline and eventually become self-disciplined, responsible adults.

One very helpful method of discipline is the concept of natural and logical consequences which is espoused by Rudolf Dreikurs. This method is familiar to us because God dealt with the children of Israel in a similar way. God's people had to face the consequences of their choices and behaviors. The blessing of the covenant was conditional in that they reaped what they sowed (although his gift of love and grace was unconditional). God has laid down laws such as the Ten Commandments; if we abide by these laws, we will find meaning in our lives, since God has our best interests in mind. On the other hand, there are consequences to be reckoned with when we disobey.

In the same way, children learn best through the consequences of their behavior, especially if they realize that the rules are a product of their parents' love and concern for them. This is in contrast to training children primarily by punishing their negative behavior, an approach which puts all the responsibility on the parents—they alone make the decision to wield punitive power when they are displeased. It is more helpful for children to come to understand that their misbehavior has specific consequences and that the ultimate responsibility rests with them.

Take the example of five-year-old June in a rocking chair. Rocking back and forth brings pleasure and joy, but if she rocks too hard or becomes too rambunctious, the chair will fall over and she will suffer the consequences of her action. This experience will help her monitor herself the next time she rocks in the chair. Children find their own limits through these consequences. As they self-correct and set appropriate boundaries for themselves, they are taking responsibility for their actions.

How should parents go about the business of setting up fair and reasonable rules (logical consequences) to help their children learn limits and eventually become responsible for their own behavior? Basically, children should be given a limit which is reasonable and told that a specific consequence will be applied whenever they go beyond that limit. For example, to prevent Bobby from running into the street, his parents might tell him not to go beyond an imaginary line in the yard; if he does so, he will have to come into the house for a certain amount of time. At first one of the parents must stay close by. As soon as Bobby tests the limits of the rule (puts his foot over the line), the parent must firmly let Bobby know that he has overstepped the limit and therefore the consequence applies (he must come into the house).

Notice how the consequence is logically related to the misbehavior and carried out in a clear and pleasant manner. There is no need for a verbal reprimand, which might well lead parent and child into a useless power

ALBERT AND I JUST LOVE TO TEACH THE CHILDREN
BY MEANS OF NATURAL CONSEQUENCES.

struggle and would also sidetrack attention from the child's responsibility for the consequence. The main point is that the parent does not need to scold or punish, but to see to it that the child becomes fully aware of the consequences of the behavior. This allows the child to accept limits and eventually to achieve self-discipline.

Obviously a crucial point is how the consequences are set up and carried out. The consequences should, of course, be appropriate to the child's age and maturity. Also, parents should not be unduly restrictive and punitive by making rules and regulations which seem unfair or unreasonable to the children.

This is where the idea of the family council comes into play. It is recommended that when children are old enough, they be included in the setting up of the rules and the consequences of failing to keep them. The family decides together what are reasonable rules and expectations for all. It must be an equitable arrangement! For example, if the family rule is "no dishes are to be left in the sink after supper," then every family member must submit to the consequence. Therefore, if the father forgets, he, like any other family member, must wash the dishes the next morning.

When assigning chores, wise parents will be flexible and listen to every family member. Perhaps someone is too fussy about how the beds are made, and another too careless in mowing the lawn. These matters need to be discussed together openly in the family council. This is the time and place to set up assignments which are age-appropriate and fair. The family council provides an opportunity for children to learn the democratic principles of equality, freedom of speech, and fairness. All members should have input as to whether the emotional needs of the family are being met. Even the youngest child can point out that the family is not spending enough time together having fun and give suggestions as to how that might be remedied. Or the teenagers may need to point out that since they are older and can handle more independence, it is time to make some changes in policies.

The mode of discipline we have suggested entails personal empowering. The ultimate goal is mutual empowering between all family members. Of course, the onus of responsibility will initially be on the parents. They will need to take time with the family, listen to each member, and consider the uniqueness of each child. The parents must be willing to forgive and be forgiven, set an example by submitting to the same requirements asked of the others, and model love and caring behavior, fairness, and consistency. Wise parents will allow a child the right to choose a behavior in spite of the consequence to be faced. They will know when to step back and allow the consequence to do the correcting, as well as when to step in to prevent a destructive consequence from exacting its toll.

These principles of the empowering process have to do with serving and being served. They are built on a foundation of unconditional loving and commitment, operate most successfully in an atmosphere of acceptance and forgiving grace, and result in intimacy through deep knowledge of and communication with one another. People who have been empowered have a competence and self-esteem which they can share both in the family and outside the family with their community, society, and the world at large.

Once again God's covenant serves as an analogy. Unconditional faithfulness and love form the foundation. Even though we deserve the consequence of our failure and sin, God offers grace and forgiveness as we fail to meet expectations. Moreover, God provides the Holy Spirit to encourage, empower, and enable us to live according to the law so that the blessing may be ours. Finally, we are renewed and revitalized by the hope of intimacy and relationship with the Almighty One. As we grow in this circle of covenant, grace, empowering, and intimacy, we experience a deeper and more intense level of God's love and of our love for one another. And so too does the love within a family deepen as its members implement the empowering process.

8

Adolescence and Midlife:
Seedbeds for Stress and Conflict

The greatest conflicts within the family are likely to occur when children are in their adolescence. One reason for this is that at the very time children are in the difficult period of adolescence, their parents are likely to be reaching midlife. Recent research on adult development has shown that reaching midlife is very often a crisis. So the conflict that frequently occurs during the strain of adolescence must be viewed in light of the parental strain as well. Both the children and the parents are likely to be undergoing a great deal of developmental stress.

In a systemic understanding of family life, adolescent stress does not merely add to parental midlife stress, but multiplies it. So too for the effect of midlife strain on adolescent strain. The two must be seen as interactive. Whenever more than one family member are going through a period of great personal anxiety, the potential for conflict in the family increases geometrically.

This chapter will present the stressful aspects of adolescence and mid-life separately, and then consider the special problems which arise when the two occur simultaneously. Our starting point will be an examination of the factors which have contributed to the rise of adolescent and midlife strain in our society. "What's the big deal?" the reader may be asking. "People pass through adolescence and midlife in every society. Why make such an issue about them?" But this is not, in fact, the case. True, people in every society pass through the chronological ages which correspond to adolescence and midlife, but these are not distinct stages of life in most societies. We will attempt to explain why our society seems to produce more adolescent and midlife strain than do most others.

Adolescence

The Origin of the Adolescent Stage

Prior to the Industrial Revolution, youth were viewed as young adults. To recognize this, one need only recall how children appear in medieval paintings. They are commonly depicted as miniature adults, with adult-like arms, legs, and general physical features. In addition, we know that the Puritans treated their children like adults—they were expected to sit still for long hours at church, and then to exhibit the same disciplined behavior at dinner.

It is only within the last three hundred years that childhood has come to be recognized as a distinct stage of development. During that time children have come to be viewed as being qualitatively and not just quantitatively different from adults. They do not think like adults, they do not have a mature conscience, nor do they view reality in the same way.

After the recognition of childhood, Western societies initially had the cultural equivalent of puberty rites. Prior to the Industrial Revolution, youth learned to farm or acquired a trade by developing skills through the apprenticeship system. As they both lived with and worked under the watchful eye of the master craftsman, apprentices occupied very clear-cut positions. Once the skills were mastered, one was ready for adulthood and marriage. Mastering the skills of what was to be one's trade was the rite of passage into adulthood.

Urbanization and industrialization have resulted in a slower and more ambiguous passage into adulthood. With the development of factories, the apprenticeship system declined. Factory work did not require a high degree of skill, so youth could begin working independently of a master craftsman very early in life. Children began to leave their homes in order to work in urban factories. Because of the very low pay, most of them lived in slum apartments. As they became alienated from the rest of society, they increasingly became a problem. Disenfranchised from adult life, an adolescent culture emerged.

What in the beginning included just a few urban youth for a brief period of their lives has grown to include virtually all the youth in our society. In addition, the period of time involved—the gap between childhood and adulthood which we call adolescence—has expanded. There are a number of reasons for this phenomenon. First, as our society has increasingly become technologically oriented, more jobs have been created at the highly skilled level and fewer at the lower level. This means that youth must continue in their education and delay their entrance into the full-time work which would award them adult status.

Second, most work is now done outside the home (the exception being farm families). This means that parents are unable to provide a visible work model for their children, which further alienates them from the everyday functioning of society. This isolation is aggravated by the high degree of mobility. The average American moves so often that there is a lack of community control and support behind the family structure.

Third, the extended family has been replaced by the nuclear family because of this high mobility. The nuclear family is a small, fragile unit isolated from relatives who could give youth a sense of stability and belonging. In many families divorce, separation, or the need for parents to work long hours in the marketplace further complicates the situation.

A fourth factor which has contributed to the expansion of adolescence is the affluence of youth in Western societies today. Either because they earn their own money or because their parents give them money, many youth possess a degree of independence unexperienced by any previous generation. The greater independence of youth today goes hand in hand with a loss of parental and societal control. Although these factors did not produce adolescence, they have been very instrumental in furthering it.

Adolescence came about because social structures developed which retard the movement of youth toward adult status. Concomitant with this arrested development is a lack of meaning in the lives of youth today. Being locked out of adulthood, their lives are void of the meaning which is a part of adult roles. It is from this vantage that the creation of adolescent subcultures can best be understood.

But what about other societies? "Why adolescence?" is the precise question which anthropologist Margaret Mead tried to answer when she reported on her years of research among peoples of the South Sea Islands. In *Coming of Age in Samoa* (1928) and *Growing Up in New Guinea* (1935) she stated that these societies were free from the adolescent stress and strain of Western cultures. There was, in fact, no adolescent! Rather, there were only two categories of people—children and adults.

In the cultures Mead studied, children were treated like children, free from adult responsibilities and excluded from making adult decisions. Adults were treated like adults, having both rights and responsibilities which were not a part of childhood. There was no question as to who were children and who were adults. For when the children in New Guinea or Samoa reached puberty, between the ages of eleven and thirteen, they were put through a series of puberty rites. For our purposes, what went on at these puberty rites is unimportant, since activities varied from society to society. What is important is that successful passage through these rites was an infallible indication that one was no longer a child, but rather an adult. They can be thought of as the initiation into adulthood. Youngsters left the village as children and returned as adults. To have completed puberty rites was tantamount to wearing a sign which read "Adult."

What is absent from these and most other Eastern societies is the ambiguity which is associated with being a teenager in the United States. Being a teenager in our society is like being Alice in Wonderland—not knowing what the rules and expectations are. If asked whether a teenager is a child or an adult, most people will say, "Both," or "Neither." The underlying element here is that the beginning of adulthood has not been clearly defined.

Formal attempts to define the beginning of adulthood in contemporary society do very little to clear up this confusion. For example, the age at which one may marry (with parental consent) is variously defined in the United States, ranging all the way from thirteen for women in one state to eighteen for men in others. In terms of voting privileges and military service, an eighteen-year-old is judged to be an adult. In most states a sixteen-year-old is permitted to drive. It is enlightening to note the age at which a person is regarded as an adult when financial profit is involved. Movie theaters, airlines, and most public establishments which require an admission fee consider a twelve-year-old to be an adult. Teenagers are asked to pay adult prices, but when it comes to seeking adult privileges, they are told to wait until they grow up.

To grow up in the United States can be an absurd experience. It can be compared to a jam session where jazz musicians play without a score. They simply improvise as they go along. With no clear cultural norms, adolescents similarly improvise new ways of behavior. This explains the rapid change in adolescent fashion and style, whether it be clothes, hairdos, or language.

Adolescence as an Identity Crisis

Although adolescence can be explained as arising out of the social conditions of Western cultures, its effect is most profound at the individual level, where it is often experienced as an identity crisis. In societies in which youth are given meaningful, clearly defined roles to play, such as those cultures described by Margaret Mead, youth have a clear sense of who they are. Similarly, some youth in our society never do experience the stress and strain of adolescence because they have a clear sense of identity. This is likely to be true of youth who have a consuming pre-occupation, such as a dedication to being an outstanding athlete, musician, or scholar. Others do not experience an identity crisis because they are given an adult status at a very young age; farm youths, for example, begin to take on adult responsibilities in their teens.

The creation of an adolescent subculture is an attempt to establish identity. One learns from peer groups to wear the right clothes, affect the right hairstyle, play the in music, speak the in language. The greater the adolescent's insecurity, the greater the slavish obedience to doing all the right things as sanctioned by the peer group.

The generation gap of which we often speak can be understood as the result of the identity crisis faced by most adolescents. The task of establishing one's identity in today's society might be compared to driving a car. Many teenagers are restless because their parents are still in the driver's seat, running their children's lives. These parents fear that their children's restlessness and rebellion against established norms are a sign of rejecting them and their values. In most instances, however, the children want nothing other than to get behind the wheel—to gain more control over their life and to share in determining where it's going. Parents hesitate to give up control to their teenage children for fear they will make bad decisions, while the children wonder how they are supposed to learn to make decisions if they are not given the chance. The solution to this dilemma is to be found in appropriate parental empowering of teenage children, an issue which we will address at the close of this chapter.

Midlife

Recent research has revealed that adults continue to pass through individual stages of development throughout their lifetime (Levinson 1978; Sheehy 1978). One of the most widely recognized stages is the onset of midlife, which a number of social factors often render more of a crisis than a transition. The most important factor is the rapidity of social change. Although Alvin Toffler titled his book *Future Shock* (1970), what he was really writing about was present shock. Because of the rapid social and technological change, we are shocked now as we think about the future. Personal crises develop because we are not prepared for the change that is taking place in the world.

Adults in the labor force are especially vulnerable when they realize that the job that they are trained to do, and have been doing for most of their adult life, is becoming obsolete. Automobile workers quite understandably experience a crisis when they realize that robots are beginning to do much of their work. A similar anxiety plagues management and other people in the business world. There is the fear of being overtaken by younger, better-trained college graduates.

Midlife transition may also be a crisis for people who begin to realize that they will not reach the lofty goals which were set years before, goals which represent self-acceptance and self-esteem. Others may feel that they did their best work at an earlier age and that life is now downhill and boring. The term *career burnout* has been coined to refer to such situations. Other persons compare the progress of their careers with the progress of others of a similar age and become discouraged because they have not accomplished as much. Such persons experience a crisis because they feel that they are not on schedule. Women who enter careers after their childbearing years feel there is no way to make up for lost time.

Still others who have worked long, hard hours at their jobs reach midlife only to realize that they have spent little time with their children, who are now nearly grown, and have had little actual influence over them. Some of these hardworking persons find that when they do want to relax with their family, they are unable to do so. The crisis in this case is that one has become a slave to work and career.

In his study of career-oriented men, Daniel Levinson (1978:209–44) has identified four polarities of midlife transition:

1. Youth/Age. Many men in midlife occupy a marginal status: they feel older than youth, but not ready to join the rocking-chair set. They will attempt to appear young by the way they dress or to improve their physique by running or lifting weights.
2. Destruction/Creation. Having experienced conflict on the job and being battle-scarred and hurt by others, men in midlife may resort to the same tactics. They are aware of the death of friends their age, but at the same time they have a strong desire to be creative as they enter what often prove to be the most productive years of life.
3. Masculinity/Femininity. Concern over a physically sagging body is coupled with a desire to become more nurturing.
4. Attachment/Separateness. A continued need for bonding with others is balanced by a need to prove that one can do it alone.

Levinson believes that although these polarities exist through the entire life cycle, they are accentuated during transition periods. Men who have dealt with these polarities throughout their life, having met minor crises on a regular basis, do not experience the midlife transition as a crisis period. On the other hand, men who have not dealt with these polarities are candidates for a major midlife crisis.

Although most of the research concerns men at midlife, Gail Sheehy (1978) believes that a woman may experience the same midlife tensions, especially if she has chosen a career. For the woman whose only role has been mother and wife, midlife may be traumatic for other reasons. She may feel her role is being phased out—her maturing children have less need of her, and her husband may no longer appreciate what she is doing in the home. For the woman whose whole identity and self-esteem are based upon being a supermother and superwife, this can be a devastating blow.

Parent/Adolescent Relationships

Having considered the stressful aspects of adolescence and midlife, we are now in a position to consider the interaction between them. To begin with, it should be noted that a family with older children is likely to have a double inferiority complex. Both the children and the parents feel insecure about who they are. This will have enormous impact on the parent/adolescent relationship.

In establishing their own identity, adolescents need to exert their independence. Parents who feel good about themselves can accept this; they will not be threatened by what they see as a passing need in their children. Parents who, on the other hand, are experiencing their own identity crisis will not be as psychologically prepared to handle a rejection from their children. The reverse is also true. A parent undergoing a midlife crisis may have personal needs which will put demands on the relationship with the children. The child who has already established a clear sense of self and is not in the midst of an identity crisis is in a better position to be supportive of the needy parent.

One of the chief factors in parent/adolescent conflicts may be that the parent in midlife and the adolescent are experiencing opposite physical effects. At a time when the adolescent is just beginning to develop the physical characteristics of adulthood, the parents are beginning to lose theirs. While the adolescent boy finds his muscles growing and his physical strength increasing, the father finds his muscles shrinking and his strength declining. While the adolescent girl begins to develop a nice figure, her mother is fighting hard to keep her figure intact. The one is just developing increased physical beauty and capabilities; the other is losing them. That fact strikes home when the daughter tells her mother to hold her stomach in, and the mother replies disgruntledly, "It is in!"

Parental Stimuli of Adolescent Rebellion

The evidence presented in the earlier part of this chapter leads us to believe that adolescent stress, strain, and rebellion are most likely the result of sociocultural factors existing in Western society. But while these factors are helpful in explaining the emergence of adolescence as a general

DAD, IF YOU'D JUST HIT THE BALL A LITTLE DEEPER,
I'D HAVE A HARDER TIME CHARGING THE NET.

phenomenon in Western societies, they do not entirely explain why some adolescents go through a period of rebellion and others do not. There is some evidence that structural components within the family contribute to adolescent rebellion. A study of 417 college students conducted by Jack Balswick and Clito Macrides (1975) found that parental unhappiness, unwise child-rearing practices, unsatisfactory division of authority between mother and father, and lack of an appropriate amount of cohesion within the home can stir up adolescent rebellion.

Parental unhappiness. The finding in the Balswick and Macrides study that rebellion is more likely to occur in unhappy homes than in happy homes should not be surprising, especially in light of the evidence that unhappy homes are related to juvenile delinquency (Glueck and Glueck 1950; Monahan 1957) and mental illness (Nye 1957). Parental unhappiness may produce frustrations in the child, resulting in rebellion. When parents are perceived as being unhappy in their marital relationship, the child is likely to discount them as a source of authority and may even see an opportunity to conquer the divided. A child may find it easy to justify a defiant attitude toward parents who have not shown themselves to be models of contentment. Their unhappiness usually involves a certain amount of verbal or physical abuse, thus providing the child with a model of aggression. Applicable here is Albert Bandura and Richard Walters's (1959) theory that aggressiveness on the part of a child is an imitation of parental aggressiveness. Also, children may rebel as a way of separating themselves from their unhappy parents.

According to a systemic perspective on the family, the teenager may be rebelling in an effort to unite unhappy parents. The idea here is that if the parents share concern over the misbehavior of their teenager, they may well forget about their own problems. There is, indeed, ample research to indicate that many rebellious teenagers come from disengaged families, and that the rebellion may be an effort to pull the family together (Lewis, Beavers, Gossett, and Phillips 1976). On the other hand, if the parents are experiencing their own crises of trying to separate and individuate, the teenager's rebellion may be counterproductive and result in further chaos rather than in unifying and stabilizing the family.

Unwise child-rearing practices. The relationship between parental restrictiveness and adolescent rebellion is not simple. As can be seen in figure 14, adolescent rebellion is highest in very permissive and very restrictive homes, and lowest in homes with a balanced approach. This fact may be related to a basic principle of the family-therapy literature: the main task with which adolescents must deal in relationship to their parents is differentiation. Differentiation is the process of separating from one's parents. Adolescents have the psychological task of becoming their own person, taking on or letting go of their parents' attitudes, beliefs, and values. There is also the physical task of leaving home.

Ideally, the child moves from complete dependence upon the parents to semidependence to relative independence from them. The change from dependence to independence tends to proceed smoothly if the parents are moderate in their disciplinary practices. Overly restrictive parents hold the reins too tight upon their children, and do not allow for a gradual development of independence. This tight hold creates a situation where independence can be achieved only by a drastic break from the parents. Restrictiveness leads to frustration in children. These children may become aggressive toward their parents and sometimes toward society in general; this aggressiveness is interpreted as rebellion.

On the other hand, some teens from restrictive homes find even more dysfunctional ways to individuate. Such families are often so enmeshed that breaking away comes through subtle controlling techniques, including psychosomatic disorders such as anorexia nervosa. In effect the child is saying, "I'm in control, and you can't do anything about my behavior!" This is indeed a drastic form of rebellion, since it can lead to bodily harm and even death. Parents are totally helpless to deal with such subtle re-

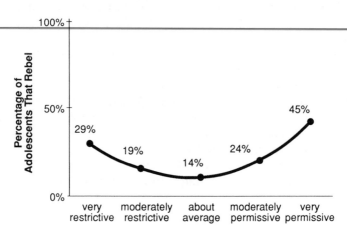

FIGURE 14 **Parental Restrictiveness and Adolescent Rebellion**

bellion. Again, such behavior may actually be an effort by the child to unite the parents.

The extremely permissive home may produce a state of confusion in the child, for the parents may be so indulgent that the child does not perceive any clearly defined rules for behavior. Extremely permissive parents not only allow their child to make basic decisions, but also fail to set limits for the child's behavior. Benjamin Spock regrets that his book *Baby and Child Care* (1968) has been grossly misinterpreted by modern parents. Whereas he did argue for greater permissiveness in the sense that children should be free to begin making their own decisions, he did not intend that parents set absolutely no limits for their children.

When parents do not clearly state rules and limits, the child has no option but to behave in increasingly extreme ways in an attempt to discover precisely what the rules and limits are. In a permissive home there is a great deal of ambiguity about how the child is expected to behave. This ambiguity produces behavior which may be looked on as rebellious, but which in fact is a search for norms.

Teenage children have a great need to know what the rules are, even though they may not agree with those rules. They interpret permissiveness as lack of interest in them. Having reached such a conclusion, teenagers often rebel as a way of gaining attention from their parents.

Why is the incidence of teenage rebellion high in restrictive and permissive homes and low where there is a balanced approach? We believe the answer can be found in the nature of family life in restrictive and permissive homes. Restrictiveness is likely to be a reflection of a low degree of adaptability in the home. Parents who are very restrictive in rearing their children tend to be rigid in the application of family norms. This rigidity causes a feeling of frustration in children. Younger children need more structure and may not feel as frustrated in such a home; but when they become teenagers, they will feel the need for more breathing space. If parents continue to be very restrictive, adolescents are likely to rebel in frustration.

Permissiveness is likely to be a reflection of a high degree of adaptability in the home. There are very few set patterns of behavior. To the outsider (to say nothing about the view of some insiders) the family life seems chaotic. There is a lack of family norms and clearly defined ways of doing things. This type of situation can also lead to frustration. Teenagers in chaotic homes with very permissive parents feel frustration because they do not know what their parents expect. Without guidelines adolescents will try almost anything, behavior which is usually viewed as rebellious.

Unsatisfactory division of parental authority. It is no secret that our society is currently questioning gender roles. The traditional American family has been patriarchal: the husband and father was the head of the home. There is currently much controversy as to the best authority pattern for the home. In this connection figure 15 presents some very interesting and confusing data on the relationship between the division of parental authority and adolescent rebellion.

The incidence of rebellion is high in homes where either the father or

Figure 15 **Parental Authority and Adolescent Rebellion**

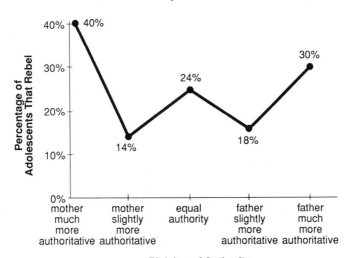

Division of Authority

mother is dominant, moderate where they share equal authority, and low where one parent has slightly more authority. We believe that extreme inequality in parental authority results in a state of confusion for the teen: Just what is the nature of the disciplinarian role of the subordinate parent? When authority is perceived as being primarily in the hands of one parent, the child may have problems interacting with both parents as authority figures. Rebellion may be the best solution to this confused situation. Excessive authority on the part of one parent may also mean domination over the child. Such domination is frustrating to the child and may result in aggressiveness.

A different type of confusion may be experienced in the egalitarian home, where the problem for the child is an inability to identify in whom the ultimate authority resides. Or the child may pit one parent against the other, so that they do not present a unified position. Nonetheless, on the whole the egalitarian home presents a healthy situation. Dolores Curran (1983:35–36) reports that in healthy families there is an unusual equality between parents. When children in such families are asked, "Who is boss in your home?" they will usually respond, "Sometimes Dad and sometimes Mom." There is a balance of parental power in these healthy family systems. This goes along with the findings of many family therapists: there must be an equality in the parental subsystem and a clear boundary between the parental and the child subsystems. A key factor is that parents present a united front even though they will sometimes act separately in disciplining their children.

It has also been discovered that there is less rebellion in homes in which one of the parents clearly takes authority and makes final decisions when there is a question of how to handle a situation. This is an agreed-upon policy which does not demean or put down the other parent, but rather provides a clear-cut authority structure which children cannot disrupt. When one spouse takes the tie-breaker role, there is no possibility of uncertainty.

Lack of an appropriate amount of cohesion. Cohesion is an important dimension of parent/adolescent relationships. Clinical evidence suggests that adolescent rebellion will be highest under conditions of extremely low or extremely high cohesion. It will be recalled that cohesion refers to the degree of closeness or social and psychological involvement which family members have with one another (pp. 44–45). A family with a low degree of cohesion is said to be disengaged, while a family with a high degree is enmeshed. The ideal pattern entails a moderate amount of cohesion. This enables a teenager to work through the process of differentiation.

Differentiation takes place throughout life. It is during the teenage period, however, that the process of differentiation is most important. In disengaged families adolescents lack the depth of bonding with parents which is vitally needed in order to establish a separate identity. There is no basis or standard against which to construct one's own self-structure. In many cases the result will be unstructured, that is, rebellious behavior.

In the enmeshed home it is difficult for an adolescent to break away to establish a separate identity. In this case, the bonding between parents and children is like a permanent glue which prevents children from establishing any space between themselves and their parents. Family therapists use the term *ego enmeshment* to refer to the family in which each member's ego or sense of self is so tightly bound up with the family as a whole that no one can make a distinction between one's personal self and the others. In such a family the teenager will have a hard time establishing a separate identity. Rebellion may be the only way in which children from an enmeshed home are able to become differentiated. Some will, in fact, not differentiate and will spend a lifetime enmeshed with their family of origin. It will be especially difficult for them to establish their own separate homes and families without constant involvement with and dependence on their family of origin. Such a situation disrupts the spousal subsystem, for without leaving one's parents there can be no real cleaving to one's mate nor establishment of a new and independent family.

In the differentiated home, one with an appropriate degree of cohesion, the adolescent will have already begun the differentiation process. Adolescence is merely a period in which this process is accelerated. Of course, the need for differentiation works both ways—children from parents and parents from children. Parents who are themselves in a period of crisis will find it difficult to allow their children the needed space to successfully work through the differentiation process. They will either hang on to their teenagers, or throw them out of the house before they are ready to leave! In the latter case, physical separation is no guarantee that there is differentiation in an emotional sense.

Family therapists agree that a child should not leave home until both the child and the parents are ready. Sometimes the child leaves in a bit of a huff; in such cases anger helps both parents and teens to make the break. This is often a difficult time, since it is hard to give up the familiar roles of parent and child. Nevertheless, differentiation must be accomplished if teenagers are to proceed to new stages of growth and development.

Empowering Adolescent Children

The model of Christian parenting which was presented earlier (pp. 101–8) helps us understand why empowering may be difficult when children reach the teenage years. In the ideal parent/child relationship, teenage children are well on their way toward being empowered. As parents model behavior to their teenage children, they will have eased up on the telling and teaching, and will have begun to delegate responsibility to them. This is the ideal; and when it happens, the result is an empowered teenager who assumes responsibility and control over her or his own life.

In reality, however, many parent/adolescent relationships do not resemble this ideal. We suggested earlier that parents need to change their parenting style as their children mature. Inability or refusal to do so will hinder the empowering process. As long as parents are limited to telling, teaching, and participating, they feel secure in the power and control they have over their children. But when it comes time to delegate responsibility to their children, they may begin to feel anxiety over their loss of control. To trust one's children to make the right choices and decisions and to act responsibly may be one of the hardest things a parent is called upon to do. Parents suffer anxiety for two reasons: (1) the child's reaction to the delegation of responsibility is a true test of whether the child is mature; and (2) it is also a true test of the parents' success in the empowering process. We suggest that the latter is the greater cause for parental anxiety. Parents are afraid to let go of their children because of the potential negative reflection upon themselves if the children make mistakes.

Children will, of course, make mistakes; this is part of the learning process. But because of the prevalence of parental determinism—the view that good parenting can ensure that children will turn out well—many parents feel unwarranted guilt when their children do make mistakes. If parental love and discipline could ensure that children will turn out well, God would have nothing but perfect children.

The failure of parents to adapt their parenting style to the changing needs of their maturing children is only half of the empowering problem—the other is the lack of opportunities for children to exercise responsibility. Part of the reason for this is the nature of modern technological society, which to a large extent has disenfranchised youth. Our entire society needs to be reoriented so that youth can participate earlier and more meaningfully. This is no less necessary in the church than in any other social institution. The youth programs of many churches do a good job of entertaining the young people and keeping them busy, but do little in the way of bringing them into responsible positions within the church community.

The success of adolescent empowerment depends upon both parents and children. Parents giving responsibility and adolescents acting responsibly will mutually reinforce each other. The reverse is also true—adolescents acting irresponsibly and parents failing to give responsibility will mutually reinforce each other. We should bear in mind that attitudes toward adolescents often act as self-fulfilling prophecies. The belief that youth are incapable of acting responsibly actually brings about irresponsible behavior; on the other hand, the belief that teenagers are capable and responsible will usually be confirmed.

The empowering process will be most successful, we believe, in parent/child relationships which are based upon covenant commitments. The true test of parental unconditional love occurs when the child reaches adolescence. Where unconditional love prevails, the family will live in an atmosphere of grace. Where there is grace, there are room for failure and the assurance that one will be forgiven and afforded the opportunity to try again. This deepens the intimacy between young people and their parents and makes mutual empowering possible.

PART 4

Sexuality:
Identity in Family Life

Introduction

This section focuses on two major sources of personal identity—one's gender and one's sexuality. In chapter 9 we indicate the impact of changing gender roles on the family in our society. We will examine various current explanations of gender differences and then offer a Christian viewpoint. There will also be some practical ideas on how Christian families and the church can provide leadership in this area.

In chapter 10 we expound on the fact that God created us as sexual beings and pronounced this very good. God intended that we be authentic and whole in our sexual relationships. After noting sociocultural influences on the development of our sexuality, we will present a theological understanding. Finally, focusing on four important areas of sexual expression—sex and singlehood, masturbation, sexual preference, and marital sexuality—we offer some practical guidelines for Christians who are attempting to achieve wholeness in a broken world.

9

Changing Gender Roles:
The Effect on Family Life

In most societies throughout history, being a man or woman was taken for granted. Males and females developed into their respective roles quite naturally. This is not the case today! Our society is embroiled in debates over what constitutes masculinity and femininity, and what the appropriate roles are for each gender. This redefinition of gender roles has caused disruption in the family.

The marital dyad, where husbands and wives are struggling with conflicting definitions of marital roles, has suffered the most. Disruption in the family also extends to parent/child relationships as parents come to grips with how to raise their sons to be men and their daughters to be women in an age when traditional definitions of manhood and womanhood are being challenged.

The fact that more than half of all married women work outside of the home today raises a concern over the adequacy of parenting. This is a crucial concern since the family is the arena in which a child's personal character and gender identity are formed. A little boy learns how to be a man by observing not only the behavior of his father and older brother(s), but also what is expected of him by his mother and sisters. Likewise, a little girl learns how to be a woman by viewing the behavior and expectations of family members of both sexes. It is for this reason that we have chosen the family as the context for our discussion of changing sex roles.

The Christian community is currently far from united in its evaluation of the change in gender roles. Some say that women should return to their rightful place in the home, while others argue for increased participation by women in all occupations, including the ordained ministry. It is important for us to grasp hold of the intentions God had in mind in creating humanity as distinctly male and female (Gen. 1–2). We must be aware that social and cultural definitions have expanded this distinction in ways that were not intended by the Creator. Keeping this in view, let us examine the reasons why gender roles are changing today and then consider some of the explanations for gender differences. Finally, we will explore the effect which the redefinition of gender roles has on the family.

Why Gender Roles Are Changing

There are several reasons why traditional definitions of sexual roles are currently being called into question. The social sciences have demonstrated that many of the traditional characteristics of masculinity and femininity, formerly assumed to be the result of natural development, are in reality a result of cultural conditioning. Increased observation and dialogue with people from various parts of the world have also informed us that most differences between masculinity and femininity are culture-bound.

The explosion of technological culture is another reason gender roles are changing. Before the machine age, the physiological differences between the sexes determined one's work role. Being larger and stronger than women, men were expected to do most of the heavy work. Since women give birth to babies and nurse them during infancy, they were more involved with child care. With the emergence of electronics and computers, however, the most valued work is no longer manual labor, but rather work that demands the development of the mind. That males and females are equally qualified in this realm has opened up the job market for women. In addition, the development of contraceptives has freed women from giving birth to large numbers of children.

Explanations of Gender Differences

For years there has been an argument as to whether gender differences are due to environment or heredity. This controversy began with the emergence of modern science. With the development of the biological sciences it was discovered that genetics plays a key role in determining the nature of both plants and animals. Furthermore, not only physical features, but traits of temperament were traced to the genetic packages

I CAN OPEN MY OWN DOOR, MACHO MAN!

which children inherit from their parents. Although each individual genetic package was understood to be unique, males and females were thought to possess decidedly distinctive genetic packages.

Behavioral scientists challenged this notion, explaining that gender differences are acquired after birth as a result of cultural conditioning. Both sides of the debate initially assumed an either/or approach, arguing that gender differences are either a result of hereditary factors or a result of environmental factors.

As the dividing lines between scientific disciplines have broken down, explanations for gender differences have become less of an all-or-nothing proposition. Contemporary explanations of gender differences are much more complex, and both sides point to the interactive effect between heredity and environment. Let us look at some of these explanations and then at some of the theories propounded by the women's movement of the 1970s.

Sociobiology

Sociobiology explains the differences between the sexes in terms of the gene pools which have developed through a natural-selection process over thousands of years. According to one version of sociobiology (Tiger 1969; Tiger and Fox 1971), men bonded together because of the need to hunt wild animals. In the process they also developed a sense of adventurousness and protectiveness toward their family. Women, on the other hand, developed nurturing abilities because of their need to bear and rear children.

One may ask, What prevented women from going with the men on the hunt? Research indicates that some women did in fact hunt, and that the offspring of these women were not likely to survive. Additionally, women who spent their time at home giving birth to and caring for children were more desirable as marriage partners. Consequently, these were the women whose genes were passed on to future generations.

The men who were desired as marriage partners did not stay around the compound and care for children, but rather were successful on the hunt. Thus, it was not the men with nurturing tendencies who contributed to the gene pool, but rather those who acted on their hunting instinct.

The result, according to the sociobiologist, is that men and women have different genetic packages. Women are perceived as more capable of emotional bonding with small children. Men are perceived as more adventurous, strong, and protective of their families. The differences in temperament between the sexes are explained in the same way. While sociobiologists admit that we no longer live in a society dependent upon hunting dangerous animals, and that the differences between the sexes are no longer a matter of our prime function in life, they continue to argue that these genetically produced differences are real and cannot be dismissed.

Christians differ in their assessment of sociobiology as an explanation of the temperamental differences between the sexes. Some are rather favorably disposed; others categorically reject any attempt to explain these differences; still others believe that the temperamental differences between the sexes were determined by God's act of creation. The dialogue continues today.

A toned-down version of sociobiology, which in actuality synthesizes genetic and environmental factors, is offered by Alice Rossi. She writes, "Organisms are not passive objects acted upon by internal genetic forces, as some sociobiologists claim, nor are they passive objects acted upon by external environmental forces, as some social scientists claim . . . genes, organisms, and environment interpenetrate and mutually determine each other" (1984:11). Rossi finds five compelling evidences that biological factors account for some gender differences: (1) correlations between the social behavior and the physiological attributes of each sex; (2) gender differences in infants and young children prior to socialization; (3) the emergence of gender differences with the onset of puberty, when body physiology and hormonal secretion change rapidly; (4) stability of gender differences across cultures; and (5) similar gender differences among the higher primates.

Rossi also cites evidence indicating that females have a head start in developing the capacity to care for children. Already in infancy females have a higher degree of sensitivity to touch, sound, and odor; they are more drawn to human faces and exhibit a greater responsiveness to the nuances of facial expression. In addition, girls develop more quickly than boys in the areas of language, verbal fluency, memory, sensitivity to context, and picking up and processing peripheral information. Whereas these findings may seem to reinforce traditional gender stereotypes, they do not deny that these tendencies are accentuated through the socialization process.

Socialization Theory

The socialization theory holds that from the time children are born, they are taught both explicitly and implicitly how to be a man or how to be a woman. In learning to be a man, boys in American society come to value masculinity as expressed through physical courage, toughness, competitiveness, strength, control, dominance, and aggressiveness. In learning to be a woman, girls begin to value gentleness, expressiveness, responsiveness, sensitivity, and compliance. When parents rigidly enforce these values, male children will fear being caught doing anything which has been traditionally defined as feminine. Girls will avoid appearing too aggressive, boisterous, or tomboyish, for fear of being branded unladylike.

Peer groups continue to perpetuate the gender stereotypes as well. According to studies of male subcultures such as school groups or street-corner gangs, if a male is affectionate, gentle, or compassionate toward others, he is not invited to be one of the boys. Girls are ostracized in a similar manner. In addition, the mass media, including magazines, television, and movies, reinforce the traditional stereotypes in subtle yet powerful ways.

The message of how to be female or male is deeply imprinted in the cultural patterns of every society. The family, peer groups, and the media converge to persuade young females and males to take on stereotypical behaviors. By the time they reach adulthood, they have been socialized into clearly defined sexual roles.

Neopsychoanalytic Theory

Nancy Chodorow, in her book *The Reproduction of Mothering: Psychoanalysis and the Sociology of Gender* (1978), presents an explanation of gender differences which is consistent with both Freudian theory and feminist thinking. She believes that women rather than men do most of the parenting as a result of social structures rather than as an unmediated product of physiology.

Chodorow contends that while the mothering process enhances a girl's nurturing capacity, it inhibits a boy's. Both boys and girls begin their lives with an emotional attachment to their mother, but boys must learn to identify with their father by denying this special attachment to their mother. Girls, on the other hand, can continue to identify with and attach to their mother in a natural way.

A girl's relationship to her mother and a boy's relationship to his father are significantly different. The girl is likely to be continually involved with her mother in the home. That the father is probably absent from the home for most of the day means that the boy must derive notions about masculinity from his mother and the culture at large, rather than from a personal ongoing relationship with his father. One might say that girls get an inside look at what their role in the family will eventually be; boys, on the other hand, must learn their role from the outside. As a result, females will take an active part in family life; males will see themselves somewhat as outsiders.

The close ties developed with their mothers means that girls will most likely desire to be nurturers. Boys are not closely tied to their fathers, and must deny the attachment to their mother for the sake of defining their own masculinity. Consequently, when they become fathers, they will probably be emotionally distant from their children.

In summary, neopsychoanalytic theory, which is a specialized type of socialization theory, explains that gender differences are a result of girls' experiencing a warm, close relationship with their mother and boys' experiencing a cool, distant relationship with their father. Male and female temperament can be expected to change with an increased emphasis upon fathering.

Feminist Theories

Liberal Feminism

The women's movement has generated several feminist theories, each of which attempts to explain the conscious as well as unconscious dominance of males over females. The majority wing of the movement consists of liberal feminists who generally explain gender differences in terms of the socialization theory.

Liberal feminists emphasize that inequality of opportunity has been perpetuated by a social structure in which men are the dominant class and women are the underclass. Although liberal feminists do not deny some innate dissimilarities between the sexes, they believe that most of the difference is socially determined. They believe that every individual has unique skills and abilities which have nothing to do with sex.

On the basis of an assumption of equal potential, liberal feminists believe that gender should not be a factor in determining involvement in any familial or societal task. All individuals should be allowed to pursue their own goals, irrespective of gender, and to participate in any task or activity they choose.

Liberal feminists argue that a variety of family forms is a constructive and healthy consequence of modernity. It is desirable for a society to honor different family arrangements in which individuals of both sexes have a free choice in their wage-earning and housekeeping roles. For example, a couple may decide on any one of three options: male wage-earner/female housekeeper; female wage-earner/male housekeeper; or dual wage-earners/dual housekeepers. Every couple should be allowed and encouraged to develop the type of living arrangement that is best for them. Liberal feminists abhor the bondage and constriction of family life dictated by rigid definitions of female and male roles.

In the area of sexuality, the active male/passive female dichotomy is viewed as culturally determined. Liberal feminists would elevate the role of both females and males, believing that both genders are responsible for their own sexuality and sexual fulfilment.

Marxist Feminism

Advocates of Marxist feminism believe that gender equality is possible only in a classless society. In their view, class differences and the concomitants of those differences, such as private property, perpetuate the oppression of women. Within capitalism upper-class women are reduced to useless, perfunctory roles. They are viewed only as beautiful objects to be adorned with fine cloth and costly jewelry, thereby remaining helplessly dependent on the men who provide for them. At the same time, lower-class women are overworked, exploited, and made to bear the worst of the burden.

Marxist feminists believe that if capitalism is defeated, women will gain equal jobs. To accomplish this, women need to join men in the labor force in the struggle to overthrow capitalism. At the same time housework needs to be valued and esteemed as the economically productive activity it is.

Although Marxist feminists accept the sexual and emotional aspects of monogamy, they would eliminate its economic aspects. As an instrument for channeling wealth and power from one generation to the next, monogamy helps perpetuate upper-class dominance. This means of keeping women economically oppressed must, they say, be put to an end!

Radical Feminism

Radical feminists argue that the oppression of women is inherent in the nature of male/female relationships and predates the emergence of private property. Contrary to Marxist feminism, radical feminists do not believe that the abolition of class-based societies will do away with the oppression of women. Rather, sexism is understood to be rooted in the very fabric of all societies; consequently, it will not diminish apart from radical structural change.

Radical feminists seek change in at least three areas. (1) Presently held in economic bondage to men in a society which is geared to reward the male rather than the female, women must form their own economic associations and businesses. Women's progress to date is seen as mere tokenism—only a few females have been given premier positions in the business structure. Capitalist organizations controlled by men freeze the economic subordination of women. (2) Women must be allowed to be sexually free and to establish spontaneous relationships with those they choose. This means putting an end to the hypocritical double standard which gives much more sexual freedom to men. (3) Women need to be freed from the burden of rearing and caring for children. This task should be shared by society as a whole.

Socialist Feminism

Accepting the major arguments in both Marxist and radical feminism, but rejecting the exclusivity of each, socialist feminists argue that both economic oppression and the fundamental structure of male/female relationships are primary causes of sexism. Like Marxists, socialist feminists reject the dichotomy between homemaking and work. They believe that domestic work must be considered real work, that is, it must be considered productive work. The lower-class wife, in releasing her husband from housework, is contributing to what Marxists call surplus value. Accordingly, housewives should be paid a wage by the state.

The family in its present form must be eliminated, because it represents the private sphere and functions to aid capitalism and perpetuate sexism. Only by eliminating the existing familial and societal structures can the dual evils of economic and sexual oppression be eradicated.

Socialist feminists see an additional dimension in the problem of sexism. They argue that although all women are oppressed, they are oppressed in different ways. Working-class and Third World women are more oppressed than upper-class women. The most oppressed persons are the lower-class women living in the poor societies of the world, for they must bear both international economic exploitation and sexism.

Biblical Feminism

Biblical feminists are women and men who advocate legal and social changes which would establish the political, economic, and social equality of the sexes. They are committed to enabling women to identify, develop, and use their gifts for the advancement of God's reign on earth. This is to be done responsibly and without regard to sexual stereotypes. Biblical feminists are concerned about establishing justice and living one's faith.

In her book *Sex, Sin and Grace* (1980), Judith Plaskow broadens the definition of sin and argues that women's sin has been self-denigration and lack of self-affirmation, which have led to excessive dependency and powerlessness. Sin manifests itself in the social and political systems of patriarchy, which keeps women dependent on men. Sexism, like racism, is embedded in a sinful social system that perpetuates practices that discriminate against women and keep them subordinate. Sexism is sinful and needs to be eradicated through changes not only in individual attitudes and behaviors, but also in the social and institutional systems themselves.

Biblical feminists are committed to raising the consciousness of people within the Christian tradition. They challenge the inequality of hierarchical structures by promoting the ordination of women and inclusive language, by attending to the special needs of the disadvantaged poor, and by fighting against the physical and sexual abuse of women and children.

Christian feminists seek reform in and through the church. They urge Christian communities to acknowledge the human suffering of women and to come up with solutions. They demand that the church encourage all persons, regardless of gender, to recognize and affirm that they are endowed by God with gifts and responsibilities to strive for love and justice through service to one another in all realms of life and in all parts of the world.

All these feminist theories have in common (1) the fervent goal of eliminating sexism and (2) the view that gender differences are the product of the fabric of society and culture. Patriarchy has been an obstacle throughout history, blocking the affirmation of women as persons. Frustrated by this obstacle, feminists see the necessity of altering the social and institutional structures which perpetuate the subordinate status of women.

Toward an Integrated View of Gender Differences

On the basis of both physiological and social-science research, it may be said that males and females are born with general dispositions, but not directional predispositions. These genetic tendencies are then exaggerated by patterns of socialization to fit in with the prevailing definition of masculinity and femininity. (See figure 16, where the distance between the horizontal lines represents the difference between male and female behavior.) We would suggest that it is culture and not biology which molds males to exhibit primarily dominant and rational characteristics and shapes females to appear submissive and emotional. It is essential for Christians to keep this in mind when they ask the fundamental question, "What is God's intention for the development of full manhood and womanhood in modern society?"

As Christians we must take care not to defend cultural images of gender differences. This is precisely what happens when we argue for the preservation of traditional gender roles! It is also important to guard against a wholehearted embracing of the modern androgynous ideal. What we must do is accept the evidence of biology and social science, and then interpret those data in light of the biblical pronouncements.

Genesis 1:27 records the creation of Adam and Eve: "God created man in his own image; in the image of God he created him; male and female he created them" (NEB). One important implication of this verse is that God created male and female as distinct human beings. We are left to determine exactly what that means and how such differences are to be expressed in male/female relationships. We must turn to the Scriptures for further elaboration on this distinctiveness and then interpret what we find there in light of the social-science findings on gender differences.

When we examine the Bible, we see little evidence that God desires there to be sharp normative differences in temperament and behavior between males and females. Those Christians who argue for rigidly separate roles for men and women can do so only by misconstruing the overall message of Scripture. Some use a proof-texting method that ignores the context of the verses cited. Another faulty use of Scripture is to view historical descriptions of gender roles as if they were normative.

The Bible has more to say about Christian temperament in general than it does about distinctions between female and male temperament. Paul writes in Galatians 5:22–23: "The fruit of the Spirit is love, joy, peace, patience, kindness, goodness, faithfulness, gentleness and self-control" (NIV). It is noteworthy that our culture considers these attributes to be feminine. On the basis of these verses, we would argue not only that males and females should be more alike, but that males need to develop the qualities which have traditionally been defined as feminine.

FIGURE 16 **Differences Between Male and Female Behavior**

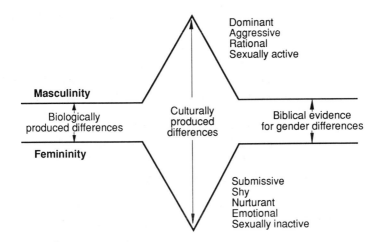

Still another means of viewing gender roles from a Christian perspective is to examine the person of Jesus during his earthly ministry. That is to say, what was Jesus really like as a human? To begin with, we read about a person who experienced a wide range of emotions, but compassion and love were pervasive. Jesus' compassion is seen in his relationships with the blind man, the lepers, the bereaved widow, the woman at the well, and the children. Consider also his actions toward people in need—feeding the hungry, healing the sick, and reaching out to the lost as to sheep without a shepherd.

The compassion of Jesus was also expressed in his sorrowful emotions during experiences of despair and loss. Jesus wept over Jerusalem because of the unbelief of its people. When he saw Mary and Martha grieving over the death of Lazarus, he openly cried and expressed his own sadness. At other times Jesus was elated and expressed great joy. When the seventy he had sent out to witness returned, Jesus "rejoiced in the Holy Spirit" (Luke 10:21 RSV). He also told his disciples that if they would abide in his love, his joy would be in them (John 15:10–11).

In addition to meekness, Jesus openly expressed anger and indignation. In a world under the curse of sin, he responded appropriately with anger. When he witnessed unbelief, hypocrisy, and acts of inhumanity, he took action. Jesus openly expressed his emotions, whether it was to nurture the little children or to overturn the tables in the temple.

The picture that emerges is that Jesus was not traditionally masculine or feminine by current cultural standards but, rather, distinctively human. He incorporated the characteristics of both masculinity and femininity and presented to the world a model of an integrated and whole person.

Changing Gender Roles and Family Life

As we mentioned earlier, the current redefinition of gender roles is causing confusion and disruption in family life. In response, some Christians have retreated out of fear to a traditional patriarchal form of family life in which gender roles are sharply separated. While it may be tempting to return to a time that appears to have been less disruptive, this course of action offers a false sense of comfort, for women had a very difficult life in the past. Christians need to see the present disruption as an opportunity to put in place a more biblically based form of family life. In doing so we must avoid both excessive individualism, which can culminate in a cult of self-fulfilment, and an overemphasis on the group, which can lead to a worshiping of the family.

Women in Family Life

In our society, females have traditionally acquired status through being wives and mothers. However, this situation is rapidly changing as women assume extrafamilial responsibilities, particularly in the work force. Many women experience contradictory expectations when they begin to pursue professional careers or work full-time outside of the home. Magazines, films, and television add to the confusion by encouraging romance, marriage, and childbearing, and at the same time glorifying the independent, career-oriented woman.

The message given to women is that they must have it all! In an effort to do it all, they become superwomen who suffer stress and frustration. Whereas men may encourage the women to do it all, they often do not pick up the slack, so the woman is left with a double-duty workload. The result has been confusion and disruption for the women, the men, and their families.

We feel that Christians should pursue a path of moderation in all of this. They should be on the cutting edge in working for the liberation of women from suppressive societal conditions which have kept them from having equal opportunity with men. At the same time Christians must be on guard against the philosophy which induces women to overextend themselves.

Men in Family Life

The traditional definition of the male role encourages toughness, inexpressiveness, and competitiveness. During recent years much evidence has accumulated demonstrating that this traditional definition of manhood is very costly for women, children, and men themselves. The tragedy for women has been documented in several books.

In *Women Who Love Too Much*, Robin Norwood (1985) describes the dilemma facing women who have emotionally invested themselves in a relationship with a man only to find that his masculine restrictiveness does not allow him to fully love back. In *Men Who Hate Women and the Women Who Love Them*, Susan Forward and Joan Torres (1986) write of women who are caught up in relationships with men who love them, yet cause them tremendous pain. These men may, for example, intimidate by yelling or withdraw into angry silence. They may switch from charm to anger without warning; belittle a woman's opinions, feelings, and accomplishments, and even humiliate her in front of others; or withhold sex, love, money, or approval as a form of punishment or control.

In a report on male intimacy which is based on responses from 737 males and 646 females, Michael McGill concludes, "Most wives live with and love men who are in some very fundamental ways strangers to them— men who withhold themselves and, in doing so, withhold their loving. These wives may be loved, but they do not feel loved because they do not know their husbands" (1985:74). Even in relationships with other women, where a man can be "revealing without risk, caring without commitment or loss of control, honest without being hassled, men are not completely self-disclosing. As a result, rarely does anyone really know a man, rarely does anyone know his love and feel loved by him" (pp. 115–16).

Lillian Rubin goes as far as to title her book on modern marriage *Intimate Strangers: Men and Women Together* (1983). Rubin asserts that for women intimacy means sharing thoughts and feelings, for men it means being in the same room.

The cost of traditional masculinity can be equally devastating on men's relationships with their children. McGill concludes that the average father is more of a "phantom man" than a "family man," for even when he is present he is absent—he is there in body, but in every other respect he is removed from the family. Present or absent, the father is reliant on his spouse to relate to the children for him. Whatever closeness he has with his daughter is more likely to be based on imagery and illusion than on substantive information about himself. His relationship with his son is circumscribed by competition, where "proving oneself is more important than presenting oneself" (McGill 1985:184).

Men do not fare much better in their relationships with other men, which McGill finds to be superficial, even shallow. In summarizing what a boy can expect to learn from his father, Perry Garfinkel states, "If he has learned well—about the importance of power, achievement, competition, and emotional expressiveness—he will enter relationships with other men with great caution and distrust" (1985:43).

Perhaps the most discouraging statement on fathering is Samuel Osherson's *Finding Our Fathers: The Unfinished Business of Manhood*. On the basis of an in-depth longitudinal study of 370 men, Osherson concludes that "boys grow into manhood with a *wounded* father within, a conflicted inner sense of masculinity rooted in men's experience of their fathers as rejecting, incompetent, or absent" (1986:3). As a result of a distant relationship with their fathers,

> men carry around as adults a burden of vulnerability, dependency, or emptiness within themselves, still grieving, reliving a time when going to mother for help as they wanted to was inappropriate, and they wouldn't or couldn't go to father with the confusion, anger, or sadness they felt. When men are put in touch with their pain today, they respond ambivalently—with rage or shame, attempting to prove their independence, as well as with curiosity and a desire to deal with the wounds they feel. [pp. 6–7]

Garfinkel believes that such patterns or rules of behavior govern and are reinforced in fraternal relationships. A boy learns from his brother that "rivalry rules. He who comes in first—who is born first, scores higher, earns more—is better. Like an endless game of one-upmanship from cradle to coffin. The lessons of competition and emotional inexpressiveness come through the brother bond as well" (1985:95). Some men join clubs as a retreat from the competitive, nonnurturing society at large. Garfinkel finds that "once inside, however, they are faced with similar struggles and competitions for power and control. . . . A man comes away from his men's club and fraternity experience with mixed feelings. His need to belong is fulfilled but his need for closeness to men may not be" (p. 107).

All this evidence should cause us to challenge the traditional definition of manhood, which some misguided persons have even labeled "Christian." Hypermasculinity cripples men, preventing them from establishing bonds of intimacy with their children, with their wives, and with their male friends. If men are to become the complete persons God meant them to be, there is a need for structural changes in two important areas: (1) parenting within the home, and (2) the demands of the workplace.

At present most parenting is, in reality, mothering. Fathers need to be jointly involved in child-rearing efforts. The contribution made by the father must be significant enough to establish deep emotional bonding with his children. Research has shown (Chodorow 1978) that the more exclusively a boy is parented by his mother, the greater his need to be superior to women and eliminate any behavior which appears to be feminine.

Psychologist Dorothy Dinnerstein (1977) makes deductions about the origins of sexual warfare between men and women, which she regards as a repercussion of early mother/child conflicts. Children demand nurturance and respond with extreme rage when the mother cannot or does not supply all they require. This negative experience with the person who is regarded as the sole (or primary) caregiver carries over into adult relationships, distorting the ability of men and women to love each other. Dinnerstein also feels that the view of women as totally responsible for child rearing has resulted in inequality of opportunity and deep strains of discontent between women and men. The pain, fear, and hate which are generated between the sexes will continue until "men and women raise their children together" (Viorst 1986:217).

Fathers who become involved in the parenting process will likely find that their socioemotional and relational sides develop. This will have a positive effect on the sons as well, for when fathers set an example of expressing their feelings, their sons also become more expressive (Balswick 1988:101–19). In contrast to the world of work outside the home, where decisions are expected to be based on the rational rather than the emotional, taking care of children inclines men to consider personal and emotional issues. This will impact their work roles as well.

It may very well be that as a result of the Industrial Revolution, and the attendant separation between work and family, fathers are less emotionally bonded with their children today than they were in the past. Most men are fully able to commit themselves to a lifetime of hard work and economic support of their family. This is part of the ethic of traditional masculinity. What they have trouble doing is meeting the relational and emotional needs of their wives and children.

If we take seriously the evidence suggesting that modern society has become increasingly cold, heartless, and impersonal, then the need for the family to be an intimate, nurturing, and caring environment becomes even more obvious. Fathers do daily battle in this impersonal and heartless society, and they often return battered and bruised to the confines of their self-contained, emotionally isolated nuclear family. At the same time the social supports for family members—extended families, neighborhood networks, community embeddedness—have been largely eroded by the cultural move toward modernity. The result is that the nuclear family is often the sole source for meeting its members' emotional needs. Because of all these social and cultural changes, men need and are emotionally needed by their family more than ever before.

Family roles cannot be altered without altering work roles. Therefore the second type of structural change needed has to do with the demands which the workplace makes on men. In working full-time outside of the home, most fathers have little opportunity to establish a deep bonding with their children, even if they so desire. Fathers must usually crowd any attempts at establishing intimacy with their children into a few hours at the end of the workday (when their emotional resources for doing so are probably lowest) or into increasingly busy weekends. Their efforts are typically limited to excursions for milkshakes after dinner, quick-ending games, jokes, and bedtime stories.

By playing down the father-child relationship the legal system sets up further barriers to the development of deep, meaningful bonding between a father and his children. Fatherhood is not a legally acceptable reason for being deferred from the military draft. Divorce courts usually give the mother custody of the children and relegate the father to the position of periodic visitor. Fathers can be brought into court for failing to support their children financially, but little is done about the absence of emotional support from fathers. It will take a prodigious effort to overcome all of these various obstacles to effective fathering.

The traditional pattern of segregated gender roles—women in the home and men in the workplace—serves to keep males and females dependent upon each other. While women are kept economically dependent upon men, men are emotionally dependent upon women. Christians need to encourage men to devote more time to those tasks which require emotional input. If men committed only half as much time to relating to their children as their wives do, their relational ability and sensitivity would be greatly enhanced, not to mention the effect on their children. Some of the needed structural changes have already been initiated by women redefining their roles in society. Now is the time for men to commit greater amounts of their energy to activities which will produce deeper emotional bonding.

The current clash between the traditional and modern definitions of gender roles confuses women and men alike. The anxiety produced tempts many Christians to react defensively against the current redefinition. But the present situation should be viewed as an opportunity—an opportunity for both females and males to become more fully developed human beings as God intended. Such change will benefit children, families, society, and the individual men and women themselves.

We feel that Christians should be actively working to liberate males from traditional definitions of masculinity which have hindered them from developing healthy male/female, male/male, and father/child relationships. In order for there to be a true liberation of women, there must also be a liberation of men. When they are secure in their masculinity, they can support increased freedom for women.

Secure Christian manhood means that one is mature enough that he doesn't need to confirm his masculinity at a woman's expense. Such a man will work with women as equals as well as under their supervision. Within the family he will be willing to be equally involved in household chores and child care. Secure Christian womanhood means that one is mature enough not to succumb to the male world and try to be better than men, but to establish her own identity, priorities, and personal values in the workplace and at home.

True Christian womanhood and manhood are not mere reflections of traditional definitions of femininity and masculinity. To help achieve the ideal of true manhood and womanhood, cultures can continue to recognize the distinctions between men and women and at the same time encourage individuals to meet their potentials and goals in life through equal opportunities and responsibilities. The Scripture proclaims, "There is no such thing as Jew and Greek, slave and freeman, male and female; for you are all one person in Christ Jesus" (Gal. 3:28 NEB). The essential question that we should be asking is at what points our cultural norms prevent both males and females from becoming the fully human persons God intended them to be.

Once again our theology of relationships is pertinent. Men and women must be willing to interact with one another in a cycle of covenant, grace, empowering, and intimacy. There must be a joint commitment to each other in a covenant of love working toward the goal of equality. This will entail a willingness to forgive and be forgiven of the oppression and antagonism that have gone on between the sexes. It will take grace to acknowledge and accept differences of opinion in this area. Another element is a mutual serving and empowering of one another. Women and men are both in need of liberation from the gender stereotypes which have hindered growth in personhood. Finally, men and women will achieve intimacy in same-sex and opposite-sex relationships as they become free to know and be known to each other. This requires communication and a desire to understand the other in order that we may cherish and value who we are as brothers and sisters in Christ. As we become fully developed men and women, others will know from our love for one another that we are Christians.

10

Authentic Sexuality

The search for authentic sexuality often starts with an attempt to understand how we are to behave as sexual persons. Achieving authentic sexuality, however, depends more on understanding who God created us to be as sexual persons. How we behave sexually certainly influences how we define ourselves as sexual beings, and vice versa. However, an understanding of what it means to be created as sexual persons in God's image involves much more than a simple assent to or an ability to live according to specified behavioral standards.

Sexuality includes such factors as biology, gender, feelings, behaviors, attitudes, and values. Authentic human sexuality is not something that just develops naturally. The word *authentic* is defined as "real, genuine, believable, and trustworthy." We use the term to indicate that sexuality is meant to be a congruent and integral part of a person's total being. Our sexuality must be a real, genuine, believable, and trustworthy part of ourselves, so that we can embrace what God has created and declared to be "very good."

Our sexuality is a product of God's design, but it bears the taint of our fallen nature. In a multitude of ways this good gift of sex has become perverted and warped in our world. The inauthentic sexuality which is inherent in our fallen human condition is shaped by an interplay of societal attitudes and beliefs, cultural structures, and biological factors. In this chapter we will examine some societal and cultural influences on the development of our sexuality. We will also present some ideas on how Christians can become more authentic in their sexual personhood and expression.

Societal Attitudes Toward Sexuality

Human sexuality is profoundly affected by prevailing societal attitudes. The predominant attitude in the United States has changed throughout history. Our past is often looked at as a time when sexuality was repressed; modern Americans by contrast have attempted to throw off sexual inhibitions.

The Puritans have traditionally been blamed for some of the tenseness of past generations. By the standards of seventeenth-century European culture, however, the Puritans had quite a healthy view of sexuality. They did of course hold to a standard of celibacy for the unmarried and monogamy for married persons, but they advocated a wholesome sexual expression in the marriage relationship. An example comes from the Groton church in 1675. When a husband announced that he would abstain from having sexual relations with his wife for a year as a personal penance for disobeying God, the church leaders pronounced that he had no right to deny his wife her rights to sexual fulfilment. Sexual expression between spouses was regarded as good, natural, and desirable, and therefore not to be withheld. This is in accord with 1 Corinthians 7:1–5.

The Victorians, on the other hand, held many sexual taboos, so it may be more valid to blame some of the negative attitudes toward sex on them. The Victorian philosophy was to repress anything that appeared to be sexual. For example, not only were people required to cover their arms and legs in public, but even the legs of the living-room sofa and chairs were covered with little skirts. Bare legs on furniture were considered a symbol of sexual immodesty.

The Victorians also drew a sharp line between sexual desire and love. A virtuous man was encouraged to wed a woman for whom he had pure thoughts, which meant no sexual desire. Husbands were told that if they really loved their wife, they would refrain from having sex with her too often; for even in marriage sexual relationships were considered to be degrading to women.

The expert medical opinion of the day asserted that any sexual desire in a young woman was pathological. In 1867 the surgeon general of the United States proclaimed that nine-tenths of the time decent women do not feel the slightest pleasure in sexual intercourse. John Cowan, the Ann Landers of the day, wrote this wisdom in his advice column: "The more a woman yields to the demands of animal passion in her husband, the more he loses his love and respect for her."

It is not coincidental that one of the most popular songs at the turn of the century began, "I want a girl just like the girl that married dear old Dad." The dichotomy between sexual desire and love led to a dual arrangement: a man had his sexual needs met by a bad woman, but would marry only a good woman. During the first half of the twentieth century, especially during the 1920s, shifting attitudes issued in an era of permissiveness with affection—it was perfectly acceptable to fulfil one's sexual desires, provided some affection was involved.

In the years following World War II, there was a period which can be described only as preoccupied with sex. This began with the publication of the Kinsey reports: *Sexual Behavior in the Human Male* (1948) and *Sexual Behavior in the Human Female* (1952). Later Hugh Hefner left his job as a copy editor at *Fortune* magazine and started *Playboy. Playboy* found an eager audience of young adult males who were ready to jump on the sexual-freedom bandwagon. By denying the multiple facets of womanhood, they proceeded to reduce woman to a single dimension—the sex object! *Playboy* had great appeal to insecure males who were terrified at the thought of relating to a multidimensional woman. They were told how to dress, what music to play on the stereo, how to mix a drink, and when to turn the lights down. In short, the message was how to get the woman into bed and emerge free of any emotional attachments.

C. S. Lewis (1960b:75) has compared a society obsessed with sex to a hypothetical society in which people pay good money to view a covered platter sitting on a table. At an assigned time and to the beat of drums, the cover is very slowly lifted and the object underneath is exposed for all to see. To everyone's great delight a pork chop is revealed. Something is obviously wrong with a society so obsessed by food. The point is well taken! Something is radically wrong with a society obsessed by sex.

Modern American society actually goes a step further in that the platter is no longer covered. In many ways our society is saturated with sex. Sex is front-page news. We hear it in contemporary music; we see it in advertisements, movies, and soap operas. We are just now beginning to witness the backlash from such overexposure.

In the 1980s a trend toward a new virginity emerged. Women began to question what they had bought into with their newfound sexual freedom; many felt their desire for emotional intimacy had been completely sabotaged. College students wore large red buttons declaring NO to casual sex. Cable television experienced a sharp drop-off in the audience for X-rated movies. Raw, explicit sex had lost its appeal as a shock and stimulus, and people began rebelling against the use of sex for entertainment purposes and recreation. There was a retreat from free sex as many people took a second look at how sexual freedom undermines relationships. The fear of AIDS reinforced the current trend to stop promiscuous sex and begin safe practices. Many are promoting monogamous relationships as the sane and healthy way to express sexuality today.

A Sociocultural Explanation of Human Sexuality

Social scientists believe that our sexuality develops as we come to learn cultural definitions of acceptable sexual behavior. In his book *Journey into Sexuality* (1986b), Ira Reiss presents a sociological explanation of sexuality. He makes the assumption that sexuality is not natural, but is learned in a societal context. Basically, people learn about sexuality in the same way that they learn about friendship or love. The sexual relationship is the most potent because of the bonding that is created by the physical pleasure and personal self-disclosure which accompany the sexual encounter.

Reiss suggests that there are three elements which help determine the particular expression of sexuality in any given society: (1) The institution of marriage serves as a boundary protecting the sexual relationship. Jealous spouses will protect their marriage by inhibiting others from crossing that boundary. (2) Gender roles also affect the expression of sexuality in a society. Since males usually have more power, they will tend to demand and possess greater sexual rights than will females. (3) Beliefs about normality and human nature also determine the expression of sexuality. The prevailing belief today is that male and female sexual rights should be equal. Reiss points out that because women in the United States are gaining power, our culture is moving toward a greater sexual equality. This is reflected in the emphasis upon foreplay and mutual orgasm. These are rights that women are insisting upon as they become more powerful in relationships.

In Reiss's theory, normality in sexuality is culturally defined. He cautions that a sexual act we deem unacceptable may be acceptable in another culture; accordingly, his definition of sexual abnormality is restricted to those sexual acts that are unacceptable in all cultures. Reiss also argues that what exists in all cultures is normal, and that what is normal is right. We must, however, distinguish between Reiss's sociological analysis of the formation of human sexuality and the values inherent in his interpretation. It is possible to accept his contention that behavior found in all cultures is normal without accepting the premise that what is normal is right.

From social-science research it seems evident that our sexuality is a reflection of the culture within which we are socialized. We are taught to respond sexually to certain objects and symbols in our environment, and this determines how we define ourselves sexually. From society we learn to view a beautiful body and certain body parts as symbols of sexuality.

Sociocultural factors are responsible for many of the differences between male and female sexuality. In Western societies women have been regarded as less sexual largely because culture places more restraints on females than on males. Parents take a more protective stance toward their daughters. Girls are warned to show modesty in their apparel; they are instructed to keep their dress down, their breasts covered, and to guard themselves against sexual advances by boys.

The message boys receive from their parents and society is generally much less restrictive. Boys are given more freedom to uncover their bodies and explore themselves physically. As boys grow into puberty, they often enter adolescent male subcultures which encourage them to make sexual advances toward girls as a sign of masculinity. Within this subculture they describe sexual encounters as "scoring" or "making it." The boy who fails to score is in danger of having his sexuality called into question. By adulthood, males have been conditioned to be sexually active, while females have been conditioned to resist sexual stimuli and advances.

It is also through their culture that males and females come to regard certain objects, including body parts, as sexual. This can be illustrated by an experience of a female missionary on her first term in the field. When she walked through a rural village for the first time, the men whistled at her. Surprised, she asked a more experienced missionary to explain. It seems that men in this particular culture are sexually attracted to women with plump thighs, which have no sexual connotation in her own country. This is evidence that each culture has its own set of objects that elicit arousal.

The extent to which human sexual responsiveness is culturally conditioned can also be detected by considering the changes in women's bathing suits over the last one hundred years. During Victorian times men and women were not even permitted to bathe together at a public beach. When mixed bathing came to be culturally acceptable (around the turn of the century), bathing suits covered the woman's body to her ankles and wrists. As cultural norms have changed throughout the twentieth century, more of the female (and male) human body has become exposed.

The gradual exposure of the body has diminished the capacity of various body parts to generate arousal. While a bare knee would have caused quite a stir around the turn of the century, it is not the focus of erotic attention today. To emphasize this point, let us suppose that a young man living at the turn of the century could be placed in a time capsule and transported to a typical bathing beach in the United States today. Conditioned to the modesty of dress and sexual conventions of the 1890s, he would be shocked—proof that sexual response is largely determined by social and cultural conditioning.

Toward a Theological Understanding of Sexuality

Humanistic explanations of our sexuality, which rely on biological and sociocultural investigations, are important but nevertheless incomplete. Moving directly from this type of information to value judgments about sexuality is a premature leap. It is one thing to examine sexual behaviors and norms, and quite another to make decisions and judgments about moral issues. It is vital that we first deliberate the spiritual and theological implications of sexual behavior.

Three types of determinism have been advanced as explanations of human sexuality. Determinism is an approach which attributes an effect to one (and only one) cause. Determinism is sometimes referred to as "nothing-but-ery," since it proposes that the particular factor in view is necessary and sufficient to explain a phenomenon (MacKay 1974). Ira Reiss's theory is an example of social determinism—he attributes the development of human sexuality solely to sociocultural factors. Biological determinism defines human sexuality in purely natural (genetic) terms. Theistic determinism holds that human beings are created by God as innately sexual; therefore a person's sexuality is independent of sociocultural and biological factors. Each of these views is partial and incomplete.

Figure 17 shows that theological, sociocultural, and biological factors all contribute to human sexuality. Christians need not feel uneasy when the evidence points to sociocultural and biological factors, for such evidence does not take away the role of God as the Creator of human sexuality. It is our view that God has chosen to use sociocultural and biological factors to shape human sexuality. Note that in the figure these two factors interact to affect sexuality (the two-way arrow between Nurture and Nature).

It is enlightening to note the relationship between one's theological position and the relative credence given to sociocultural and biological explanations of human sexuality. In general, persons with a conservative Christian theology tend to emphasize biological factors when explaining male/female differences; they believe that God uses biology to imprint different sexual codes in females and males. But these same people tend to emphasize environmental factors and discount any genetic explanations when they make value judgments about homosexual behavior.

On the other hand, persons with liberal theologies tend to do the reverse. They de-emphasize genetic explanations for male/female differences, but embrace genetic explanations when addressing homosexual orientation and behavior. It is important to be consistent in regard to the credence one grants to social and biological explanations of sexuality.

Theologically, human sexuality can be understood as a reflection of God's design for creation. Genesis 1:27–28 declares: "So God created man

FIGURE 17 **An Explanation of Human Sexuality**

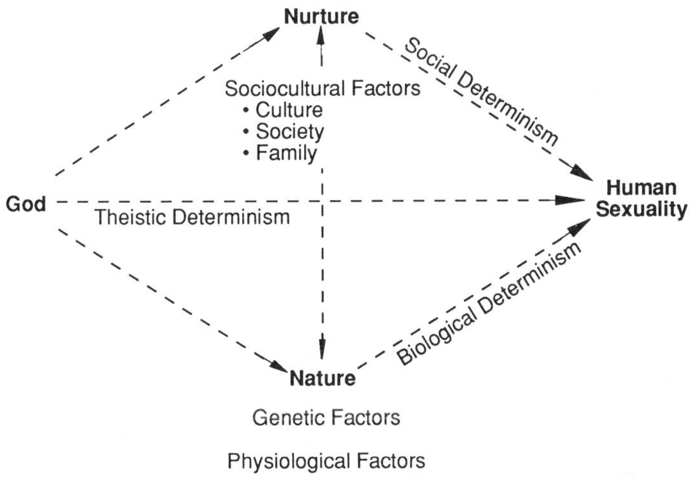

in his own image; in the image of God he created him; male and female he created them. God blessed them and said to them, 'Be fruitful and increase, fill the earth and subdue it, rule over the fish in the sea, the birds of heaven, and every living thing that moves upon the earth' " (NEB). This passage shows that males and females are distinct in God's design, yet they are equal and united as sexual beings in God's sight. They are both commanded to be fruitful, to subdue the earth, and to rule over the rest of God's creation. God created us as sexual beings and pronounced this creation very good! Acceptance of one's sexuality begins with the ability to acknowledge and be thankful for it as part of God's design and intention. Our sexuality is good in God's sight!

In the beginning Adam and Eve were perfect sexual beings just as God created them to be, yet they fell from that perfect state. All human beings inherit this fallen nature, which includes inauthentic sexuality. It is clear from the Genesis account that the fall has affected both sociocultural and biological life. Ever afterward humankind have faced physical death and various other biological consequences such as pain in childbirth and physical exertion in work as predicted in Genesis 3:17–19: "Accursed shall be the ground on your account. With labour you shall win your food from it all the days of your life. It will grow thorns and thistles for you, none but wild plants for you to eat. You shall gain your bread by the sweat of your brow until you return to the ground; for from it you were taken. Dust you are, to dust you shall return" (NEB).

Sociocultural factors were also drastically affected by the fall and, as a result, human relationships are broken. Brokenness is evidenced in the home, the place where sexual attitudes are established. Family structures, along with other social and community structures, all play their part in contributing to the distortion of a person's sexuality. It becomes difficult to achieve an authentic sexuality in the midst of these distorting influences. The comprehensiveness of the fall means that achieving an authentic sexuality involves conflict and struggle for everyone.

God has allowed human sexuality to develop through sociocultural and biological factors; because these systems are imperfect, we are all imperfect in our sexuality. Some suffer from deficiencies in the genetic package they have inherited; some lack a sexual wholeness because of inadequate socialization in the home and community; some are victims of sexual abuse and rape. Everyone at some level has to deal with the sexual distortions of the fallen world.

Despite all the obstacles, the sexual authenticity God intended for us is a goal worth striving for. Authentic sexuality is most attainable by individuals who are born with a normal genetic and physiological makeup, who are socialized in a home where parents display healthy attitudes regarding sexuality, and who live where the community and societal values are consistent with the biblical message.

Inauthentic sexuality can take a variety of forms, which are the result of differing combinations of sociocultural, biological, and spiritual factors. Everyone of course lacks spiritual wholeness. Some have the additional disadvantage of living through circumstances which result in a devastating sexual brokenness. This is especially true when sexual encounters have been deeply harmful, creating scars that make healing a long-term process. The good news of the gospel is that we can find hope and wholeness in Jesus Christ, who is himself the wounded healer.

Sexual Wholeness in a Broken World

The preceding analysis has indicated that the development of sexuality is a complex process affected by many factors. Figuring out how to achieve sexual authenticity in a broken world is even more complex. In the remainder of this chapter we will address four aspects of sexual expression which are important concerns to the Christian community: sex and singlehood, masturbation, sexual preference, and marital sexuality.

Sex and Singlehood

Not wanting to wrestle with the difficult question of sex and singleness, churches sometimes seek an easy out either by declaring that single persons should deny their sexuality, or by completely ignoring the question. Christian singles are often left with insufficient guidance as to how they are to live as sexual persons in a singles' subculture which endorses standards that often contradict biblical standards.

As a starting point, we present the three principles of sexuality introduced by Lewis B. Smedes in his helpful book *Sex for Christians* (1976:42):

1. The sexuality of every person is meant to be woven into the whole character of that person and integrated into his (her) quest for human values.
2. The sexuality of every person is meant to be an urge toward and a means of expressing a deep personal relationship with another person.
3. The sexuality of every person is meant to move him (her) toward a heterosexual union of committed love.

Living out these principles keeps sexuality and personhood connected at every level. It also calls to mind our theology of relationships. Sexuality is to be exercised within a context of covenant, an unconditional commitment to a personal relationship. We are challenged to work toward deepening this personal relationship by establishing an atmosphere of grace (acceptance and forgiveness), empowering one another, and increasing the level of intimacy. As Smedes suggests, "Sexual fulfillment is achieved when a personal relationship underpins the genital experience, supports it, and sustains a human sexual relationship after it" (1976:39). This will serve as our basic premise in discussing premarital sexual relationships.

In the United States today there are four major philosophies on the subject of premarital sex: (1) sexual abstinence, (2) the double standard, (3) permissiveness with affection, and (4) permissiveness without affection. Although sexual abstinence is the traditional Christian standard, it is no longer embraced by the majority of our society. It does remain one of the two strongest positions, however. The double standard, which allows premarital intercourse for males but not for females, has declined during the last sixty years. Permissiveness with affection is the viewpoint with the greatest number of proponents in the United States today. Permissiveness without affection, which allows casual and recreational sex between two consenting adults, has been growing during the last twenty years. However, the recent AIDS epidemic has caused a drastic reduction in the number of single persons willing to live by this philosophy. The risks involved have led formerly promiscuous persons to declare, "I like sex, but I'm not willing to die for it."

We believe that Christians should celebrate their freedom in Christ and be bound by no rules other than those given in Scripture. Starting with the Ten Commandments, it is clear that the biblical view holds adultery to be contrary to God's will. While the term *adultery* is usually defined as sexual intercourse between a married person and a partner other than the lawful husband or wife, most theologians argue that the term is broader in intent, referring to any intercourse between two people who are not married to each other.

The New Testament word *porneia,* which is translated "fornication" or "immorality," has traditionally been interpreted as sex outside of marriage. Those holding to the position of situational ethics (the guiding principle of which is to maximize love) argue that "fornication" refers to a depersonalized, body-centered sex. Such a definition allows one the freedom to engage in sex as long as it is not depersonalizing. But although the word may have this meaning in a few passages, it almost always refers to any sexual intercourse outside the marriage union.

We interpret the Bible as restricting sexual intercourse to the marital relationship. Depending on how engagement and betrothal are defined, specific application of this principle may vary from one society to the next. Historically, girls were often very young at the time of engagement. In contemporary society, however, the trend is to marry at a later age, making it more difficult for single people to meet the biblical standard.

Another contrast with the past is that societal structures used to help youth meet the standards, but in modern society persons of all ages are bombarded daily with explicit sexual stimuli. The mass media sanction sexual expression before marriage. An unrealistic situation is thereby created. At the very height of their sexual urges, people who have committed themselves to abstinence before marriage are besieged by constant sexual stimulation. This is a most difficult situation.

To add to the confusion, singles must grapple with the gray areas of determining the amount of physical and sexual involvement they will engage in during dating and courtship. This can mean anything from merely holding hands to genital contact just short of sexual intercourse. While the Bible advocates physical affection between Christians in the form of greeting one another with a holy kiss, it does not tell us what makes a kiss holy or how to express affection in a relationship that goes beyond friendship. It is indeed difficult to set up hard and fast rules regarding premarital sexual involvement since many factors enter into the situation, such as the persons' age and maturity, the level of their commitment, the length of the engagement, and the closeness to the marriage ceremony.

It is natural and good for single persons to physically express affection for the one they love. We all need to be affirmed and touched by others. Touching is a means of communicating acceptance, love, and care. We learn this from children, who feel free to express themselves through touch and to ask others to touch them. Adults, however, are often fearful

BUT, CAROLYN, PAUL WROTE IN SECOND
CORINTHIANS THAT WE SHOULD GREET ONE
ANOTHER WITH A HOLY KISS.

of touching and withhold this expression of love, thus depriving their loved ones of an important means of affirmation.

The crisis comes at the point when physical touch becomes sexually arousing. It is essential at this point that the individuals involved decide if this is what they want, whether it is appropriate, and to what degree they will continue to be involved. To assist in making these decisions, we present the following principles as guidelines:

1. The degree of sexual intimacy should correspond to the degree of love and commitment present in the relationship. Where there is no love

or commitment, a high degree of sexual intimacy is inappropriate because the focus is on the physical dimension rather than the relationship. Physical intimacy is meant to enhance the expression of love and commitment. When the personhood of the other is the primary focus, the sexual expression is merely a by-product, as C. S. Lewis observes in *The Four Loves* (1960a:132–38). Where there is commitment, being with the other person is more important than the pleasure that comes from the physical intimacy. In covenant love, commitment to the person and the relationship takes precedence over sexual expression.

2. The law of diminishing returns is as applicable in sexuality as in physics. This law states that in order to achieve an effect a second time, a stronger force must be applied. Think of the effect of one's very first kiss! It is an exhilarating experience. However, as time passes and one becomes used to kissing, the effect diminishes. We tend to desire increased intensity in physical lovemaking and progress to more intimate expressions in order to be stimulated. The ultimate sexual expression is orgasm. The closer a couple gets to that point, the harder it is to retreat to a previous level. The couple needs to be aware of this fact so that they can determine appropriate limits for their physical involvement. These limits should reflect their level of commitment and the stage of the relationship (as our first principle stated).

3. Both partners must test their personal motives for the physical involvement and activity. Is the motive for physical involvement to express affection or to sexually excite one's partner and oneself? It does something for the ego of both men and women to know that they can sexually excite another person. Most people feel a sense of power and control when they get another person to the point where they cannot be resisted. As the motive behind physical involvement, such ego gratification has a way of separating sex from personhood, since the goal is not a deeper personal relationship, but satisfaction of one's selfish needs.

4. The two persons involved must continually communicate about all areas of the relationship. A couple should tread cautiously when the physical dimension develops out of proportion to the social, emotional, psychological, and spiritual dimensions. When the sexual aspect dominates, the other important dimensions are undernourished, and the relationship becomes lopsided, vulnerable, and weak. A full relationship requires a communication process in which both partners share and get to know all aspects of each other's lives. Getting to know another person intimately requires that one listen and come to appreciate all dimensions of the beloved. The relationship itself is strengthened through such intimate sharing together. This includes learning to play together, to plan and dream together, to work toward future goals together. Spiritual oneness

will come as the couple seeks God's presence and blessing in their current togetherness and future union.

5. Both partners should take responsibility for establishing guidelines and setting physical limits. Christian males must reject the societal norm that males should go as far as they can sexually, since it is up to the female to set the limits. Both partners are responsible for their sexual involvement. This needs to be discussed early on when the couple is able to rationally set up clear guidelines. There is to be a mutual keeping of the boundaries. When one partner wavers, the other can call for accountability to the agreed-upon limits. There will be little need to argue about the standard, since the commitment was made at a prior time. This eliminates the possibility that in the heat of passion one partner will give in to the other—an action both partners will later regret.

There may be times when a couple will want to rethink an established boundary or to set a more stringent limit. They will need to find a place and time to look honestly at the pros and cons of the proposed change in standards. In this way there will be mutual agreement and commitment through a clear decision-making process in which both views are respected and taken into consideration. Once again the relationship will have priority.

6. The two people involved must agree to abide by the limits proposed by the partner with the more stringent standards. Such an attitude of respect and caring places the person above the desire for sexual activity. In an authentic relationship there will be a willingness to honestly express one's own ideas about standards and to find out what a particular limit means to one's partner. Neither person will try to dominate by judging the other's standards as prudish. In the end, honoring the limitation shows that the partner is valued and cherished. This will bring about a deepening of emotional intimacy.

It is also important that the partner with less rigorous standards not be judged. The essential thing is that each partner be willing to listen to and try to understand the other. Recognizing and accepting differences in one another will help the couple to make whatever adjustments may be necessary for the relationship to succeed.

To sum up our guidelines: the sexual dimension must be put in proper perspective. In 1 Corinthians 6:12–13 Paul says: "I can do anything I want to if Christ has not said no, but some of these things aren't good for me. Even if I am allowed to do them, I'll refuse to if I think they might get such a grip on me that I can't easily stop when I want to. 'Food is for the belly and the belly for food.' . . . But it is not true that the body is for lust; it is for the Lord—and the Lord for the body" (LB and NEB). There are, then, no hard and fast laws to govern premarital sexual involvement;

rather, there is a freedom in Christ to make responsible decisions that are in accordance with God's Word. We must bear in mind that not everything is good or beneficial for us; this is especially true of behavior which comes to have a grip on us. Once again, if sexual involvement becomes the overriding concern, it can lead to the demise of a relationship.

In thinking about premarital sexual involvement, it is important that a due amount of attention be given to the matter of sexual lust and sin. That is to say, we must neither ignore the subject nor overconcentrate on it. When Paul speaks out against fornication and immorality, he does so in a list of sins which includes greed and overeating. Some people make the mistake of magnifying sexual sin out of proportion. To them it is the great unpardonable sin; this is not the biblical view! On the other hand, others yield to the ethics of secular society and minimize sexual sin. It is not easy being single in a sexually oriented society which promotes norms that are inconsistent with the Bible. Single persons need to be enfolded into family and community life in ways that accept them as sexual persons with needs for love and intimacy. They will in turn have much to contribute to the community, as they struggle along with everyone else to realize the full potential of their humanity, which includes the sexual nature with which God has endowed them.

In a mature relationship there is a mutual responsibility for sexual behavior. This mutuality helps each partner control sexual reaction and expression. Leaving the matter up to chance is irresponsible. As single people set limits for themselves, their level of maturity should be taken into consideration. There is a great difference between junior-high students, senior-high students, college students, older adults, and single individuals who were formerly married. Chronological age does not always coincide with maturity, but it is a general indicator of one's ego development and individual autonomy. The younger the person, the more underdeveloped one's sexuality, and the more confusing sexual involvement can be.

Mutual commitment allows single adults to respond to each other with maturity and respect. A mature sexual relationship will incorporate the elements of covenant, grace, empowering, and intimacy in an ever-deepening cycle that continues throughout life. Persons who achieve authentic sexuality do not separate sex and personhood, but understand that their sexuality is an integral part of who they are. They will express themselves sexually only in the context of a covenant with and permanent commitment to their partner.

Masturbation

In the most extensive study of human sexual behavior ever conducted, Alfred Kinsey found that prior to marriage 92–96 percent of males and 60 percent of females have masturbated to orgasm (1948:499; 1952:141–42).

This study was conducted in a relatively inhibited period. Recent studies have revealed percentages to be even higher. Masturbation seems to be a nearly universal practice for both males and females.

In the past there were various attempts to discourage people from masturbating. Folk wisdom claimed that masturbation has unpleasant consequences: hair loss, warts, pimples, even blindness or impotence. Many youth lived not only with the fear of these physical consequences, but also with intense guilt.

How are Christians to view masturbation, and what should parents teach their children about it? Obviously, parents should alleviate the fears and guilt which the myths of the past may have perpetuated. It is very natural for children to explore their physical bodies and come to have an awareness of their anatomy. They need to feel positive about their bodies and the sensations they experience when they touch themselves. Healthy attitudes about sexuality begin in the home. Children who get a good start there will grow up with an appreciation to God for the gift of sexuality.

It is important to recognize that the Bible is completely silent on the topic of masturbation and that any case which a person builds either for or against it is based on inference. There are three major opinions about the place of masturbation in a Christian's life. The restrictive position is that masturbation under any circumstance is sinful. The permissive position holds that masturbation under any circumstance is healthy and morally permissible; harmful to no one, it is a good way to be aware of ourselves as sexual beings. The moderate view holds that masturbation can be both healthy and morally appropriate, but that it has the potential to be unhealthy and morally inappropriate as well.

The moderate position seems to be the most reasonable. Masturbation can be a healthy way for a person without a marital partner to experience sexual gratification. God has created humans as sexual beings, and masturbation is one means of making them aware of their sexuality. Accordingly, many Christians need to be released from the guilt feelings they have about masturbation. Furthermore, masturbation can be used to relieve tension and frustration. Studies have shown that the incidence of masturbation greatly increases among college students just before final exams.

But masturbation is not always psychologically and morally healthy. Compulsive masturbation can lead to addictive, self-defeating patterns. Within marriage, masturbation is a negative factor if it deprives one's spouse of sexual fulfilment or is used as a way of evading relationship problems. On the other hand, when married partners have different desires regarding the frequency of intercourse, masturbation can be a healthy and loving solution. The relationship must always have the priority, however, and the couple needs to face sexual problems rather than try to escape them.

Another issue to contemplate is the connection between masturbation, fantasizing, and lust. Jesus touches on this in Matthew 5:27–28: "You have heard that it was said, 'Do not commit adultery.' But I tell you that anyone who looks at a woman lustfully has already committed adultery with her in his heart" (NIV). Lusting after a particular person may lead to acting out one's desire outside the bonds of marriage. This is adultery, and adultery is sin. Lusting should not necessarily be equated with fantasizing, however. Most people fantasize about future possibilities, and masturbating with one's spouse or future spouse in mind can in fact be a helpful practice. Lusting has more to do with inordinate, inappropriate desire and finding ways to fulfil it. In fantasy, on the other hand, one's wish is more general, and there is usually no specific attempt to achieve it. The difference is usually known by the one who is doing the lusting or fantasizing.

If an inappropriate fantasy turns into lusting, there is real trouble. The pedophile, for example, who masturbates while fantasizing about having sex with young children may soon lust for and find a young victim with whom to act out the fantasy. Obviously this is a sinful act, and the fantasy was its precursor. It behooves us to pay attention to our fantasies, so that we can keep them within God's intended purpose.

It may be that a person who craves power fantasizes about sexual conquest. Bringing such a fantasy to awareness makes it possible to consider whether this is God's intended purpose. This particular fantasy disregards God's commandment to love others and not to do them harm. In the same way, persons who masturbate while viewing erotic pictures ought to consider the moral question of sexual exploitation and to judge whether the dehumanizing aspect of the erotic material is in keeping with God's intention for humanity. The rising concern about pornography has to do with these issues, since the distorted attitudes about women and sex in our culture may lead to an increase in rape and other violent crimes. Again, the Bible admonishes us to cherish and value one another rather than to degrade others.

These are the kinds of issues which Christians must consider when trying to work out what one is free to do and what is good to do. Each one of us must determine the appropriateness of our fantasies and the effect they have on our whole life. It is possible to monitor our thoughts in the area of sexuality, just as it is possible to make choices about which other things we allow to impact us. A person who experiences a romantic fantasy needs to consider whether it takes away from the spouse and the marital relationship, or increases responsiveness and receptiveness to the spouse in a positive way. The single person needs to decide whether a particular fantasy enhances the hope for a future relationship with a partner whom God has intended, or overidealizes to the point where there is no possibility of meeting a person who can fulfil one's expectations. The main thing is that we be able to admit when what we fantasize is not in keeping with God's intention, and to change it to what is in keeping with God's plan for creation.

In the past the Christian community has magnified the sins of the flesh out of proportion to other wrongs and given the erroneous impression that sexual sins are far worse than any other sins. It is important to remember that we have been created in the image of God, and we are the children of God who have been made righteous through the blood of Christ. All our sins are forgivable. Regardless of what our past sexual life has been, we can come before God, ask forgiveness, and claim sexual purity in Christ. At the same time we are responsible for our behavior and must earnestly seek God's help to become whole persons in every aspect of our lives, including sexuality.

Sexual Preference

Although most people have a preference for the opposite sex, it is estimated that approximately one out of every twenty persons in the United States has a preference for the same sex. On the basis of biblical texts like Leviticus 20:13; Romans 1:26–27; and 1 Corinthians 6:9–11, the Christian community has traditionally condemned homosexuality as sin. Today, however, many Christians feel that homosexual orientation is not to be condemned, although they do condemn homosexual behavior. Other Christians are tolerant of monogamous homosexual expression between consenting adults, but contend that it is not what God initially intended. A few even place homosexual expression on a par with heterosexual expression and advocate a marriage arrangement for homosexual couples. They believe that sexual orientation is determined quite early in life and is beyond a person's choice. Therefore, it is "natural" for homosexuals to express themselves sexually to a member of the same sex. The scriptural passages that condemn "unnatural" affections do not, it is alleged, apply in such cases.

Most Christians who tolerate homosexual behavior hold to a standard of committed monogamy for both heterosexual and homosexual couples, as opposed to casual sex or a promiscuous lifestyle. The AIDS epidemic has reinforced this position, so many homosexuals, as well as heterosexuals, are promoting the monogamous lifestyle. Both homosexuals and heterosexuals are choosing between celibacy and commitment to only one person.

A simple definition of homosexuality is a sexual attraction and orientation toward members of the same sex. At a young age homosexuals come to feel that they are different from their peers, and many do not conform with traditional gender roles. This can be a very painful time, for such children have a great fear of being different and are often cruelly labeled "queer" by their peers. Identification as gay or lesbian occurs over considerable time.

There may be a period when homosexuals hide their orientation and have great fear of being discovered. This is an understandable fear, because our society exhibits considerable hatred of and contempt for homosexual men and women. Homophobia is an excessive or compulsive hatred or fear of homosexuals. Homophobic reactions often stem from an insecurity about one's own sexuality or from ignorance about homosexuality and homosexuals. It is important for Christians to understand the great pain many homosexuals have experienced in our homophobic society, and to be compassionate to them.

Homosexuality, at least in part, may have a biological base. Where biological factors do play a role, they undoubtedly contribute to general tendencies rather than determine sexual preference. Researchers report that while there is no firm evidence establishing the origin of homosexuality, the data we do possess "are not inconsistent with what one would expect to find if, indeed, there were a biological basis for sexual preference" (Bell, Weinberg, and Hammersmith 1981:216). If there is a biological factor, it most certainly acts in concert with cultural factors.

Most attempts to explain homosexuality concentrate on sociocultural factors. The most popular contemporary explanation of homosexuality comes from the field of psychoanalysis. According to this theory, preference for members of the same sex stems from an aberrant psychosexual development during the genital stage, when children are working through the Oedipus and Electra complexes. At this time they wish to defeat the parent of the same sex and thus gain exclusive access to the parent of the opposite sex. When this type of attachment is encouraged by the parent of the opposite sex and coupled with a cool and distant relationship with the parent of the same sex, a child may take on the sexual identity of the parent of the opposite sex. Neither tested nor proven, this theory remains inconclusive.

The most complete attempt to identify the factors in homosexual orientation is reported in *Sexual Preference: Its Development in Men and Women* (Bell, Weinberg, and Hammersmith 1981). Data from interviews with 979 homosexual and 477 heterosexual men and women do not support the psychoanalytic explanation of homosexuality. Nor do they support such sociopsychological explanations as a lack of adequate heterosexual experiences during childhood, negative episodes with members of the opposite sex, or early contact with homosexuals.

The one sociopsychological factor which was found to be somewhat important is that homosexual men, more than heterosexual men, report that their fathers were cold and detached. Another finding is that a quarter of the gay males did not engage in typical boyish behavior. They report a childhood preference for girls' activities, coupled with the feeling that they were not very masculine. Lesbians report having engaged in homosexual activity during adolescence; they also exhibited dissatisfaction or nonconformity with traditional female roles.

In a recent review of the literature, George Rekers (1986:18) says:

> In light of the contradictory conclusions, and lack of good evidence, we believe that it is premature to dogmatically state any explanation of homosexuality which rules out a variety of factors. What actually causes sexual preferences is open to question. Our present understanding of human behavior would suggest that very little of that which we call human behavior is the exclusive product of either biology or culture, but in reality is a result of the interaction between the two.

Christians need to acknowledge the lack of clear evidence explaining how homosexual orientation develops and to come up with an approach to homosexuality that is based on a theological and biblical perspective.

We began this book with our theology of relationships, which is built on the premise that the original intention of God's creation was heterosexuality. In the Genesis account the ideal is a complementarity of the male and female: they become one flesh for the purpose of intimacy and procreation. However, since the whole human race is fallen, none of us achieves sexual wholeness in accordance with God's high ideal. Everyone falls short. Homosexuals and heterosexuals alike must strive to find a wholeness in their lives in a less than ideal world. We all struggle in our own ways for sexual authenticity. We believe that God can lead each one of us closer to sexual wholeness. This will of course be a more painful and difficult process for some than for others, but Christ is willing to grant to all the privilege of walking through that process with him.

Marital Sexuality

Sexuality is only a part of the marriage relationship. It is authentic and healthy when it is well integrated into a comprehensive pattern of intimacy between the partners. Several principles will prove helpful for couples who want to achieve authentic sexuality in their marriage.

1. The foundation for authentic sexuality in marriage is mutuality. This idea is presented in 1 Corinthians 7:4–5: "For the wife does not rule over her own body, but the husband does; likewise the husband does not rule over his own body, but the wife does. Do not refuse one another except perhaps by agreement for a season, that you may devote yourselves to

prayer; but then come together again, lest Satan tempt you through lack of self-control" (RSV). Here we see that the Bible urges full mutuality. "By agreement" is a translation of the Greek phrase *ek symphōnou,* which literally means "with one voice" (cf. the English word *symphony*). The mutuality mentioned in verse 5 is consonant with Ephesians 5:21, where husbands and wives are told to "be subject to one another out of reverence for Christ" (RSV).

Authentic marital sexuality can be achieved only if husband and wife are in agreement about their sexual interaction. There is no room for the misguided view that the husband initiates and dominates while the wife submits in obedience. Rather, 1 Corinthians 7:4–5 and Ephesians 5:21 assume mutual desire for and interest in lovemaking. This requires sensitive communication between the couple about their sexual desires. Just as an orchestra plays "with one voice" when each instrument contributes its own unique part and the music is brought together in harmony, so a married couple reaches sexual harmony through communication and sensitive understanding of each other's needs.

2. Husband and wife need to verbally communicate their sexual feelings and desires. Each spouse needs to know what the other desires sexually—this is not the time for guessing games. Although sexual desire can be communicated nonverbally, the communication will need to be verbal as well. It is important for couples to find a way and a right time to communicate about how they can best fulfil each other's sexual needs and desires.

Guiding each other through touch and brief words of encouragement during the sexual encounter can be helpful. However, it is also essential that the couple take time to talk about their sexual relationship, so they can evaluate how each is feeling and what may need changing. This is difficult for most couples to do, but if it is not done, dissatisfactions are never addressed and may take on more destructive and dysfunctional forms. Open discussion about sexual matters will help the couple find ways to improve or simply to reinforce what is already contributing to the sexual enjoyment. Obviously the couple will need to put in time and effort to work together on matters which will enhance the sexual relationship.

3. There must be no game playing in the sexual encounter. Total openness is essential. There must be no hiding of one's true sexual feelings and desires for the sake of personal advantage. Much of the game playing which plagues relationships is motivated by an inadequate sense of self-esteem. Thus, individuals who do not feel attractive may continually bait their partner into affirming them in this area. Another kind of game playing is alternately showing signs of sexual interest and disinterest in

one's partner. This is often motivated by the need to be pursued or the desire to be in control of the relationship. Yet another form of game playing is sexual teasing. One partner teases about desiring sex and then resists or is very passive when the other responds with sexual advances. These games do not enhance the relationship and end up having a negative impact.

4. Marital sexuality should include an element of playfulness. Although game playing is destructive, a sexual relationship benefits from a sense of fun and playful interaction, which depend on a lack of self-consciousness or embarrassment about nudity and sexual involvement. Honesty in communication, a healthy view of oneself and one's body, and comfortableness with one's partner are vital ingredients of being free to bring playfulness into a sexual encounter. Accordingly, the level of fun in a relationship is often a good measure of the degree of intimacy.

One of the benefits of playfulness is that it prevents couples from making a production out of sex. Controlling the sexual encounter in such a way that it becomes contrived and serious makes it impossible to respond to one another freely. A spirit of fun, on the other hand, keeps the sexual encounter spontaneous and relaxed.

5. It is essential not to become spectators in the sexual encounter. When partners assume a spectator role during coitus, they tend to be less able to make spontaneous sexual responses. This is a particular problem in a technologically oriented society which emphasizes the importance of using the right methods. Being sexually intimate is sometimes reduced to little more than an exercise in techniques. When this happens, sex is similar to the once-popular paint-by-number kits. The detailed instructions of a sex manual virtually dictate a couple's lovemaking. Just picture a scene in which the wife turns to her husband during lovemaking and says, "Turn back a page, Henry! We must have missed a step because I'm not responding." The whole experience is inauthentic because there is no creative and spontaneous interaction between the spouses. In a very real sense, the personhood of each spouse is lost in the effort to make love by the book. Naturalness between lovers has been replaced by an effort to be technically correct.

When partners take on a spectator role, they separate themselves from their sexuality. They are so concerned and overly conscious about their performance that they fail to be involved in the lovemaking experience. This removal of self from the sexual event defeats the whole purpose. There is no interaction.

In authentic sexuality, by contrast, the partners allow natural feelings, inclinations, and actions to occur without a conscious evaluation of the performance. Both husband and wife are spontaneously involved, relaxed, and active in the sexual encounter. Good sex cannot occur unless both partners are personally involved and able to lose themselves in the moment. Only if each one actively participates by giving to and receiving from the other will the couple truly become one flesh.

6. The greater the sensory pleasure in a relationship exclusive of coitus, the greater the sexual adequacy. This refers to the pleasure that is derived from foreplay, which involves the stimulation of specific erogenous zones of the body prior to coitus. The lyrics of a popular song express this principle: "I want a man with a slow hand; I want a lover with an easy touch." Authentic sexuality is much more than intercourse; it involves the use of touch to communicate tenderness, affection, solace, understanding, desire, warmth, comfort, and excitement. When a couple takes time to touch in ways that invite and increase responsiveness, they will find more mutual satisfaction.

7. The more secure the partners feel in their commitment to each other, the more complete the sexual response will be. Research shows that women are most able to invest themselves sexually when they feel secure about the relationship. Inversely, women who do not trust their spouse, or have fears that they may lose or be rejected by him, are less able to make an adequate sexual response. When security is lacking in a relationship, there is a tendency for the sexual aspects to involve game playing.

Shere Hite (1976) has found that men are also desirous of security in their sexual relationships. They want a sexual involvement which makes them feel warm and secure, and confirms their masculinity. Here again we see that trust helps bring about sexual responsiveness and authenticity.

These principles regarding marital sexuality call to mind our theology of relationships. A commitment gives a couple a basis of security so they can be open and responsive to each other sexually. Such trust is a necessary foundation for healthy marital sexuality. The dimension of forgiveness and grace is also crucial. To accept each other's unique sexual needs and desires and to work through different sexual preferences take an attitude of grace. And any disruptions in the sexual relationship which cause disappointment or anger will require a forgiving attitude.

Spouses ought not make unreasonable demands on each other sexually, but should instead find ways to empower each other through a loving process of giving and receiving. Learning together and being willing to be empowered by the other will make for increased pleasure in the sexual union.

Finally, understanding, valuing, and cherishing one another lead to deeper intimacy. This includes acceptance of each other's views and limitations, a desire to know and be known by each other, and the ability to be vulnerable. All these aspects of sexual intimacy come through covenant commitment, which leads to emotional closeness and oneness. Sexual satisfaction is a wonderful by-product of a total relationship. As a marriage grows in commitment, grace, service, and intimacy, the couple will move ever closer to God's ideal of authentic sexuality.

PART 5

Communication:
The Heart of Family Life

Introduction

This section deals with the important dimension of communication. This is the heart of family life in that family members interact through verbal and nonverbal exchanges to express their core emotions. By their expressions of love and intimacy as well as anger and conflict family members come to know each other in very intimate ways. It is basically by communicating and expressing thoughts and feelings that family relationships grow and deepen.

Without the ability to communicate effectively, the family unit will quickly become merely a collection of individuals whose thoughts, feelings, and desires are nobody's but their own. With an increase in ability to communicate, though, the family can become a healthy, vibrant community whose members love and care for each other. It is in this sense that communication is truly the heart of family life, for growing families are those whose members have both the freedom and the ability to effectively communicate with each other.

Chapter 11 begins with a discussion of why the expression of love is so important to family intimacy. We indicate the effects of communicating love and also deal with the obstacles that often make it difficult for family members to do so. Having focused on some of the dynamics of parent/child and marital relationships, we conclude by briefly examining a biblical model of expressiveness.

Chapter 12 deals with the important topic of conflict in families. Conflict is a normal part of life. There are both destructive and constructive ways to handle and work through these conflicts. We will present some rules for fair fighting and offer a brief outline of the stages of conflict resolution. We will look at the major styles for handling conflict and note that there are appropriate times and places for each. We conclude by describing the type of family which is best able to deal with conflict.

11

Expressing Love—Achieving Intimacy

Feelings are an important dimension of being human, and the expression of feelings of love and affection is an essential ingredient in achieving intimacy in family life. We have been stressing the importance of building intimacy in family relationships. This is one of the most difficult things for people to do. Expressing emotional feelings to one another, even to members of one's own family, is often threatening because we feel vulnerable and fear rejection when we do so. Yet family members must express feelings of love to each other if they are to achieve intimacy.

For a variety of reasons, intimacy is probably more crucial to family life today than in the past. A number of characteristics of modern society have increased the sense of alienation and loneliness. First there is mechanization; machines have nearly taken over the affairs of daily life. Not only have machines taken over a large share of the workload, but also life itself is ordered, regulated, and routinized according to a mechanistic timetable.

The prevalence of anonymity and impersonalization in our society likewise contributes to our relating to each other in superficial ways. Thousands of people live together on the same city block, but most of them know very little about their neighbors, and certainly fail to establish any semblance of intimacy with them. Business transactions such as buying clothing, groceries, or gasoline are conducted on a highly formalized and impersonal plane. So we learn to relate on a superficial level with the various people we encounter.

Finally, mass society is characterized by bureaucratization; the specialized tasks of individuals are coordinated by monolithic social structures. Bureaucracies order people into neat hierarchical relationships, and the individual's rights and responsibilities are defined in terms of one's position in the organizational chain of command. A result of bureaucracy is that we often view each other as objects occupying a position rather than as human personalities. Impersonalness is even encouraged in the name of objectivity.

Because of mechanization, anonymity, and bureaucratization, relationships today are usually conducted on an impersonal level, resulting in loneliness and alienation. We become part of a faceless crowd, being recognized and treated as mere numbers. David Riesman, writing about modern society as far back as 1950, aptly titled his book *The Lonely Crowd*. People desire intimacy because so much of life is impersonal. In the face of this heartless world, the family becomes a refuge where we can retreat for comfort, care, and intimacy.

In the past, the demands placed on marriage and family relationships to provide intimacy were not as heavy. In the institutional marriage of one hundred years ago, husbands and wives were expected to simply perform the tasks of earning a living and taking care of the children. Institutional marriage was replaced by companionship marriage: each spouse was expected to gratify the ego needs of the other. Today, however, both marital and parent/child relationships are expected to be intimate in a way which was unheard of in most societies in the past.

Intimacy is desirable in marriage and family relationships not only as a refuge from the impersonality of society, but also as a reflection of the biblical ideal. A persuasive prescription for marital intimacy is found in Genesis 2:24–25: "For this reason a man will leave his father and mother and be united to his wife, and they will become one flesh. The man and his wife were both naked, and they felt no shame" (NIV). In their nakedness husband and wife emotionally shared their fears, sorrows, joys, and desires with each other. This is an example for us to follow in our Christian marriages. Similarly, a model for intimacy within the family is God's relationship with the children of Israel. God intends the family to be a haven where we are able to express our feelings openly with each other without shame or embarrassment.

Expressing Feelings of Love

It is ironic that the three little words "I love you," which ought to be the most effortless and pleasurable phrase for us to say to those we love, are actually very difficult for most people to utter. Everyone surely knows that nothing would make another person happier than to hear such an expression, and yet even family members feel strangely uncomfortable when speaking of their love for each other.

The Effects of Expressing Love

Why is it so important to express love to other family members? First, it benefits the person who makes the gesture. It is physically and psychologically unhealthy to keep one's feelings bottled up. Physically, repressing one's emotions can lead to ulcers or other ailments. Psychologically, holding in emotions can result in losing touch with one's entire being.

The extent of emotional inexpressiveness is evident in the following illustration. One afternoon the movie *Romeo and Juliet* was shown to a crowded auditorium of high-school students. The roles of Romeo and Juliet were played by sixteen-year-olds, and many of the students could identify with the tragedy of young love impeded by family relationships. However, during the death scene it was surprising to hear laughter among the males, intermingled with the tears of most of the females. Obviously, the emotional impact was being sidetracked in order to cover up what adolescent males have been conditioned not to express.

Articulating our feelings helps us acknowledge and accept those emotions. When they are not articulated, we remain uncertain and unclear about them. Just as talking over a problem with someone is a way to get a better understanding of that problem, articulating emotions helps us to conceptualize what we are feeling.

A second reason why it is important to express love is to affirm the persons we love. Human beings need to hear and receive overt expressions of love from the time they are born until the day they die. Studies of infant deprivation suggest that babies who do not receive expressions of love will be unable to receive or express love during their entire lifetime. Many children who are not given sufficient affection, even though they may receive adequate physical care, suffer from marasmus, a disease in which the body simply wastes away. Marasmus is prevalent among war victims and orphans. A child with marasmus fails to develop socially, psychologically, and physically; death is frequently the outcome. What is most important for our purposes is the cause of marasmus: a deprivation of love. This fact makes it clear that children need to be held, cuddled, caressed, kissed, and hugged.

It is well established that children develop their self-image on the basis of their perceptions of how others view them. Children are able to love themselves if their parents have expressed love to them both verbally and physically. No one ever outgrows the need for affection and love. As we mature from infancy to adulthood, we have an increased need for verbal affirmation and physical expressions of love.

Third, expressing love is important for our relationships. Just as mutual commitment (covenant) is the basis of a mature family relationship, so communication is the process whereby the relationship is maintained and enhanced. The communication needs to be two-way. Expressive persons often make valiant efforts to sustain a relationship which is endangered by the unwillingness or inability of inexpressive persons to share their feelings. In many marriages inexpressiveness is matter-of-factly explained away: "men are like that" or "my wife comes from a very inexpressive background." But the lack of emotional sharing develops into a pattern of stifled communication. The possibility of intimacy is crushed, and the couple stagnates emotionally. Sometimes a spouse will try to satisfy emotional needs outside the marriage.

There is another way in which failure to express love can hold back intimacy in family relationships. A family member who expresses feelings and never gets any feedback will begin to express less and less. Intimacy depends very much on reciprocity. The result of one-way communication is a lack of security. For instance, when a father never expresses love for his son, the son soon wonders where he stands with his father. Such insecurity often produces manipulative behavior which is designed to evoke some kind of response from the inexpressive person. That behavior is often of such a nature as to elicit a negative reaction. Children consistently will settle for negative attention (e.g., a parent's anger) if they are not being attended to in positive ways.

Nonverbal Expressions of Love

Individuals who have difficulty expressing feelings verbally may ask, "Can't body language, physical actions, or symbolic gestures be used to show love?" It is assuring to know that there are alternative means of expressing love. Family members can express feelings for each other in a number of ways. A person can show affection with a hug, a pat on the back, or some other symbolic gesture, as well as through written language. In fact we are often unaware of what our facial expressions, posture, and general body movement communicate to others. Research on family discussions has discovered, for instance, that open- or closed-mindedness is communicated through body language. A person who assumes an open and relaxed body posture is likely to be open-minded about the ideas being discussed by the family. A family member who sits stiffly upright, tense, with legs crossed and arms folded, is likely to be closed-minded and defensive.

It is possible, then, to express love in other ways, but we must also ask the question, "How far can any of these nonverbal types of communication carry a love relationship?" The answer to this question is complex. If one family member is communicating only by nonverbal means, it is imperative that the others be able to read the hidden meaning in the nonverbal messages. When a conscious effort is made, they may be quite successful in interpreting the real meaning in a physical gesture. A grunt, sigh, cough, or glance may carry significant messages to the skilled interpreter who has spent a lifetime deciphering the wishes and feelings of an inexpressive person. The obvious problem with nonverbal expressions of love is that ambiguous messages will often result in guessing games and misunderstandings. Also, the inexpressive persons never learn to be direct and are therefore deprived of a deep level of intimacy with those whom they love.

Gestures of love are certainly appropriate: a dozen roses, a card, or two tickets to a concert often accurately represent the love and affection of the giver. Symbolic gestures are a normal and expected part of most family relationships. Love can also be expressed in literary form: a letter, poem, or song. Although it may be disastrous as art, family members will usually cherish a poem written especially for them. Moreover, expressing love in written form may instill the courage to express oneself verbally.

Family relationships can profit, then, from a variety of expressions of love. Accordingly, persons who find the verbal communication of feelings difficult may be tempted to argue that nonverbal forms of communication are sufficient in family relationships. It should be pointed out, however, that verbal communication has two distinct advantages: preciseness and personalness.

Body language, physical actions, and symbolic gestures are ways to communicate with others, but they lack the degree of preciseness which characterizes verbal communication. Body language, for example, can be misread. The receiver of the message may wonder, "What does that gleam in her eye really mean?" Physical expressions can be misinterpreted as well. A parent may question, "Is my son hugging me so tightly because he loves me, or does he want to delay my sending him to bed, or could he be afraid of something?" Symbolic expressions may conjure up suspicion: "Why did he send me these flowers? What has he done now?" or "I wonder what's behind all this special attention I'm getting from her tonight." Obviously, these nonverbal messages will need to be checked out if the receiver wants to be certain of having come up with the correct interpretation.

Although a high degree of precision can be obtained, it is hard to achieve personalness through written communication. Expressing love through writing makes an immediate exchange of feelings difficult. By their very nature, written expressions of love are usually read when the

writer is not present. This is not to suggest that verbal communication is immune from misinterpretation, or that it cannot be insincere, but only that feelings of love and affection are communicated more completely, personally, and precisely by verbal means.

Love has been compared to a finely cut diamond which can be appreciated in its entirety only if it is seen from many angles. Each angle gives a different view and shows a different facet of the unique beauty of the diamond, and yet the diamond is only one piece. The same may be said about love. The depth and dimensions of love are communicated by body language, physical actions, symbolic gestures, writings, *and* verbal communication. Although all expressions of love are important, the verbal message is the most likely to be accurate and to enhance intimacy.

Obstacles to Expressing Love

There are a number of reasons why family members—and males in particular—have difficulty expressing feelings of love. After considering some of the general reasons for inexpressiveness, we shall consider why males are less likely than females to show tenderness and love.

Unlikely though it may seem, fear is one reason why family members do not express love to each other. When we express love, we open ourselves up to another person. It is not just our feelings in general that we reveal, but our feelings for the other person. When we communicate love, we place ourselves in a vulnerable position. It is as if we are emotionally naked, as if we have stripped off all that is superficial and allowed another to see our bare emotions. When we place ourselves in this position, we begin to fear that our expression of love will be rejected, ignored, unacknowledged, or, worst of all, unrequited. An experience of rejection in the past makes it difficult to express love in the present.

The fear of expressing love is in part a symptom of low self-esteem. Persons with low self-esteem believe that they have little love to give and that their expressions of love have no worth. Where self-esteem is extremely low, there may be an inability to love oneself. And when self-love is difficult, loving someone else is also difficult. Even if love is felt, persons with low self-esteem may have difficulty expressing it.

Another obstacle to the expressing of love in families is the potential for embarrassment. This is especially true of a long-term relationship in which love has never been expressed. When certain patterns have been established, it is awkward to try to introduce new ways of communicating. Parents who have verbally communicated love from the day their children were born generally have no trouble communicating love when the children are grown. Parents who have not established such a pattern feel embarrassed about verbally expressing their love when their children are grown. Although grown children may want to tell aging parents of their love, the experience will prove embarrassing if there have been no previous verbal expressions of love.

Some family members are so embarrassed by the prospect of talking about intimate matters that they devise various ploys to avoid it. Talking about trivia is an example. Continual chatter may likewise be a defense mechanism which serves to keep a person from communicating on a deep emotional level. Another defense is the practice of intellectualizing feelings. Some people become very skilled at analyzing or talking about feelings, and in so doing never express their innermost emotions.

Another reason why family members neglect the expression of love to one another is the amount of time that is entailed. Feelings of love are usually verbalized when people are spending quality time together. Cultivating an intimacy within which love can be expressed comfortably takes much time and emotional effort. Expressions of love will likely seem forced where the individuals involved have not invested a part of themselves and a fair amount of time in each other's lives. In fact, a verbal expression of love without a substantial investment of time in the relationship comes across as superficial—and perhaps even false. It is difficult to believe and accept such an expression.

Still another reason why some people never express love is that they are not in touch with their feelings. While they may actually feel an emotion, they have such a weak grasp of its nature that they cannot identify, acknowledge, or express it. When they do attempt to express a feeling toward a loved one, they are most likely to express it indirectly. An inexpressive husband who feels love for his wife, but has trouble identifying the feeling as love, may say something like, "I guess I knew what I was doing when I picked you." This is an indirect way of saying how much he loves his wife; he will never, on the other hand, make a direct statement to that effect. Some individuals are so out of touch with their feelings that they recognize them only as good or bad vibrations. Such people lack the self-awareness which is necessary for intimate relationships.

Finally, traditional cultural expectations serve to inhibit males from expressing love. This may in fact be the most significant factor. There is some biological evidence that males have a harder time than females in verbalizing feelings (Rossi 1984:13). But while this may explain the origin of the problem of male inexpressiveness, it does not speak to the magnitude of the difference between the sexes. What usually happens is that in the socialization process parents inadvertently accentuate tendencies which already exist in their children. An inborn tendency becomes a label, so to speak, for the child, who then proceeds to behave as expected. Thus, an inborn tendency toward inexpressiveness becomes part of the child's self-image and a self-fulfilling prophecy.

Boys in our society come to value so-called expressions of masculinity and to eschew expressions of femininity. They are taught that love, tenderness, and gentleness are feminine. When a young boy expresses his emotions through crying, his parents are often quick to assert, "You're a big boy, and big boys don't cry!" or "Don't be such a sissy; be a man!" In various ways they indicate to their son that a real man does not show emotion. They will also use the expression, "He's all boy," in reference to aggressive or mischievous behavior.

As the boy moves out from the family and into the sphere of male peer groups, the taboo against displaying any of the feelings characteristic of girls is reinforced and continued. To be affectionate, gentle, and expressive toward others is to forfeit becoming "one of the boys." The mass media convey a similar message. In movies, television, and advertising, the male image does not usually include affection and softhearted behavior.

While it is true that many females also grow up in environments which inhibit the verbal expression of love, the male gets messages from society as a whole which reinforce his inexpressiveness and tie it to his identity as a male. This needs to be combated in family and society if change is to be accomplished.

The Expression of Love in Parent/Child Relationships

The emotional bond between child and parent is the most important factor in the development of a child. Children who are denied a strong emotional bond with their mother and father must go through life compensating for this lack. In reality, the most extensive problem for both boys and girls is the lack of a strong emotional bonding with their father.

Up until the time of the Industrial Revolution, the family was the basic unit of economic production. The mother and father were likely to participate together in the work that needed to be done and in the care of the children. With the emergence of industrialization, the household was separated; fathers were given the responsibility of working outside the home while mothers were given the responsibility of caring for the children within the home (Parsons and Bales 1955). As a result, females were encouraged to cultivate expressiveness while males were encouraged to adopt a more pragmatic and hardheaded approach to life (Belsky, Lerner, and Spanier 1984:71–74).

In keeping with their distinct societal roles, mothers and fathers differ in relating to their children. There is evidence that these differences begin very early and increase through the child-rearing period. Studies show, for example, that mothers tend to directly engage their babies, to stimulate responses, and to display affection, while fathers tend to read to or watch television with an infant (Belsky, Gilstrap, and Rovine 1984). In addition, mothers are more likely than fathers to hold, smile at, and speak to their infant (Lamb et al. 1982).

Parents, especially fathers, have been found to treat their sons and daughters differently. Fathers set narrower boundaries of sex-appropriate play for twelve-month-old boys than for girls (Snow, Jacklin, and Maccoby 1983). It has also been found that the disparity in the father's treatment of sons and daughters is greater when the mother is present (Gjerde 1986).

All these findings suggest that boys and girls come to have different capacities for expressiveness because of their parents' role modeling and expectations. Research consistently shows that adolescent and adult females are more expressive of their feelings of love than are males. Research also indicates, however, that males whose fathers were very expressive are just as expressive as females (Balswick 1988:101–19). Expressive parents produce expressive children.

The pattern which seems to emerge from the research on parenting is that mothers are more evenhanded in the affection they show to daughters and sons, while fathers treat sons and daughters in accord with the sexual stereotypes. Further, while the disparity in the father's approach toward sons and daughters begins when the children are still infants, it increases as they grow older. By the time children reach their teenage years, fathers view a daughter as someone to be treated in a gentle manner, held, hugged, and affirmed, while a son is treated in a standoffish way. It is not surprising that more daughters than sons rate their fathers high in the giving of nurturance and affection. Fathers seem to be preoccupied with the masculine development of their sons while they encourage femininity in their daughters.

We are reminded here once again of Samuel Osherson's negative evaluation of fathering (see p. 166). Men struggle with intimacy because they did not experience warm relationships with their fathers. The process of individuation is particularly difficult for boys because they must first psychologically separate from their mother and then identify and bond with their father, who in all too many cases is rejecting, incompetent, or absent. Discouraged from going to mother for help and turned aside by a cool and distant father, many boys are forced to deal with their confused feelings and problems all by themselves. It comes as no surprise, then, that when these boys grow to manhood, they find it difficult to share their feelings with others.

The Expression of Love in Marriage

When it comes to expressing love in a marital relationship, men face a dilemma. On the one hand, society teaches that to be masculine is to be inexpressive; on the other, marriage requires a sharing of affection and companionship, the ability to communicate and express feelings.

Research has shown that the greater the expression of positive feelings between a husband and wife, the better adjusted the marriage. A number of studies also indicate that husbands tend to be less expressive than their wives. More-recent research shows that when husband and wife express feelings about equally, the marriage tends to be well adjusted (Balswick 1988:151–71). Regardless of the total amount, similar levels of self-disclosure point to a healthy marriage. A marriage in which both partners disclose little is about as well adjusted as one in which both disclose much. Great dissatisfaction and problems are likely to emerge when there is an imbalance in the amount of self-disclosure.

While the husband is typically more inexpressive than his wife, there are some factors which work against a wife's being open and sharing. First, if an expression of love is not reciprocated, it will probably not continue to be offered. Over a period of time, lack of positive reinforcement may diminish the wife's verbal expression of love. Many a wife begins marriage with expansive declarations of love for her husband; but if after some years there is no reciprocal expression from him, she will express her feelings less.

A second factor in inequality is the level of vulnerability. When a wife reveals herself to her husband and he stands aloof, refusing to make himself equally vulnerable, she will eventually no longer be willing to take the risk. She will no longer unilaterally reveal her feelings. Without mutual sharing there can be no real intimacy between a couple.

A third possible factor is the birth of a child. Carrying this additional emotional burden, the wife may express herself less to her husband. As time passes, the child may be able to fill some of the emotional needs of the mother. It is tempting for a mother to express herself to a child who does return love rather than to a husband who rarely returns affection.

Wives may also become less expressive of their tender feelings in a bid for power in their marriage. Although commitment is the ideal basis for marriage, in actuality marriage is often more of an ongoing struggle for control. Sociologist Jack Sattel (1976) has suggested that male inexpressiveness is a form of sexual politics: men deliberately hide their feelings in an attempt to control the marital relationship. If a wife perceives that her husband's inexpressiveness is a conscious effort to control her, she may be tempted to withhold her expression of affection as well. That is, she may decide to withhold affection until her husband gives up the need to be in control and expresses affection for her.

The preceding scenario is most likely to occur in a situation in which the husband is relatively disinterested in the marriage and the wife overdependent on it. The wife will not dare make too many demands for fear that her husband will terminate the relationship. He can often have his way by being demanding and by threatening to leave unless she yields. In a relationship of this type, her expressions of love amount to a loss of power. Saying "I love you" is interpreted as a sign of dependence. When a disinterested husband can take his wife's love for granted, she is powerless. The wife who finds herself in such a situation might be very tempted to stop communicating her love. She may even pretend disinterest in the marriage in an attempt to gain some power.

A Biblical Model of Expressiveness

In our first chapter we pointed out that the last recorded exchange between Jesus and Peter (John 21) is a perfect picture of the intimacy desirable in family relationships. It is also a model of expressiveness and the communication of love. Peter and some of the other disciples had been fishing during the night on the Sea of Galilee. They came to shore just as day was breaking, and found Jesus with a charcoal fire ready. He invited them to join him for breakfast. Jesus then began a curious quizzing of Peter about his love. Three times Jesus asked Peter, "Do you love me?" After each query, Peter replied, "Yes, you know that I love you." We are told that Peter was grieved after Jesus asked him this question the third time.

Jesus had a definite reason for posing the question three times: Peter had earlier denied Jesus three times; Jesus was now giving Peter the opportunity to assert what he had previously denied and to reaffirm his love three times. We have no way of knowing whether Peter had asked forgiveness for his denial, but Jesus did offer Peter at this time both an opportunity to express his feelings of love and forgiveness. Peter certainly had a need to express these feelings and to reaffirm his love. For he would soon be one of a small group left on earth to carry on the work which Christ had started. Jesus cared for Peter; and because he did, he drew Peter out to the point where he was able to share his feelings of love toward Jesus.

With this experience Peter changed: from an intimidated coward during Christ's crucifixion he became a fearless witness after Jesus' ascension. People struggling today to find intimacy in an impersonal society need to realize that they, too, can change by expressing love. For as the Word of God teaches, "There is no fear in love, but perfect love casts out fear. For fear has to do with punishment, and he who fears is not perfected in love. We love, because he first loved us" (1 John 4:18–19 RSV).

12

Expressing Anger—
Dealing with Conflict

S trong families are not those which never experience conflict, but rather those which successfully manage conflict when it does arise. When we meet a couple who tell us that they never have any conflicts, we assume one of several possibilities—they have not been married very long, they don't know each other very well, they don't talk to each other very much, or they are lying. Conflict is a normal part of intimate relationships.

Simply put, a conflict is a difference in opinion. Family conflict can be individual (i.e., between two family members) or collective (i.e., between two sets of family members). Individual conflict can arise within a family subsystem (e.g., between a husband and a wife) or between subsystems (e.g., a father in conflict with a son). Collective conflicts can occur between family subsystems (parents against children) or irrespective of subsystems (e.g., mother and daughter in conflict with father and son).

Although family conflict stems from differences between individuals, it is usually related to the ways in which those individuals are tied into the family system and subsystems. That is to say, most family conflict is systemic in nature, centering around either the formation of or changes within the family system. Marital conflict, for example, is most likely to occur during the early years when the system is being formed or during transitional periods of family restructuring. Parent/child conflict is less likely when the parental and sibling subsystems are on solid footings, and more likely when these two subsystems are in flux, such as when children reach their teenage years and parents midlife.

It should also be noted that conflict between subsystems can cause secondary conflict within the individual subsystems. As an example, parent/teenager conflict can intensify conflict between the husband and wife over the issue of how to parent their teenager. It is also true that conflict between subsystems can unify each subsystem, such as when conflict with parents leads children to agree not to fight each other in order to present a united front in the battle against their parents.

A common pattern is for a conflict between two family members to entangle the others. Strong emotional ties and the effect which the outcome of the conflict may have on all family members make it difficult for the others to stay out of the fight. A triangle is formed when noninvolved family members are brought into a conflict to help one person win the argument. This tends to complicate the situation, since the matter of the third party's loyalty is added to the points already in dispute.

A Destructive Approach to Conflict: Denial

While conflict in itself is neither good nor bad, the way in which it is handled can be either destructive or constructive. Denying or failing to deal with conflict is invariably destructive to family relationships. Denial of conflict is like sweeping dirt under a rug. It only appears to eliminate the problem; it does nothing about the behavior which brought about the conflict in the first place. The problem, like the addictive use of drugs, will intensify because the conflict-producing behavior never gets changed. Denial is destructive not only on the relational level, but also on the personal level, since those who deny the conflict are also forced to deny their feelings of hurt, disappointment, and anger.

There are several ways in which family members can deny conflict. One common method is displacement: a family member angered or disturbed by another conveniently vents frustrations on a third member. The comic strip "Family Circle" once depicted an excellent example of displacement: the boss lashing out at the husband, the husband coming home and shouting at his wife, the wife scolding the teenage daughter, the daughter crabbing at her younger brother, and the brother bawling out the dog. The string of displaced conflict ended with the dog chasing the cat, and the cat catching and eating a mouse. There was a victim in the end who suffered the final blow.

Powerful family members use displacement to take out their frustrations on the less powerful. The younger members on the receiving end often come to the mistaken belief that they are bad and deserve punishment.

Another common form of denial in the family is disengagement. In this case family members avoid conflict by sidestepping sensitive and controversial issues. Disengagement might be initiated by a burst of anger followed by withdrawal, such as when a husband gets mad at his wife, storms out of the house and away in the car, and then returns two hours later as if nothing had happened. The husband and wife never talk about what caused the blowup and collude in the cover-up. Disengagement serves as a barrier to growth in the relationship, and the unresolved conflict may well lead to a severe crisis later on.

A more subtle form of denial is disqualification, a quick discounting of one's angry reaction. A mother may get mad at her children only to disqualify the legitimacy of her angry feelings by reasoning that she would not have gotten mad if she had slept better the night before. Disqualifiers tend to cover up angry emotions rather than admit them. Like the other forms of denial, disqualification is a barrier to growth and is destructive to family relationships.

Constructive Approaches

The first step in dealing constructively with conflict is to admit that the conflict exists. The second step is to decide how the conflict is to be handled. While there is little disagreement regarding the need to recognize and admit angry feelings, opinions differ as to how to go about resolving the anger. There are three basic constructive approaches: fair fighting, conflict resolution, and conflict management.

In 1968 George Bach and Peter Wyden wrote a book entitled *The Intimate Enemy: How to Fight Fair in Love and Marriage*. They suggested that conflict be handled in a fair fight. Perhaps because of the seeming contradiction in terms like "constructive conflict" and "fair fighting," many have vehemently reacted to this proposal; they feel that fighting is always destructive. Others have found the analogy of a fair fight to be helpful.

The second constructive approach is conflict resolution. Its advocates wholeheartedly accept many of the rules of fair fighting, but reject the concept itself because of the negative connotation of words like "fighting." It can be dangerous to endorse such terms in a society like ours where there is so much physical abuse in families.

The third constructive approach is conflict management. It emerged in reaction to conflict resolution, which suggests that there is an end to conflict. It is argued that a more realistic model views conflict in human relationships as an unending process which involves constant change.

There is a sense in which conflict will never be completely resolved but will need continuous management.

Fair Fighting

Before the concept of fair fighting was introduced, there was a tendency to view all conflict as destructive and undesirable. Fair fighting developed as a reaction to the opposite extremes of denial and avoidance on the one hand, and confrontation and attack on the other. We believe there is wisdom in reviewing the rules of fair fighting (see table 6). We have made no attempt to identify the source of each rule; some appear in Bach and Wyden's original work, some have been formulated by a number of other writers over the past twenty years, and some are our own reformulations.

1. *Identify the issue.* The first rule in fair fighting is to identify the real issue in a conflict. This can be a very difficult task, because most family conflicts involve more than a single issue. There is also the likelihood that family members will differ as to what the central issue really is. Little progress can be made until each person involved knows how the others define the conflict. Where there are multiple issues, the first task is to agree on which one to tackle first and to try to understand how they are all interrelated.

2. *Choose the right time.* If time is available, and if emotional intensity does not preclude a reasonable argument, some conflicts can be construc-

TABLE 6
Rules for a Fair Fight

1.	Identify the issue.
2.	Choose the right time.
3.	Choose the right place.
4.	Begin with a positive stroke.
5.	Stick to the issue.
6.	Do not bring up the past.
7.	Do not hit below the belt.
8.	Take the other seriously.
9.	Express anger nonabusively.
10.	Do not play games.
11.	Do not be passively aggressive.
12.	Avoid asking for explanations of behavior.
13.	Avoid labeling and name calling.
14.	Avoid triangles.

tively resolved when they arise. In most cases, however, family members need a period for cooling off and must schedule the main event for a time which will be mutually convenient for everyone involved. If a sixteen-year-old son arrives home at midnight, one hour past his deadline, the parents would be well advised to wait to deal with the issue, for they will be tired and angry. Perhaps a brief explanation from the son together with an expression of concern by the parents and a promise to discuss the issue the next day is the best plan of action.

In our own marriage, we have learned never to schedule a fight for the early morning as Judy is barely functioning then. Likewise, to schedule a fight late at night is to risk Jack's noninvolvement. Through our many years of marriage, we have learned to schedule our conflict discussions for early evenings.

3. *Choose the right place.* Fair fighting needs to take place on neutral territory. The father's workshop is an inappropriate place, as is the wife's study or the child's room. Seek out a neutral area where all parties involved are on equal footing and where the family can be free of interruptions.

4. *Begin with a positive stroke.* The discussion will proceed much more smoothly if one begins by giving a positive stroke. For example, suppose that Sally has been remiss lately about hanging up towels and picking up her clothes when she uses the family bathroom. Her parents might confront her by saying, "Sally, we're tired of your throwing towels and dirty clothes all over the bathroom floor; so shape up!" Or they could begin with a positive stroke: "Sally, you are generally very good at following the family rules, but you seem to have forgotten the agreement regarding bathroom tidiness. We would really appreciate it if you would pick up your clothes and hang up the towels after you bathe." This is a clear indication of discontent as well as an honest request, but the positive stroke gives Sally the benefit of the doubt and does not label her actions as intentional or antagonistic. There is no need to berate her for the infraction of the rule, and the positive stroke may well elicit a positive feeling and response.

5. *Stick to the issue.* Once conversation has begun, it is essential to stick to the issue. This may be hard to do, especially when someone brings up a related point. If that point is truly pertinent to the issue at hand, the discussion may need to be widened. However, no one is to be allowed to diffuse or sidetrack the major issue. Left-field issues, since they only muddy the water and forestall resolution of the problem, should immediately be declared off-limits.

When the family gathers to work out a conflict, it is important that everyone participate. The group has come together to listen to each member and to try to understand one another's involvement in the conflict.

Each person needs to ask how he or she is contributing to the problem and what can be done individually and collectively to solve it.

6. *Do not bring up the past.* In the heat of an argument it is tempting to dredge up past hurts and complaints. Some people have a habit of storing all their anger and frustrations rather than dealing with them directly. This is sometimes called gunnysacking. These individuals will unload their past anger and disappointment on others during a fight. The experience of being dumped on is devastating and will, in fact, negate any progress toward conflict resolution.

7. *Do not hit below the belt.* In a fair fight verbal attacks on areas of personal sensitivity are prohibited. Each of us has emotionally vulnerable areas where even a mild punch would be a shattering blow. Family members generally know each other's sensitive areas. For example, a reference to weight may be a hit below the belt. So too a reference to stinginess. On the other hand, some family members are so overly touchy that important issues cannot be addressed without their calling foul. These persons wear their belt around their neck!

8. *Take the other seriously.* Ridiculing or laughing at another family member during a fight is inappropriate. Such behavior does not take the other person seriously and gives the message that the other's opinion is worthless, stupid, and not worth considering. This obviously precludes any problem solving.

9. *Express anger nonabusively.* It is important to be reminded that the Bible does not say that anger is a sin. Ephesians 4:26 reads, "Be angry but do not sin; do not let the sun go down on your anger" (RSV). There are two ways, however, in which our anger can become sin. First, if we deny our anger or hold it in, never expressing it to the one with whom we are angry, it will smolder and build within us. This is allowing the anger to become sin. Unexpressed anger can lead to resentment, hate, and revenge.

Second, anger becomes sin when it is expressed in abusive ways, either verbally or physically. Physical abuse is, without doubt, sinful behavior. But it is also true that verbal abuse is psychologically damaging and sinful. The familiar saying, "Sticks and stones may break my bones, but words will never hurt me," is clearly not true, for abusive words certainly do hurt.

A healthy expression of anger includes a clear statement of just how one is feeling. It is important to use the first person. Thus one would say, "*I* am angry because of such and such," rather than, "*You* make me feel so angry!" When we can admit our anger, we take personal responsibility for our feelings rather than blame them on others. The party being addressed is not made to feel defensive nor wounded by a personal accusation. Clear first-person statements make it possible for the individuals

ARE YOU SURE "DO NOT LET THE SUN GO DOWN ON YOUR ANGER" IS TO BE TAKEN LITERALLY?

involved to work together on the behaviors or situations which are contributing to the anger.

10. *Do not play games.* Game playing is a barrier to fair fighting. One of the most common games is to play the martyr. In response to criticism a person may cry, "I just can't do anything right," or "I guess it's all my fault." Another common game is to feign weakness, inability, or neediness and thus trick others into doing favors. Some family members like to play the "poor me" game or "kick me" game in order to get sympathy or assistance.

11. *Do not be passively aggressive.* Passive aggressiveness, which aims at getting back at another person in indirect, devious ways, is one of the

more effective methods of sabotaging fair fighting. Picture a Sunday morning when Mom and Dad are trying to hurry everyone so the family will not be late for church. Dad has managed to herd everyone to the car except Greg, who happens to be mad at his parents. In response to Dad's call, "Hurry up or you will make all of us late!" Greg very slowly walks to the car, placing one foot in front of the other as if they were made of lead. This is an example of passive aggressiveness—denying one's anger while acting it out in an indirect manner. Since others cannot deal with the anger openly, no resolution is possible, and the anger continues to be acted out in passive ways. The person who behaves in this manner will wield a great deal of control in the family.

12. *Avoid asking for explanations of behavior.* Asking others to vindicate themselves is counterproductive in fair fighting. More often than not, such questions are construed as attempts to place blame. It is frequently the case that the person being quizzed cannot give a satisfactory explanation. In this situation it is better to back off from the question and try instead to work on solutions.

13. *Avoid labeling and name calling.* A sure way to antagonize another person and destroy any chance of reasonable discussion is to engage in labeling or name calling. Examples include calling another person stupid, ignorant, silly, dumb, square, childish, spoiled, compulsive, conceited, or some other derogatory adjective. Using such labels traps people in a box or category from which they cannot escape. It is disrespectful and prohibits any serious efforts to deal with the conflict.

14. *Avoid triangles.* Suppose thirteen-year-old Kathy and fifteen-year-old Chad are arguing at the supper table. Kathy turns to her mother for support: "Isn't that so, Mom?" She has just attempted to entangle her mother in the argument she is having with her brother. If the mother is wise, she will not allow herself to be drawn into the argument. It is a common practice for two people who are fighting to attempt to bring in a third party in order to gain an advantage in the argument. In some homes this has developed into a fine art which thoroughly disrupts the family.

Now that we have reviewed the basic rules of fair fighting, the question arises: Should parents fight in front of their children? Raise this question with a group of parents, and a variety of answers will be forthcoming. Some parents carefully monitor their disagreements so that their children do not hear the slightest word of conflict between them. Others openly argue with each other even if children who may be emotionally stressed by the conflict are present.

We are of the opinion that children should be exposed to fair fighting by their parents. Children learn to accept conflict as a natural part of relationships when they observe their parents in the process of working out their differences. Obviously, it is best when children learn effective ways of resolving conflict. Unfortunately, parents often model ineffective or destructive ways of dealing with conflict. It can be very frightening and unsettling for children to watch their father refuse to talk and angrily walk out of the house in a huff every time he has a disagreement with their mother. Worse still, those children are likely to imitate that behavior in their own disagreements. Keeping all arguments behind closed doors can be equally frightening and disruptive, because children do have an uncanny sense of what is happening when in their presence parents give each other the silent treatment. Such behavior can have destructive effects.

We offer two qualifications to our general position that it is healthy for parents to fight in front of their children. (1) The parents must engage in constructive dialogue rather than destructive bickering. (2) Certain matters are strictly personal and should not be shared with the children. Especially when children are very young, it is best not to burden them with financial worries as they may easily misunderstand the nature of the problem. Conflicts concerning sexual matters and other highly personal concerns should, as a rule, be private. However, some of these adult matters may be discussed with the family after the parents have dealt with them satisfactorily. For example, financial difficulties can be openly explained in a way that will remove the mystery surrounding problems which children tend to sense and worry about at their own level. Bringing the children in on the problems at an appropriate time allows them to participate and contribute to the problem-solving process.

Conflict Resolution

Conflict resolution is in many ways a systemization of fair fighting under another name. Research on conflict resolution suggests that it is a process which moves through several stages (Filley 1975:7–19; Turner 1970:137). In applying this research to the family, Kathleen Galvin and Bernard Brommel (1986:169–72) identify six:

1. *Prior-conditions stage*—the problem arises
2. *Frustration-awareness stage*—a family member comes to realize that satisfaction of some need or concern is being blocked by another family member
3. *Conflict stage*—a series of verbal and nonverbal messages is exchanged
4. *Solution (or nonsolution) stage*—the problem is resolved (or an impasse agreed on)
5. *Follow-up stage*—the conflict reerupts, or hurt feelings and grudges develop
6. *Resolve stage*—the conflict no longer affects the family system

Conflict Management

We believe that conflict management is the most realistic approach to family disputes. Family life is too complex to be understood in neat cause-and-effect terms. And conflict is so much a part of this system that it cannot be viewed simply as something which arises within and is then purged from the family. Rather, conflict continually feeds back into the system as a whole. It is, therefore, more realistic to think of conflict as a process to be managed rather than a situation to be resolved.

As can be seen in figure 18, there are five major styles of conflict management: (1) Avoidance, which involves a low degree of both co-operation and assertiveness, is characteristic of individuals we might describe as withdrawers. (2) Accommodation, which involves a high degree of cooperation and a low degree of assertiveness, is characteristic of yielders. (3) Competition, which involves a low degree of cooperation and a high degree of assertiveness, is characteristic of winners. (4) Collaboration, which involves a high degree of cooperation and assertiveness, is characteristic of resolvers. (5) Compromise, which involves a moderate degree of cooperation and assertiveness, is characteristic of compromisers. It should be noted that these five styles of conflict management are

FIGURE 18 **Styles of Conflict Management**

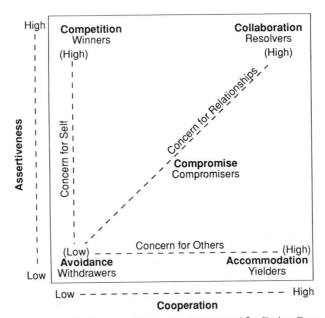

Adapted from R. Kilmann and K. Thomas, "Interpersonal Conflict-handling Behavior as Reflections of Jungian Personality Dimensions," *Psychological Reports* 37 (1975): 971–80; and Joyce Hocker and William Wilmot, *Interpersonal Conflict* (Dabuque, Iowa: William C. Brown, 1985), pp. 40, 52.

basic theoretical types. In the real world, styles of conflict management can fall at any point in the figure.

Each style of conflict management entails specific levels of concern for oneself, for other family members, and for family relationships. The style of conflict management which evidences little cooperation and little assertiveness (avoidance) shows little concern for self, others, and relationships. The style with a high degree of cooperation and a low degree of assertiveness (accommodation) shows high concern for others, less concern for relationships, and little concern for self. The competitive approach shows high concern for self, less concern for relationships, and little concern for others. The collaborative approach shows high concern for relationships and, accordingly, a balanced concern for self and others.

Much research has accumulated in support of the ideas depicted in figure 18. Unfortunately, most of the research has been based on bureaucratic organizations which are larger and far less personal than a family. Two questions need to be asked at this point: (1) Are the data consistent with the biblical view of how to handle conflict? and (2) Are they applicable to family conflict?

In answer to the first question, we believe the data on conflict management to be consistent with what the Bible says about how Christians are to handle conflict. The Bible most directly addresses this issue in Ephesians 4:25–29:

> Therefore each of you must put off falsehood and speak truthfully to his neighbor, for we are all members of one body. "In your anger do not sin." Do not let the sun go down while you are still angry. . . . Do not let any unwholesome talk come out of your mouths, but only what is helpful for building others up according to their needs, that it may benefit those who listen. [NIV]

Contained in these verses is support for assertiveness. We are told that when there is conflict, we should speak truthfully with our neighbor. The implication is that Christians will neither withdraw ("Do not let the sun go down while you are still angry") nor become aggressive (" 'In your anger do not sin.' . . . Do not let any unwholesome talk come out of your mouths"). The text lends support to a direct confrontational style which shows concern for self, the other, and the relationship.

The verses also point toward cooperation as the ideal for Christians— we should speak the truth because "we are all members of one body." If there is anything which should be characteristic of the body of Christ, it is a spirit of high cooperation or collaboration. First Corinthians 12:12 states, "The body is a unit, though it is made up of many parts; and though all its parts are many, they form one body" (NIV). The implication is that all members of the body must work together for the good of the whole.

We believe that the Bible stresses both assertiveness and cooperation. The best way to deal with conflict is a collaborative style with equal concern for self, the other, and the relationship.

How well do the data on conflict management fit the family? One way of answering this question is to examine how closely they fit with our theological model of family relationships. This model began with an emphasis on a two-way covenant commitment. The data on conflict management similarly stress the need to be concerned with both self and others. Second, just as an atmosphere of grace is essential to our theological model, reciprocal forgiving is an essential part of fruitful conflict management. Third, collaboration can be viewed as a type of mutual empowering, as two persons work together toward common goals. The fourth phase in our model is intimacy, which entails a caring and concern for one another. In conflict management, likewise, there is an emphasis on concern for the self and the other.

While we have argued that the social-science evidence on styles of conflict management is consistent with the biblical view, we also believe that different situations call for different styles. It is wrong to suggest that one style is inherently superior to another. We believe that there are times when it is appropriate to take the part of a withdrawer; at other times it is appropriate to be a winner, yielder, or compromiser. There is a dysfunction in family life when one style is the dominant or only way in which an individual can react in conflictive situations. Thus, the husband who always withdraws or the wife who always yields in a marital conflict makes it very difficult to deal with the conflict openly and adequately.

Each style of handling conflict has both advantages and disadvantages and, depending on the situation, may be more or less appropriate. As we discuss each style, we will give an example from the life of Jesus to show that he used that style. He was, variously, a withdrawer, a winner, a compromiser, a yielder, and a resolver.

Withdrawers. Although avoidance was not Jesus' usual style, at times he did withdraw. When he healed the man with the shriveled hand on the Sabbath, he greatly angered the Pharisees, who "plotted how they might kill Jesus" (Matt. 12:14 NIV). Jesus surely could have confronted the Pharisees, as he had on other occasions. But instead, when he became aware of the Pharisees' plotting, "Jesus withdrew from that place" (v. 15). There was a similar reaction during the final hours before his arrest, as Jesus anticipated the coming conflict. When he and his disciples "went out as usual to the Mount of Olives," he said to them, "Pray that you will not fall into temptation," and then "he withdrew about a stone's throw beyond them, knelt down and prayed" (Luke 22:39–41 NIV). We are also told in Luke 5:15–16 that when crowds of people pressed upon him with their needs for healing, "Jesus often withdrew to lonely places and prayed" (NIV).

There will be times when family members need to withdraw from a conflict in order to think more clearly about the issue. Sometimes emotions of anger run so high that conflict resolution is impossible. There are other times when trivial conflicts need to be set aside for the sake of more pressing family matters. Avoidance can be destructive, however, so the person who withdraws for a time needs to be called to accountability by the other family members and must promise to come back and deal with the conflict. In the absence of such a promise, withdrawing sends a signal that the individual does not care enough to work out conflicts.

Winners. At times Jesus adopted the approach of a winner. This can most clearly be seen in Matthew 21:12–13: "Jesus entered the temple area and drove out all who were buying and selling there. He overturned the tables of the money changers and the benches of those selling doves. 'It is written,' he said to them, ' "My house will be called a house of prayer," but you are making it a "den of robbers" ' " (NIV). In this situation there was no yielding, withdrawing, or compromising. Rather, Jesus acted authoritatively and decisively. The reason for this action, as Matthew makes clear, was that the law of the Lord was being violated.

There will be times when family members disagree on the basis of their principles and assume that the family is strong enough to survive the competition. The danger here is that the real issue may get lost in the battle over principles and the conflict may degenerate to a personal level at which each party feels the need to win the point to save face. Such competition between family members escalates rather than decreases conflict. It takes a strong family system to survive. Winners often win the battle (the point) but lose the war (the relationship) in the process.

Compromisers. We tend not to see Jesus as a compromiser. Yet when the Pharisees sought to trap him by asking if it was right to pay taxes to Caesar, Jesus replied, "Give to Caesar what is Caesar's, and to God what is God's" (Matt. 22:21 NIV).

Compromise can be the best way to handle conflict when there is inadequate time to work out a collaborative effort. When used too often, however, compromise is too easy an out, leaving all family members less than satisfied. Some family conflicts can be handled best by compromise, such as disagreements about when to serve the evening meal, where to go on vacation, and what television programs to watch. On other issues, compromise is not the best solution. For example, the Kakimotos are planning to move to a different region of the country. Annette wants to live in the heart of the city where they both will work, while Duane wants to find a twenty-acre plot of land in a rural area some distance from the city. To compromise by living in the suburbs would leave both spouses unhappy. They will need to work together toward a resolution that will afford both of them the essential advantages they are seeking. It will take some creative thought to find such a solution.

Yielders. In the greatest conflict Jesus had to experience in his life on earth, he yielded himself to be arrested, falsely convicted, and finally crucified. His yielding is evident in the account of his arrest in Matthew 26:50–53:

> Then the men stepped forward, seized Jesus and arrested him. With that, one of Jesus' companions reached for his sword, drew it out and struck the servant of the high priest, cutting off his ear. "Put your sword back in its place," Jesus said to him, "for all who draw the sword will die by the sword. Do you think I cannot call on my Father, and he will at once put at my disposal more than twelve legions of angels?" [NIV]

Yielding may be appropriate when an issue is far more important to one family member than to the others, or when it threatens a relationship. Yielding can also be a self-giving act of putting another person's wishes ahead of one's own. However, when yielding is motivated by a desire to show others how self-sacrificing one is, it can be a form of manipulation. Similarly, yielding out of a fear of rejection or a need to be liked can be detrimental. Yielding to another may also not be in the best interest of that person. The parent who gives in to a child's demands for more candy or wish to stay up late may be doing the child a disservice.

Resolvers. During his earthly ministry, Jesus elicited strong reactions. Toward those who reacted against him, such as the scribes, priests, and Pharisees, Jesus assumed a confrontive style. Toward those who reacted positively he assumed a collaborative style, which can best be seen in his long-term commitment to his disciples.

Since family relationships are long-term commitments, most family conflicts can best be dealt with through collaboration. The advantage of this style is that it offers maximum satisfaction to all. The disadvantage is that collaboration takes a lot of time, effort, and emotional energy. In addition, it affords a family member who is verbally skilled the advantage. In conflicts between siblings, the elder may be able to manipulate the younger one into the worse end of a deal. Five-year-old Carol may be able to resolve a conflict by offering three-year-old Eddie five big nickels for his four small dimes.

In general, family systems benefit from having at least one resolver around who will see to it that conflicts are not swept under the rug. The resolver is often very intense in working through conflicts and will be frustrated when others do not cooperate or have the same amount of determination to settle things. There may be family dysfunction if the resolver is unable to rest until there is closure on an issue. When the resolver pursues too intently, the others will distance themselves and intimacy will be impaired.

Each one of the five styles of handling conflict will prove, at one time or another, to be the most appropriate. It is imperative, then, that family members not get locked into any one particular style and thus lose their flexibility and capacity for finding creative solutions.

At the systemic level each particular combination of different types of styles produces its own chemistry and problems. Picture, for instance, a marriage between Barb, a resolver, and Mike, a withdrawer. This type of marital system, in which one partner pursues and the other withdraws, can turn into a cat-and-mouse game. In addition, each partner's style may be reinforcing the style of the other and thus perpetuating the imbalance in the relationship. The more she pursues, the more he withdraws, and vice versa. It is inevitable, of course, that every individual will tend to use the style learned in one's family of origin. The challenge is to expand one's horizon and to consider the possibility of using other styles, giving up the tendency to always select the style that comes naturally. To return to our example: Barb may get further if she stops pursuing and persuading. If she is able to relax and let go of some of her intensity, Mike may well take more initiative and work with her toward conflict resolution.

One can only imagine what the dynamics are when a yielder is married to a winner, a winner to a winner, a compromiser to a yielder, and so on. Add to this the various styles of all the individual members of the family, and there is an even greater challenge. The more complicated the situation, the greater the need to be flexible and responsive to different ways of dealing with conflict.

To this point we have considered individual styles of conflict management. This has been necessary because individual family members differ in the ways they handle conflict. Family conflict must be understood, however, as involving not only the individual members, but also the entire family system. Consider, for example, how conflict management in a disengaged family might be different from conflict management in an enmeshed family. Or consider the difference between rigid and chaotic families.

In disengaged families the bonding between members may be so weak that there will be little direct confrontation when conflict arises. Conflict is most likely to be dealt with by ignoring it and hoping it will go away. On the other hand, in the highly enmeshed family it is impossible for conflict to involve just two family members. The whole family is so intertwined that every member will quickly be drawn into the conflict. By contrast, a healthy approach to conflict is most likely to be found in families which are moderately cohesive, possessing a balance of separateness and connectedness.

In rigid families, patterns of behavior and communication are fixed, meaning that there will be little room for negotiation or a search for creative solutions when conflict arises. Conflict is likely to be handled through the existing power structure, with those who have the greatest power either dictating to or manipulating the others.

In chaotic families, the system is so unstructured that family life is an endless series of shifting negotiations and rearrangements. Given the lack of structure and of basic ground rules, there is little possibility that conflict will be well handled. Living in a chaotic family is like playing in a baseball game in which each team has its own set of rules. One team considers three strikes an out, and the other two. For one team a fly ball caught in foul territory is an out, for the other it is merely a strike. One team permits the runner to lead off base before the pitch, the other team does not. The problem in chaotic families is not that communication is cut off, but rather that there is little possibility of finding a solution since there are so many different ways of playing the game.

By contrast, family systems which are moderately adaptable are best able to handle conflict. They have both the needed structure and flexibility to successfully negotiate disputes.

Family systems, as well as individual family members, develop styles for dealing with conflict. Families which are inclined to avoidance rarely deal with their conflicts. Families with a competitive style may be a little better off, because they at least talk about their conflicts. While families with an accommodating style may appear to be healthy, there may also be many unexpressed personal wishes, opinions, and needs which go unfulfilled.

At times the needs of the family will be met at the expense of the needs of individual family members; at other times the needs of the individuals will be met at the expense of the needs of the family. Families which are characterized by compromise and collaboration are the most successful in balancing the needs of individual family members with the needs of the family as a whole. Healthy families also have the combined strengths of flexibility and structure, separateness and connectedness, as well as open and clear channels of communication which permit them to alter their approach to fit the situation.

PART 6

The Social Dynamics of Family Life

Introduction

In this section we turn our attention to the social dynamics of family life. Power within the family, stress, and divorce will be the major topics of concern.

Working out the issue of power in family relationships is a difficult process. In chapter 13 we will examine different types of power as well as where it should reside and how it ought to be exercised in family life. We argue that empowering, that is, the use of power to enable all family members to realize their potential, is the biblical prescription.

Family stress is the topic addressed in chapter 14. Every family encounters stress in one form or another. We present a model for understanding stress and will see how family members should work together to solve problems and cope with catastrophes. Christian beliefs and values are crucial resources in times of family stress, providing hope in the midst of despair.

Divorce is a stressful time for families. The high divorce rate in America means that millions will experience the pain and loss which divorce entails. Some of the factors which contribute to this breakdown in family life are discussed in chapter 15. We address the effects of divorce on both the couple and the children. After brief discussions of the single-parent family, remarriage, and the reconstituted family, we conclude with a plea for understanding and note that Christianity offers the survivors of divorce the hope of restoration and renewal.

13

Family Power and Empowering

One of the strongest human tendencies is the will to dominate, to be in control not only of oneself, but also of others. Consequently, power is a dimension which is found in all human relationships. Our desire for power undoubtedly stems from the basic self-centeredness which is a part of our human creatureliness. In formal organizations like businesses, schools, and government agencies, power is clearly charted out in elaborate hierarchies. In informal and impersonal relationships, such as interaction with a sales clerk, power is more ambiguous and perhaps less important. In intimate relationships between family members, however, a power system is present and operative even if it has not been formally established or is not officially recognized by the family.

The concept of power is important to an understanding of family relationships. Although many dimensions of the use of power within the family have been researched (Safilios-Rothschild 1970; Scanzoni 1979; McDonald 1980; and Szinovacz 1987), the concept of empowering, which we introduced in chapter 1, seems to have been neglected. The purpose of this chapter is to explore the distribution of power within the family and the effects of empowering.

Power is the ability of one person to influence or to have an effect on another person's behavior. Rightly understood, power is actually the capacity to influence and not the exercising of that capacity. A person may have a very powerful influence, for example, but choose not to exercise it directly. In fact, such an individual often does not need to act in order to be influential; for others have come to trust that he or she has their best interests at heart. The result is responsiveness, a willingness to be influenced and empowered.

We will see that power is a dynamic process which operates in both marriage and parent/child relationships. Power in the marriage relationship is an especially timely topic because of the current changes in opinion regarding marital authority. Our society has been moving from a patriarchal system, where the male is head, to an egalitarian system, in which husband and wife exercise power as partners.

Power in the parent/child relationship is also an important issue. The tensions between parenting responsibilities and the child's desire for freedom and self-determination create dilemmas throughout the stages of the child's growth. Battles often erupt over when parents should relinquish power as their children are empowered to make their own decisions.

Since the dawn of history there have been power struggles between family members. The first was the rebellion of Adam and Eve against God. And in the first recorded act of aggression, Cain killed his brother Abel out of jealousy. These power struggles remind us of the distortion that occurs in all relationships as a result of the fall. Genesis speaks of the husband's dominating and the wife's bearing children in pain; in addition, enmity would occur as a result of sin. What God had ordained and created to be perfect became broken and distorted. However, the message of restoration and renewal is seen throughout the Old and New Testaments. Through the power of the resurrection and the empowering of the Holy Spirit, God has provided a way for us to lead lives of servanthood. We are called to the building up of others; this is the task and privilege of the empowering process.

Types of Power

Authority and Dominance

One reason why there is so much confusion surrounding the issue of power in the family is that there are a number of different ways to conceptualize power. One of the most important ways to categorize it is on the basis of whether it is legitimate. Simply put, legitimate power is authority, and illegitimate power is dominance. The person whose power is sanctioned by society possesses authority. For example, most societies grant parents authority over their children until the children reach the age of majority. While the age of majority differs from culture to culture, and even from state to state, parental power is regarded as legitimate by most societies.

Dominance, on the other hand, is power which has not been sanctioned by society but, instead, taken without consensus. It is, therefore, illegitimate power. For example, some parents and some spouses go beyond the boundaries of legitimate power as given to them by society. Society then makes a second judgment, and those persons who are guilty of child neglect or spouse abuse are (at least in an ideal situation) denied further exercise of the legitimate power originally granted to them.

Authority is based upon societal sanction and possession of valued resources. In their absence a person may resort to intimidation or brute force in an attempt to influence. In *Winning Through Intimidation* (1979) Robert Ringer claims that an individual without skills and resources can gain power by intimidating others. Much of his book consists of clever tricks: dressing in a certain manner to enhance one's image, controlling the situation by meeting people on one's own turf (i.e., in one's own office), purposely making others wait a few minutes for an appointment, or prearranging with a secretary to interrupt the meeting so that the guest sees how important and powerful one is. These manipulations are designed to give one the upper hand.

The empowering model we have in mind is the direct opposite. By building others up and valuing who they are and what they contribute to the situation and relationship, a mutual respect is achieved. Parents who have the respect of their children have legitimate power (authority). Parents who do not have the respect of their children must resort to force and coercion (dominance).

In some societies, legitimate parental power is acquired merely by becoming parents. Such power is ascribed on the basis of one's position. It is not earned, but is merely possessed because one has a given status in society.

In other societies, there is a democratic view of parent/child relationships. Here the mere fact of being a parent does not automatically guarantee legitimate parental power. The possession of resources is an important condition of parental power. Such resources as money or nurturing skills, if recognized and valued by children, are the basis of parental power. Such power is achieved rather than ascribed. Power is not an automatic given with parenthood, but parents must earn it by developing and offering resources valued or needed by their children.

Traditionally, in rural societies power is ascribed; in modern urban societies it is much more likely to be achieved. Accordingly, most of the power being exercised today has been earned. It is the reward for behaving in ways that are respected and trusted by others. Obviously, there are positions of power in any society which are assigned on the basis of status, but the people in these positions must prove their worth if they are going to keep their power.

Orchestrative Power and Implemental Power

Another way of categorizing power is to distinguish between orchestrative power and implemental power. Orchestrative power involves making decisions and delegating responsibilities to others. Implemental power involves carrying out those decisions made and responsibilities delegated by the one who has orchestrative power.

In some families headed by the husband it may seem that the wife actually wields most of the power and makes the important decisions. However, she may simply have implemental power which was delegated to her by her husband, who has orchestrated her role and duties. In reality, then, he is still the seat of power.

There appears to be an inverse relationship between how powerful one is and how active one must be in order to be influential. A really powerful person can be influential without trying to be, while a less powerful person has to work very hard to be influential. For instance, some parents need only speak a request once and their children obey, whereas others must raise their voices and bark out a series of threats to bring about compliance.

Power must be understood from a systemic perspective. The individual who appears to make the important decisions is not necessarily the most powerful person in the family. There may be a hidden power in the system or a silent delegation of power. Sometimes the smallest child seems to be in charge of the whole system, or the children collude to be more powerful than their parents. These are symptoms of dysfunctional families.

It is very important for the parents to be clearly in charge and responsible for the family. When they are not, dysfunction occurs. In healthy family systems the parents are united and take on the executive function. Single parents need to take on this role as well.

Parental authority does not mean that the children are not to be involved in problem solving and decision making. Empowering parents will listen to, understand, and value the points of view of each family member. They will then incorporate these views so that the family works together for a satisfactory solution or decision.

Basic Models of Family Power

There are four basic models of family power (see table 7). The patriarchal model has been dominant in the past. But after World War II, changing social conditions, such as women working outside of the home, combined with the spread of individualistic and democratic ideals, brought forth the democratic-exchange model. The power in most American families today probably reflects a combination of the traditional patriarchal and the democratic-exchange models. The hedonistic self-interest model is a logical result of the narcissistic, hyperindividualistic emphasis which characterizes contemporary American society. The empowering model embodies biblical principles.

The Patriarchal Model

The patriarchal model is still very much present in contemporary society. Power is ascribed to the husband because of his position in the family. Ideological justifications which attempt to go beyond mere cultural tradition usually defend the patriarchal model as being God's intent. The man has been placed in the position of headship for the sake of resolving disagreements in the family.

In some extreme cultural versions of the traditional patriarchal family, the husband has dictatorial rule, ordering his wife and children around as he sees fit. In versions which have been tempered with Christianity, his rule is usually more of a benevolent dictatorship. In the most authoritarian of Christian versions, the father is placed just below God in a chain of command which extends downward to the mother and then the child. The father is in a position of absolute power over his wife and children. Children are to submit to both father and mother, the wife is to submit to her husband, and the husband is to submit to God. Noticeably absent are the concept of mutual submission and the suffering-servant role modeled by Christ (Phil. 2:5–8). In less authoritarian Christian versions of the patriarchal model, the husband is seen as head of his wife as Christ is head of the church; the husband also emulates Christ's role as the suffering servant. The husband remains head of the home, however, and he is expected to make decisions and assign responsibilities.

TABLE 7

Models of Family Power

	Basic Assumption
Traditional Patriarchal	God has determined that ultimate power resides in the role of the husband.
Democratic Exchange	Power does not reside in any one individual, but rather in the family as a whole operating as a democracy.
Hedonistic Self-Interest	Each family member watches out for self.
Empowerment	The goal of the most powerful family member(s) is to empower the less powerful.

The Democratic-Exchange Model

The democratic-exchange model, which has emerged in recent years, is based less on the notion of ascribed power than on the assumption that power resides in the family unit as a whole. The notion that power resides in one individual on the basis of his position is rejected. Family policy is determined by negotiation and bargaining. The exercise of power is understood as a balance between the democratic ideal of each family member's being given equal power and practical reality—each family member has different resources with which to bargain and negotiate for power. Thus, whereas it might be assumed that children will have as much power as do their parents, this is not truly the case because of the inequality in resources which parents and children have at their disposal. To resolve this built-in tension, some families emphasize democracy and the exchange of resources.

The issue of family power is much more complex in the democratic-exchange model than in the traditional patriarchal model, where power is ascribed. Achievement rather than ascription determines who has power. Power in the democratic-exchange model can best be analyzed in terms of its bases, processes, and outcomes (see figure 19). Analysis of the bases of power is most relevant to our purposes.

In the democratic-exchange model, every family member gets a hearing and is very much a part of the decision-making process. Power is still determined, however, by the distribution of resources within the family. The types of resources which can be converted into power are many and varied, differing according to the specific needs of family members. The most obvious type of resource which can be converted into power is economic. Being without economic resources, children are dependent upon their parents and are thus less powerful in deciding matters which have anything to do with money. When children are employed outside

FIGURE 19 **An Analysis of Family Power**

Bases	Processes	Outcomes
1. Economic resources	1. Influence	1. Decision making
2. Affective resources	2. Persuasion	2. Implementation of decisions
3. Personal resources	3. Assertiveness	3. Defining of social/family realities
4. Cognitive resources		
5. Societal definitions		

Adapted from Gerald McDonald, "Family Power: The Assessment of a Decade of Theory and Research, 1970–1979," *Journal of Marriage and the Family* 42 (1980): 844.

the home, they experience a new independence and become more powerful as a result. Likewise, a wife who does not earn money outside of the home will have less power than will her husband, who is the sole financial contributor to the family. Research demonstrates, on the other hand, that wives who work outside the home experience an increase in power and input into decision making.

But family members have needs that go far beyond the economic. Therefore resources can come in the form of emotional nurturing, support, protection, and the like. Some couples are fairly equal in power not because both make equal economic contributions to the marriage, but because one has the ability to provide the affection and nurturance that the other needs.

If the family values certain natural endowments, such as physical appearance, musical ability, athletic prowess, intelligence, or manual skills, those children who possess or develop these gifts (resources) will become powerful. On the other hand, in some dysfunctional families power may fall to someone who is sick, or perhaps to the youngest sibling, because of a systemic need to divert attention from a frightening concern. For example, if the marriage relationship is unhappy, the children and parents may collude to focus on some other family member, placing power in that person's hands in an effort to divert attention from the problem between the parents. Everyone feels more secure when distracted from the possibility of divorce which is threatening the whole family system.

The Hedonistic Self-Interest Model

The individualistic and materialistic values of modern society have led to self-interested hedonism. In family life, as in mass society, everyone watches out for self. Personal interests and needs come before any collective interests or needs of the larger system. Although this philosophy is not characteristic of cultures which value the extended family, it is espoused by many today.

In families which adopt the hedonistic self-interest model, there is no clear head; instead, everyone vies for a place of authority. Cooperation is incidental; family members work together only as a way of getting personal needs met. These homes are often chaotic because of the separation caused by individualistic thinking. They can also be described as disengaged, since there is little connectedness and support between family members.

Empowerment

Our last model of family power is empowerment. It assumes that the task of the more powerful family members is to enable the less powerful family members. Even though empowerment is rarely recognized in the sociological literature, we believe that it is exemplified in Christian family life at its best.

The Basic Nature of Empowering

The concept of empowering has to do with the use of power. Most of the research on the use of power has focused on attempts to influence or control the behavior of others. The underlying assumption has been that persons who use power are not seeking to increase the power of the person(s) whom they are trying to influence. Rather, they use power to ensure the maintenance of their own more powerful position. While we do not deny that most uses of power are essentially of this selfish nature, we also believe that some of them—specifically, those that embody the empowering principle—are not.

One way of describing empowering is that it is an attempt to develop power in another person. As we have already pointed out (p. 28), empowering does not necessarily involve yielding to the wishes of another person nor giving up one's own power to someone else. Rather, empowering is the active and intentional process of enabling another person to acquire power. The person who is empowered has gained power because of the encouragement of the other. There is an interactive process between the two.

One of the secular literature's rare recognitions of empowering can be found in Rollo May's popular book *Love and Will* (1969). He identifies five types of power: (1) exploitative—influence by brute force; (2) manipulative—influence by devious sociopsychological means; (3) competitive—influence based upon the possession and use of personal resources; (4) nutritive—influence like that of a parent on a child (this power eventually outlives its usefulness); and (5) integrative—the use of personal power for another's sake. What May identifies as nutritive power may or may not be an example of empowering—it all depends on the motives of the parent. What May calls integrative power, however, is clearly what we refer to as empowering. May points to Jesus and Gandhi as examples of persons who used integrative power. In stating his central message Jesus said, "I am come that they might have life, and that they might have it more abundantly" (John 10:10 KJV). Gandhi maintained that the goal of his nonviolent resistance was to empower not only the oppressed, but the oppressor as well.

Another recognition of empowering is found in Maximiliane Szinovacz's (1987) brief discussion of family power and the construction of family members' self-images. Building on previous descriptions of power as the potential for shaping another person's identity and self-concept (Berger and Kellner 1964; McLain and Weigert 1979), Szinovacz interprets

I SOMETIMES THINK THIS EMPOWERING THING GETS TO BE A LITTLE ONE-SIDED AT TIMES.

this shaping of another's self-image as an attempt to impose one's own values. One way to develop another's self-concept is not to tell that individual what to be, but who and what he or she is. Szinovacz concludes:

> It would seem essential that family power researchers pay more attention to such control situations. If A is able to shape and modify O's identity and self-concept, his/her control is likely to extend to a broad range of behaviors, to be long-lasting, and to involve relatively few costs since O is made to believe that [A] acts in [O's] own interests. [p. 683]

Erich Fromm (1956:79) has observed that the socialization of children is the process of getting them to want to do what they have to do. From this perspective, empowering can be understood as the process whereby external control (the wishes of the more powerful, e.g., the parent) is transferred into internal control (the child actually wants to do what the parent desires). One is left with the impression that empowering is self-ishly motivated. At best it is a type of paternalistic pronouncement: "You may think you know what is best for you, but I really know what is best, and I'll see to it that you come to feel that way also." This is an inadequate view of empowering.

Another inadequate view is the perception that power is in limited supply. Most analyses of the use of power are based upon such an assumption. The social-exchange theory (p. 84), for instance, is based upon the belief that there is a set number of power units available in any relationship. Thus power in marriage may be represented as 100 units to be divided up between the husband and wife. Now the husband may have all the power (100 units) and the wife none (0 units), or the wife may have slightly more power (60 units) than the husband (40 units), or (in the egalitarian marriage) 50 units may be allocated to each spouse. Scott Bartchy (1984) points out that in this scenario one spouse must command at least 51 power units to be in a position of control.

In promoting the ideal of empowerment, the Bible disproves the view that power is in limited supply. The message of the Bible is that the power of God is available. to all human beings in unlimited amounts. Thus the family member who empowers will benefit another and at the same time be benefited in the very act of empowering. Empowered family members mutually enable each other. Therefore, increasing another person's power will not decrease one's own, but will instead multiply one's potential for further empowering.

Empowering as a Component of Utopian Societies

A virtually unanimous finding of sociological studies is that humans use power as a means to suppress and control others. The most effective instruments of suppression and control are social structures. Some would suggest that human history can best be understood as a record of domination built on classism, racism, and sexism (Ferguson 1984).

As a dominant group begins to use power, reification takes place; the rule of the powerful comes to be regarded as justifiable and is incorporated into ideology. The subordinate group is no longer considered to be oppressed, but rather rightfully subject to the rule of the powerful because of inequality in abilities. Any attempt at building a utopian society must deal with the problem of inequality. It is noteworthy that two of the persons who originated utopian ideologies, Jesus Christ and Karl Marx, incorporate the practice of empowering into their image of an ideal society.

What Jesus taught about power was so central to his mission that it serves as an ideal for all human relationships. To the request of James and John that they be permitted to sit on his right and left hand in glory, Jesus replied, "Whoever wants to become great among you must be your servant, and whoever wants to be first must be slave of all. For even the Son of Man did not come to be served, but to serve, and to give his life as a ransom for many" (Mark 10:43–45 NIV). By his teachings and life Jesus redefined power. He rejected the use of power to control others, and instead affirmed the use of power to serve others, to lift up the fallen, to forgive, to encourage responsibility and maturity, and to enable the unable.

The relationship of Jesus to his disciples is a perfect example of empowering, which extended even beyond his ascension. When preparing his disciples for his leaving, Jesus encouraged them by promising that the Holy Spirit would come to comfort and help them accomplish their ministry (John 16). Later he assured them, "But you will receive power when the Holy Spirit comes on you" (Acts 1:8 NIV).

It is worth noting the type of community the disciples developed after Jesus' departure. It is stated in Acts 2:44–45 that "all the believers were together and had everything in common. Selling their possessions and goods, they gave to anyone as he had need" (NIV). They took seriously Jesus' message of servanthood and mutually gave up the very resources upon which conventional power is based. For Jesus had modeled a power which served rather than controlled others.

Although an avowed enemy of religion, Marx like Jesus found it necessary to radically alter the conventional definition of power. Marx believed that the traditional use of power is in fact exploitation and results in an abuse, namely, private ownership of property. Marx's solution was amazingly similar to that of the early Christians: own all things in common and give to each according to his or her needs.

Marx held that in a property-based society people inevitably seek to use power to control, but in his utopian society they would use power to build one another up. The Marxist slogan of "power to the people," rightly understood, involves empowering. In Marx's view, this empowering must begin among the underclass (proletariat) in the form of a consciousness raising, and will end only when all members of society are part of a classless whole.

Given the competitive economic system of our society, it is not surprising that power within the family is usually exercised as a self-centered social exchange. But the time has come to realize that our perception of how power is to be used is debilitating. As Szinovacz (1987:682) suggests, "To avoid interpretations that 'eternalize' present societal constraints, we may further profit from in-depth analyses of couples or families who have themselves, at least to some extent, transcended these constrictions."

Empowering and Gender Roles

As a group, men are less disposed to empowering behavior than are women. This assertion is based upon the insightful work of Nancy Chodorow (1978) and Carol Gilligan (1982). According to Chodorow, a fun-

damental personality difference between males and females results from
the fact that most parenting is done by mothers rather than fathers. Boys
and girls go through a different process of maturation. While both boys
and girls begin their lives with an emotional attachment to their mother,
boys must learn to deny this attachment and identify with their father.
Girls, on the other hand, have an easier time; to establish identity all they
need do is to emulate their mother.

Because of the close ties with their mothers, most girls desire to be
nurturers. Since boys for the sake of their masculinity must deny their
attachment to their mothers, and since most boys never become close to
their fathers, in the future they will undoubtedly keep at an emotional
distance from their own children.

In building upon Chodorow's ideas, Gilligan has found that males and
females make moral decisions on different bases. Whereas men prize
hierarchy, rights, and autonomy, women emphasize context, caring, and
attachment. While women are more optimistic that problems can be solved
relationally through frank communication, men rely on logic and abstract
rules to ensure fairness in moral decisions. The implication is that females
are more psychologically prepared than males to take an empowering role
in relationships. There is a psychological barrier within males that works
against empowering and moves them, instead, to use power as a means
of obtaining security. As Gilligan (1982:42) states, "Men feel secure alone
at the top of a hierarchy, securely separate from the challenge of others.
Women feel secure in the middle of a web of relationships; to be at the
top of a hierarchy is seen as disconnected."

Women view life as based on bonds of attachment, dependent on inter-
connections, and sustained by caring activities. This perspective serves
to direct women to empower rather than to control. The moral imperative
which men obey is an injunction to respect the rights of the individual;
concerned primarily about the right to self-fulfilment, men are inclined
to use power to control rather than to empower. Fearful of being put in
a dependent position, men reach out for more power and, when they get
it, hoard it as if it were a nonrenewable resource.

Empowering in the Family

We believe that there is something fundamentally wrong with the way
in which power is typically used in the contemporary family. The social-
exchange theory was originally proposed because it seemed to explain
the way in which family members utilize power—the aim is to maximize
personal rewards and minimize personal costs. However, the social-
exchange theory has become reified and has come to represent what is
considered the ideal way for families to operate. This is very unfortunate

because a view which emphasizes that power is to be used to control is ultimately destructive to the development of all family members to their full potential. We propose empowering as the model for the use of power in family life. It will transcend racism, classism, and sexism as they continue to have oppressive effects upon society and family life.

As a model for marriage, the concept of empowering transcends the regressive approach inherent in a system of social exchange. Every couple begins marriage with similar and dissimilar (complementary) resources and skills. In a hedonistic, self-oriented relationship, each partner will jealously guard personal resources, attempt to accumulate more power, and in the process keep the other person dependent. In an empowering relationship, on the other hand, each partner's primary concern is how best to build up and encourage the other to reach his or her potential.

Under the traditional patriarchal system, servanthood was expected only from the wife—the husband assumed the position of master. In an effort to do away with this type of oppression, our society has too often opted for hedonistic, self-centered marriages in which both partners seek to be master and want to be served by the other. An even more radical change is needed: both spouses must devote themselves to empowering.

Marital empowering might be direct, such as when one spouse shares a skill, expertise, information, or abilities with the other. One partner could teach the other how to cook, how to read a map, how to interact socially, or how to share feelings openly. The aim is to help each other overcome any personal deficiencies which may be keeping one dependent either on the partner or on some element in society.

Marital empowering might also be indirect. A spouse who does not possess the personal resources needed to empower in a specific area can encourage the partner to get some specific education or training.

The goal of empowering within marriage could conceivably be construed as bringing two persons with different skills and abilities to the point where they are mirror images of each other. This would be a mistake since God gives different gifts to different people. Moreover, part of the complementary quality of the marital relationship is the ability to appreciate and enhance one another's gifts. Empowering does not mean that each partner's strength has to be duplicated in the other, but rather that there are a willingness to build the other up and a commitment not to control or keep the other dependent.

Since chapter 6 is an in-depth statement on parental empowering of children, we will make only a few additional comments here. That children are born totally dependent upon their parents means that parents are in a position of control. While trust is one of the first things a child must learn, parents must also learn to trust their children. This is a key component of the empowering process. Parents who do not trust their children will seek to maintain control over them.

Parental trust of children can function as a self-fulfilling prophecy. The trust which parents place in their children will encourage the children to be trustworthy; in time they will also learn to trust themselves and others. A child who does not experience trust will develop a negative self-image—"I am a person who is not to be trusted."

Of course, circumstances may work out the other way—children may abuse the trust. When this happens, parents need to be mindful of the faithfulness of God. Despite the repeated failings of the children of Israel, God remained faithful, thus providing the perfect model of parental empowering. Even after the children of Israel openly rejected their heavenly Father, he refused to be a controlling parent. Instead, desiring his children to grow to spiritual maturity, God demonstrated persistent and persuasive actions of love. The hope was that one day the children would respond with similar love for their faithful parent, that the initial unilateral commitment would empower the recipients of God's love with the capacity to respond in kind, so that the unilateral unconditional commitment would become bilateral.

14

Family Stress

A ny group whose members have a strong attachment to each other, interact on a regular basis, and go through various changes together can expect to experience stress. The family is such a group. Family stress can be defined simply as an upset in the regular routine of the family. Family stress can vary from a minor irritation over someone's being late for dinner to a major crisis, such as the death of a family member. Moreover, similar events can trigger completely different reactions in different families. Thus, what is normally a minor irritation may turn into a major crisis in some families. We will also see that families handle stressful events differently.

A Model for Understanding Family Stress

Attempts to study family stress can be traced back to the Depression of the 1930s and to World War II, when millions of fathers were separated from home. In his classic study *Families Under Stress*, Reuben Hill (1949) discussed the stress in families separated because of the war. He proposed that family stress can best be analyzed by considering the interaction of three factors: (1) the stressful event itself; (2) the resources or strengths which a family possesses at the time the event occurs; and (3) the family's perception of the event. In a sense the event is the necessary cause of family stress. But it is not sufficient in and of itself to cause stress. Indeed,

245

there are some instances in which it does not create a problem. For example, when the father is a source of tension in the home, his separation from the family may be perceived as a positive event. This is especially true if there is another family member who has the resources to carry out the functions usually performed by the father.

Most models of family stress are based upon Hill's work; they simply elaborate on the various ways in which the three factors interact. The major refinement has been an endeavor to understand the coping abilities of the family when confronted by a stressful event. This has placed the focus on the family's recoverability instead of its troubles, and on the family's resources instead of the crisis itself.

Stressful Events

Before we consider how families cope, it is important to gain an understanding of the various types of stressful events which affect most families. A major distinction can be made between predictable events (usually transitions to new stages in family life) and unpredictable events. In chapter 2 we discussed various changes which can cause stress in the family. Weddings, births, and the onset of adolescence, for example, are events which can be anticipated by the family. While it is true that the predictability of an event does not eliminate the possibility of stress, families can at least make an effort to prepare for such changes.

Associated with transitions in family life are changes in the lives of individuals. In chapter 8 we suggested that one reason adolescence can be such a trying stage is that the parents often reach middle age at about the same time. The family, a system of maturing and changing individuals, is challenged by these events. The stress generated by the family system causes stress to individuals, and likewise the strains on individuals introduce tension into the family system.

Among the unexpected troubles which plague families are environmental disasters such as floods, fires, famines, and earthquakes, and societal afflictions such as war and economic depression. Over these adversities individual families have little control. These unexpected troubles may be the greatest crises because families are powerless to do anything to prevent or alleviate them. Help is needed from outside sources.

There are various other ways to classify stressful events: maturational/situational, normative/unusual, developmental/environmental, and volitional/nonvolitional. Or we might ask, Do they originate inside or outside the family? Are they chronic or acute? mild or severe? isolated or cumulative? (Boss 1987:699). But while it is important to understand the different types, it is impossible to build an understanding of family stress on that knowledge alone.

In a study of experiences which disrupt life (Holmes and Rahe 1967), forty-three stress-producing events were ranked on a scale from 0 to 100, with a score of 100 representing the greatest amount of stress. It is noteworthy that of the twelve most stressful events, eight directly involve family life (see table 8). Obviously the major source of personal stress for most people is the family.

A series of stressful events can have a cumulative effect upon the family system, especially if the family is unable or unwilling to deal with each event as it occurs. There can be stress buildup, after which a relatively minor incident can burst the floodgates. For example, a twelve-year-old boy who fails twice in one week to take the garbage out, and who regularly leaves his belongings in the living room, may meet his parents' fury when he shows up one hour late for supper. Similarly, a family under financial strain may react out of all proportion when a child has a minor accident that needs medical attention.

Resources

A family's ability to cope with stress is directly related to the resources it possesses. Some of these resources are personal in that they reside in the individual family members themselves. An obvious example is the ability to earn an income. Education is a resource that contributes to one's earning power, enhances prestige, and instills self-confidence. Personal maturity coupled with a good education can provide helpful skills in such areas as problem solving, goal setting, and strategy planning. Physical

TABLE 8
Stressful Events

	Level of Stress
1. Death of spouse	100
2. Divorce	73
3. Marital separation	65
4. Detention in jail or other institution	63
5. Death of a close family member	63
6. Major personal injury or illness	53
7. Marriage	50
8. Being fired	47
9. Marital reconciliation	45
10. Retirement	45
11. Major change in the health or behavior of a family member	44
12. Pregnancy	40

and mental health are also valuable in time of stress; they impart the needed strength to handle the situation. Personality characteristics such as self-esteem and a positive disposition are also valued resources.

The most important resources needed in coping with family stress, however, are those which reside in the family system itself. The ability of a family to handle stress is closely related to its degree of adaptability and cohesion, which we discussed in chapter 2. Healthy family systems are structured, yet flexible. Families which are excessively adaptable (chaotic) or inflexible (rigid) are ill prepared to handle stressful events. So too for family systems which are enmeshed or disengaged. Members of enmeshed families are so intertwined with each other that they lack the degree of separateness needed to perceive the stressful event objectively and to be supportive of each other. Members of disengaged families are so distant that they are unable to give the type of emotional and material support needed for the family to operate as a unit in dealing with the

HI, I'M DOING A STUDY ON FACTORS WHICH CAUSE FAMILY STRESS.

stress. Families which handle stress well are moderately cohesive: they are connected, yet separate.

Clear and open communication with each other is one of the most important strengths families can draw upon during times of crisis. Input from all members is needed if the problem is to be solved. The family must pull its resources together and work as a united front; to do so requires good communication.

Some families possess many resources, but use them so unwisely that they are of little value in times of crisis. The ability to manage resources is an invaluable tool in periods of stress.

Another essential resource is the external networks the family has established and developed. We are referring to the support systems—friends, neighbors, co-workers, church and community groups—which families can draw upon in time of special need. The necessity of cultivating such outside resources is one of the reasons why geographical stability is so important to the family system. When the family has no such resources, it is highly vulnerable to all stress that may come its way.

Family Responses to Stress

There are two general ways in which families respond to stress: coping and problem solving. Although the literature on coping is more directly related to the issue of family stress, we believe that the literature on problem solving is also helpful, because it conceptualizes the family's response to stress as taking place in stages.

Coping

Coping refers to what the family and its individual members do with their resources in the face of stress. Pauline Boss (1987:695) agrees with Hill that stress is the result of the interaction between the event, the family's resources, and their perception of the event, and adds that the degree of success in coping with stress varies significantly from family to family.

A family that is incapable of coping with stress is in crisis. To cope with stress the first step is to marshal all available resources. Coping strategies may consist of direct action aimed at changing the stressful conditions, a rethinking of the whole situation (including how the stress might be turned around into a benefit), or a combination of both of these processes. Take as an example the case of an elderly grandmother no longer able to live independently. One solution is to find a retirement home for her to live in. An alternative is for her to move in with the family. Such a change will mean stress for the family, but also an opportunity for all its members to grow. Finding creative ways for her to contribute to the family as well as for the others to help meet her special needs is the task at hand. Flexibility will be required as the system itself changes to meet the new situation. Her presence, even though initially stressful, may well result in positive interaction for the whole family. Creative solutions of this nature are examples of functional coping with stress.

An example of dysfunctional coping is a husband who, feeling frustrated and powerless in his job, abuses his wife and causes all sorts of disruption in the family system. Or again, if a family appears to be coping very well with stress, but is doing so at the cost of the wife's being depressed, the father's overworking, or a child's overeating, there is dysfunction. Functional coping involves successful management of stressful events by both the family system and each individual in the family (Boss 1987:701–8).

Coping styles will vary with cultural and ethnic identity, social class, and each stage of family life. Family therapists have noted that coping styles, whether functional or dysfunctional, are passed down from generation to generation. Most coping behavior is learned from the patterns established in one's family of origin.

Coping is a complex process; in fact, many of its mechanisms can become secondary stress factors. For example, when the mother works outside the home to alleviate the family's financial burden, the resulting vacuum in the home may cause another kind of stress. A coping strategy can begin a chain reaction in the family system; for instance, when working parents leave their children without supervision after school, the children may misbehave as a means to gain attention, and the result is additional disruption in the family system.

Problem Solving

Much research has been done in the area of problem solving within families. In a recent paper Irving Tallman and Louis Gray (1987) have suggested that five stages are involved:

1. The family becomes aware of and defines a situation as a problem. The greater the threat to the family's welfare, the more the situation will be perceived as a problem. "The most salient problems for the family as a unit will be either external threats to its ability to care for and protect its members or internal threats to its viability and functioning" (Tallman and Gray 1987:13). It is also true that the more immediate a situation, the more likely it is to be perceived as a problem. So a serious threat to the family's survival, such as spouse abuse, may temporarily have lower priority than a more immediate problem, such as a burst pipe in the bathroom. Tallman and Gray summarize these two points: "some degree of threat is necessary at least to the extent that the actor is uncomfortable

with the existing state of affairs; and the situation must be sufficiently immediate to make the action implicit and problem awareness meaningful" (1987:16). Another important factor is that families that consider themselves effective problem solvers are quick to perceive threatening situations as problems. Families that lack confidence in their ability to deal with problems are more likely to deny the seriousness of the situation.

2. The family decides to try to solve the problem. Such a decision is likely if they believe that they can really do something about the situation. The greater the family's confidence that they can solve the problem, the greater their motivation to act.

While stress is often a motivating factor in a family's decision to solve a problem, it has also been found that families are less likely to recognize and act on problems when stress is very low or very high. When stress is very high, families engage in defensive avoidance instead of constructive problem solving. Examples of defensive avoidance include selective inattention, forgetfulness, distortion of the meaning of warning messages, and wishful rationalizations which minimize the severity of the problem. During a time of severe crisis a family may panic and need someone from outside to assist in constructive problem solving.

Families are also likely to engage in problem solving if its aim is correction of a negative situation rather than improvement or betterment. Parents, for example, will be motivated to attend a seminar on parent/child communication if they think it will reduce the stress in their relationship, but not if its stated goal is a more intimate relationship. Further evidence along this line is the reluctance of couples to engage in premarital counseling. Most couples seek counseling only after marital difficulties arise. It is ironic but true that families are more motivated to act constructively if the matter is framed in negative rather than positive terms. By implication, then, ministry to families is more effective if its avowed aim is to overcome an existing problem rather than to avoid a potential one.

3. The family searches for and processes information relevant to effectively solving the problem. On the basis of the information gathered, the family decides which among the many options is the most effective way to resolve the problem. In general, they will select the solution which entails the least inconvenience, that is, the least time, money, energies, and resources. Thus, the family will not necessarily search for the best possible solution, but rather for a satisfactory one. Once they have found a satisfactory solution, they will give up their search. For example, once the parents of a rebellious teenager believe that the solution to the problem is to spend more time with their child, they will stop considering other solutions which may be directly related to the problem behavior, such as adjusting the restrictions on the teenager or changing their parenting style.

4. When the selected solution has been tried, the family evaluates its effectiveness. They may decide that the chosen strategy should be continued, revised, or discarded in favor of an alternative strategy. Many families, unfortunately, lack the patience to wait for a solution to work. The proof is that stress is usually heightened, rather than reduced, during the problem-solving process. The family simply must learn patience. For studies have shown that the greater the investment of time, money, emotional energy, and resources, the more likely it is that the problem will be solved.

5. The family either accepts the solution or returns to the second stage, once again deciding whether or not to attempt to solve the problem. Families out of touch with reality are incapable of perceiving whether the problem is being solved. Healthy families, by contrast, can gauge the situation accurately and make whatever changes are necessary.

Coping with Catastrophes

A catastrophe is a stressful event which is sudden, unexpected, and life-threatening; it is due to circumstances beyond one's control and results in an extreme sense of helplessness. Because catastrophes occur infrequently, most families are not prepared to cope with them. Wars, terrorist attacks, rapes, stock-market crashes, fires, floods, earthquakes, and tornados leave survivors devastated.

Catastrophes differ from other stress-causing events in a number of ways (Figley and McCubbin 1983:14–18): (1) a family has little or no time to prepare for a catastrophe; (2) there has been no previous experience to help the family deal with the situation; (3) there are few resources to draw on to help manage the resulting stress; (4) there are few other families that have experienced a similar disaster and can therefore provide suitable support; (5) the family is likely to spend a long time in a state of crisis; (6) the family will likely experience a loss of control and a high sense of danger, helplessness, disruption, destruction, and loss; and (7) a number of medical problems (including emotional difficulties) are likely to result.

There has been a substantial amount of research into the various emotional stages that a family in crisis goes through. Best known is Elisabeth Kübler-Ross's study (1970) of the five-stage process an individual or family typically goes through when confronted with the fact of death (see figure 20). First comes the denial stage, which is usually characterized as a state of shock. Family members may appear to be calm and collected, exhibiting emotions which are fairly inappropriate given the severity of what has happened. Before moving on to the next stage, there may be feelings of loneliness, guilt, conflict, and meaninglessness.

As family members are able to get in touch with their feelings about what has happened, they enter the anger stage. To the outside observer, the increased emotional intensity which characterizes this stage may appear to be regressive. In truth, however, it is a necessary and healthy step along the road to emotional wholeness.

After the emotional outburst of the second stage, the family enters into the bargaining stage. They are still not prepared to accept the magnitude of the loss and may seek to minimize it by bargaining (e.g., a family that has suffered financial reversal may promise to give more to the church if only God will restore a portion of what has been lost). When the family comes to realize the full extent of the catastrophe, they enter into the depression stage. Here the family reaches its lowest emotional point. Depression is actually a preparation for the last stage, acceptance. The passage from depression to acceptance is known as the angle of recovery. It can be depicted as a very steep incline, pointing to a speedy emotional upturn, or as a gradual slope, representing a long-drawn-out recovery period. The angle of recovery depends on the resources which the family has at its disposal.

On reaching the acceptance stage the family may be very different from what they were before the catastrophe occurred. Reaching the acceptance stage does not mean that family members will no longer feel any of the emotions of the other stages (denial, anger, depression), but that they will no longer be immobilized by these emotions. Having been empowered, the family will have increased self-reliance and be in a position to make adjustments and to plan for the future.

A catastrophe can happen to an individual in the family or to the whole family. When a catastrophe befalls an individual, the family should provide vital support. It is a mistake, however, for the family to become overinvolved emotionally, reacting in ways which take the crisis away from the person to whom it really belongs. Another mistake is to completely take over and do everything for the victim; this gives the message

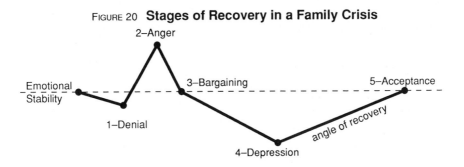

FIGURE 20 **Stages of Recovery in a Family Crisis**

that the victim is totally incapable and helpless. What such a person needs instead is encouragement to take appropriate self-empowering action.

Overreacting in anger is another response that is detrimental to the empowering process. For example, the mother of a rape victim may scream, "How can this happen to *my* daughter!" The father may threaten revenge because his honor has been undermined. Both of these reactions are self-centered and fail to show concern and support for the daughter, who is the real victim. She ends up taking care of the family rather than getting the help she needs. Obviously it is important to recognize and attend to the emotional reactions of each family member, but not at the expense of neglecting the true victim.

When an entire family is the victim of a catastrophe, its members are often drawn closer together by the common experience. In such a situation each individual, while in great emotional need, must give support to the others. The isolated nuclear family is especially vulnerable during times of catastrophe. This is why it is so crucial for the Christian community to reach out during crises. Jesus radically redefined the concept of family when he said, "Here are my mother and my brothers! Whoever does God's will is my brother and sister and mother" (Mark 3:34–35 NIV). The challenge is for us to be family to one another, so that we can offer Christ's love and support in emotional and physical ways during times of crisis.

Christian Belief and Response to Stress

Our perception of stressful events and our ability to cope with them are strongly influenced by our belief system (Boss 1987:715–18). The particular influence which Christianity has had in this regard varies over a broad continuum from passive resignation to self-reliant attempts to achieve mastery over catastrophe. At one extreme is a fatalistic view which abuses Paul's teaching that Christians should be content in whatever state they find themselves (Phil. 4:11). Most Western versions of Christianity, in contrast, are very action-oriented, stressing the responsibility and capability of the believer to take whatever action is needed to alleviate the threatening situation. These two conflicting extremes reflect the current narcissistic thinking of our society and deny the legitimacy of stress within the Christian life.

A current example of the fatalistic view is the theology of positive thinking. It comports well with the societal emphasis upon each individual's ability to mentally create his or her own perfect world. Positive thinking comes close to promising a life without any difficulties, but this is incompatible with the reality of a world tainted by sin. To live in a fallen world is to experience stress. In our humanness we are capable of causing all sorts of stressful situations for ourselves and for others.

Clichés which admonish us to "turn every stumbling stone into a stepping stone" and to "turn scars into stars" must not be used to deny the very real disruptions families face. Rightly taken, however, positive thinking can be helpful in reducing stress and keeping problems in perspective. To view scars as stars, that is, to change one's perception of a stressful event, is healthy when combined with both an awareness of the potential damage the crisis can inflict and a realistic assessment of how the family can manage with the resources available. Such an approach enables the family to take action rather than deny or be paralyzed by disaster.

No less narcissistic than positive thinking is the opposite extreme— the view that stress is the direct result of specific sin and is therefore capable of being overcome instantaneously through an act of divine healing. In reality, most of the events and conditions which distress families, including alcoholism, eating disorders, job loss, parent/child conflicts, and illness, are caused by complex physical, social, and psychological factors. In a general sense, of course, all of these stressful conditions stem from our living in a fallen world tainted by sin. But to insist that the cure lies simply in taking action against the sin in individual lives is to fail to comprehend the pervasiveness of evil and the role which social structures play in producing stress in the world.

True, to deal with stress we must take action against the sin in our lives, but we must not ignore other realities such as dysfunction within families, unjust economic systems, the oppressiveness of poverty, and so on. We must adopt a multifaceted approach which recognizes the complexity of the anxieties and pressures of life in the modern world. Awareness of this complexity will keep us extremely cautious about claims of instant healing for homosexuality, eating disorders, drug addiction, alcoholism, mental illness, and various problems in interpersonal relationships.

In our pill-oriented society, we want instant relief and cure from all that ails us. One aspirin advertisement promises relief "when you don't have time for the pain." The narcissistic emphasis in our society promotes the quick fix over the long and hard work which is required to overcome most of the stress in today's society. To become whole a healing process must take place in the believer. This healing process, which includes growth in faith and in our relationship to God and others, usually works at a gradual pace.

To think that Christians are immune to stress is not only unrealistic, but bad theology. There are numerous examples in the Scriptures where disaster falls on the just and unjust alike. We need look only at the life of Job to know that evil circumstances come to the righteous and that instant cure is not the norm. What is guaranteed is the compassion of God in every circumstance. God will be present with us through the body of Christ and in the power of the Holy Spirit.

The two extreme responses to stress which we have examined lead, respectively, to a theology of escapism, where the Christian tends to withdraw in the face of crisis, and to a theology of activism, where the Christian tends to be self-reliant to the point of rendering God a mere bystander in the process. What is the biblical response? Scripture suggests that when confronted by a crisis, Christians should not fatalistically resign themselves. For example, when Paul was arrested, he did not meekly succumb. Instead, he asserted his status as a Roman citizen in order to deliver himself. Examples from the life of David point to a balance between passivity and activism in the midst of stress. There were times when David fell upon his knees before the Lord, acknowledging that his situation was hopeless without divine intervention. At other times David took forthright action in the face of extreme difficulties. The balance between passivity and activism can be seen in the story of David and Goliath. Fully aware that without God's help he had no chance against the Philistine, David equipped himself with his sling and five smooth stones.

The same combination of passive reliance and active assertiveness can be seen in the life of Jesus. Faced with imminent arrest, trial, and crucifixion, Jesus retreated to the Garden of Gethsemane. "Deeply distressed and troubled," he told his disciples that his soul was "overwhelmed with sorrow to the point of death." In his despair Jesus prayed to his Father, "Take this cup from me. Yet not what I will, but what you will" (Mark 14:33–35 NIV).

It is important to recall that this very same Jesus had previously gone into the temple and angrily driven out the moneychangers. Enraged at the hypocrisy of the Pharisees, he called them whitewashed tombs, snakes, and a brood of vipers. His language was equally severe when he called Herod a fox, unreceptive audiences swine, and false prophets savage wolves. Nor did he restrain himself from taking direct action against the social evils of his day.

Christians need to be able to respond to stress. An unavoidable part of living in a fallen world, stress should be approached as a time to draw especially near to God and others for support. Although God has not promised an escape from stressful situations, he has promised to be our "stronghold in time of trouble" (Ps. 37:39 NIV).

It is often the case that stressful events shake up the family system in a way that disrupts the stagnant comfort of routine life. This can be an occasion for growth as Christians. It can also be a time of increased intimacy between family members and with the body of Christ as a whole. When people are vulnerable, they are often more receptive to the support and love of others. It is essential, then, in periods of adversity to choose a direction which, with God's help, will lead to deeper levels of intimacy, commitment, forgiveness, and empowering. To help achieve and maintain a balanced perspective, we might also keep in our hearts the simple yet profound prayer of Reinhold Niebuhr:

> O God, give us serenity to accept what cannot be changed,
> courage to change what should be changed,
> and wisdom to distinguish the one from the other.

15

Divorce and Remarriage

Families are amazingly resilient. In the face of challenging external pressures and the destructiveness of internal conflict, a family can continue to function as if it had a built-in survival mechanism. A family can survive in hard times because of the important needs it fulfils for its members. From an outsider's point of view, a given family may be a very poor environment in which to live; but to the members within, it may represent the only security and source of identity they have in life.

There comes a point in some families, however, when life together is no longer workable. This usually comes after a period of denial when family members pretend that no problems exist. Eugene O'Neill's play *Long Day's Journey into Night* provides a good look at a family engaged in collective denial. They keep talking about each other in totally unrealistic terms. Such defense mechanisms deflect debilitating conflict for the time being, but they ultimately have a destructive effect in that they keep the family from instituting needed change.

A theme we have emphasized in this book is that family life is a dynamic process, and a healthy family must be willing and able to adapt to meet the changing needs of its members. A family which cannot or will not adapt is a candidate for breakup. When one or more members of a family system believe that their needs can best be met elsewhere, the family is likely to break up.

In this chapter we will investigate families which have experienced divorce. Because of the large number of divorces in contemporary society, we will give special attention to single-parent families. Given the fact that most persons who divorce eventually remarry, we shall also consider remarriage and reconstituted families. We will conclude with a statement on the Christian attitude toward broken families.

Divorce

Demographics

Not only is the divorce rate higher in the United States than in any other country of the world, it is also higher than at any other time in history. As shown in figure 21, the annual divorce rate has been steadily rising from a low of 1 divorce for every 1,000 married couples in 1860 to 22.5 in 1979. In the 1980s the annual rate has leveled off at around 20 divorces for every 1,000 married couples.

Immediately following World War I there was a noticeable rise in the divorce rate; similarly, following World War II there was a dramatic rise in the divorce rate. These increases reflect both the stress put upon marriages by forced separation and the large number of unstable marriages

FIGURE 21 **Annual Divorce Rate**

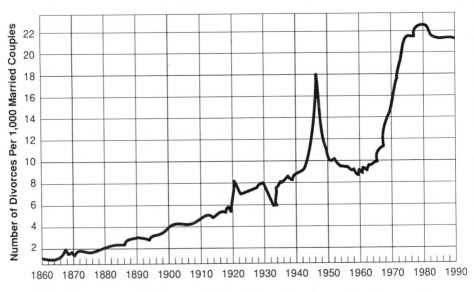

From H. Raschke, "Divorce," in *Handbook of Marriage and the Family,* ed. Marvin B. Sussman and Suzanne K. Steinmetz (New York: Plenum, 1987), p. 844; and Andrew J. Cherlin, *Marriage, Divorce, Remarriage* (Cambridge, Mass.: Harvard University Press, 1981), figure 1–4.

which were contracted during the wars. The drop in the rate during the depression years reflects the costliness of legal divorce. The most dramatic rise in the divorce rate occurred between 1965 and 1979. It was especially pronounced among persons under forty-five.

In the 1980s there have been approximately 1,200,000 divorces each year, slightly less than half the number of marriages. Caution must be taken, however, when projecting the likelihood of any one marriage ending in divorce. The best estimate is that approximately one out of every three current marriages will end in divorce, with the likelihood of divorce being lowest among those who have been married the longest. (The average length of marriages which end in divorce is seven years; the rate of divorce is highest for marriages of two to three years' duration.)

While there is no sure way of predicting whether a marriage will succeed, correlations have been found with a number of demographic factors, including education, age, ethnicity, and religion. Although income, occupation, and social class may have a greater bearing, level of education does play a role. The divorce rate is low among men with little education, increases among those who have had some high-school training, and declines among men who have a college degree.

Those who marry young, especially in their teens, are much more likely to divorce than are those who marry in their twenties. A number of interrelated factors may also be at work here. Those who marry young are typically from a lower socioeconomic class (which increases the probability of financial difficulties); they marry after a very short engagement and perhaps because of a pregnancy. Given their stage of individual development, most teenagers are socially and psychologically unprepared for a relationship as demanding as marriage. Inadequacies in role performance, unfaithfulness, disagreement, and lack of understanding and companionship have been found to contribute to divorce among those who married while very young (Booth and Edwards 1985).

Next to teenage marriages, the most unstable are those between people who marry after age thirty. Among their most common complaints are a lack of agreement and the tendency of the partner to be domineering and critical (Booth and Edwards 1985). The underlying dynamic here is that those who marry late in life have become so set in their ways that they have a hard time adjusting to the expectations of a spouse. On the other hand, people who marry in their mid-twenties tend to have the most stable marriages.

In terms of ethnic differences, the divorce rate is highest among blacks, moderate among whites, and lowest among other ethnic groups, particularly those of Far Eastern origin. In terms of religion, divorce rates are lowest among Jews, moderate among Catholics, and highest among Protestants (Chalfant, Beckley, and Palmer 1987:224–28). Finally, heterogeneous marriages are more likely to end in divorce than are homogeneous marriages. Thus divorce is more likely when there is a sizable age gap or differences in religion, social class, or ethnic origin.

Causes

There is no single cause of divorce. The causes are multiple, complex, and interrelated. Some have to do with the idiosyncrasies of the individuals; others involve social and cultural factors such as the demographics we have just examined. Other things being equal, the lower the quality of the marriage, the greater the likelihood of divorce. Therefore, absence of any of the requisites for a strong marriage (e.g., family support, differentiation, adaptability) which we discussed in chapter 4 could be listed here as an indirect cause of divorce.

Other explanations for divorce can be found in the decline of certain barriers which have traditionally discouraged people from resorting to divorce (Lewis and Spanier 1979:271–73).

1. Religious doctrine and norms have been liberalized to permit the possibility of divorce in a difficult marriage.
2. External pressures against and the social stigma of divorce have decreased; correspondingly, tolerance for divorce has increased.
3. Societal norms stressing commitment and obligation have eased.
4. Liberalization of divorce laws and the availability of legal aid make it easier for persons contemplating divorce to actually follow through.
5. Alternatives to one's present spouse become manifest as males and females increasingly work and socialize together.
6. The redefinition of gender roles has resulted in wives' being less economically dependent upon husbands, and husbands' being less emotionally dependent upon wives.

It is impossible to compile a complete list of reasons for divorce. The best we can do is to realize that there are a multitude of reasons, some direct and some indirect, some conscious and some unconscious, some personal and some societal, behind the divorce of any one couple. In particular, the conditions of modern society (see chap. 16) have contributed to the high divorce rate. These include preoccupation with individualism and self-fulfilment, loss of a community base to support family life, downplaying of the concept and practice of covenant commitment, and emergence of materialism as a dominant value.

The Process

While from a legal standpoint divorce is actually enacted on a specific date, the ending of a marriage typically stretches out over several years.

As both a public and private process, divorce is a painful and crisis-producing event. It involves the death of a relationship and, as with most deaths, pain and crisis are common by-products.

It has been suggested that the divorce process typically follows a four-stage sequence (Salts 1979; Price-Bonham and Balswick 1980). The first stage is the period before separation. Characterized as emotional divorce or the erosion of love, it may involve denial, anger, disillusionment, detachment, decision making, and bargaining. The second stage is the point of actual separation, which typically entails bargaining, depression, anger, ambivalence, guilt, and regret. The third stage, the period between the separation and the legal divorce, involves legal issues, economic readjustments, mourning, coparenting arrangements, reorientation of lifestyle, and a focus on one's own identity and emotional functioning. The final stage in the divorce process is the period of adjustment, which involves new activities and new goals. There may be a second adolescence in which one begins to date again. This is also a time of personal recovery in which people restructure their lives in order to achieve stability and autonomy.

The emotions which persons experience in the four stages of a divorce are like the emotions experienced during the stages of coming to grips with death and dying: denial, anger, bargaining, depression, and finally acceptance. This is an especially difficult time because although the marriage has died, the two individuals are still alive and continue to interact. While both suffer immensely, the man is generally affected most negatively in the sociopsychological sphere and the woman in the economic.

The Effect on Children

It is usually assumed that divorce has a detrimental effect upon children. Research suggests, however, that children may be better off in a happy one-parent home than in an unhappy two-parent home. There are less psychosomatic illness, less delinquent behavior, and better relations with parents in happy one-parent homes than in unhappy two-parent homes (Nye 1957). In such cases it is possible that divorce has removed a parent who was unable or unwilling to play the role of parent and given the child hope for a more suitable replacement.

Even so, divorce does have an adverse effect on children. A study of thirteen- to seventeen-year-old girls found that daughters of divorcées seek attention from male adults and contact with male peers, while daughters of widows tend to avoid contact with male peers (Hetherington 1972). Both groups of girls show an inability to interact in appropriate ways with males. It was also found that the younger the girl at the time of the divorce, the greater the effect upon her.

In a study of male adolescents, it was found that boys from homes where a father is not present exhibit more field dependency than do other boys. "The field-dependent individual is less differentiated in his general style of life and, among other things, seems more passive in his approach to the environment, apparently depending more upon external cues to determine his behavior. In contrast, the field-independent individual seems to rely more upon himself for cues to determine his behavior" (Barclay and Cusumano 1967:244). It was concluded that a boy from a home where a father is not present is much more likely to adopt the role of his mother—and, in so doing, have difficulty in achieving masculine identity—than is a boy from a two-parent home.

A summary of longitudinal studies which have investigated the effects of divorce on children states, "The impressive consensus of these studies is that divorce results in negative stresses for both children and parents" (Guidubaldi, Cleminshaw, Perry, Nastasi, and Lightel 1986:142). These children tend to do poorly by social, academic, and physical standards.

In addition, there is evidence that children of divorced parents are likely to experience a divorce themselves (Glenn and Kramer 1987). A suggested explanation is that children of divorced parents have a low commitment to marriage and a tendency to marry at an early age, two factors associated with a high divorce rate.

Rather than asking whether divorce has a negative effect on children, more research is needed which investigates under what conditions divorce is least troubling (Longfellow 1979). In this regard it has been reported that children adjust better when parents discuss the possibility of divorce and continue to explain matters after it has taken place (Jacobson 1978). Further, the less hostility there is between the parents, the better adjusted the child. Divorced parents who maintain an affable relationship with each other and who continue to show love and support of their children can lessen the disruptive effects of their separation. It is vital that the parent who has not been awarded custody spend time with the children. "Orderly, organized, stable, daily routines [also contribute] to adjustment" (Raschke 1987:617).

Single-Parent Families

Approximately one-fifth of all children under eighteen presently live with one parent only. Of all children born in the 1980s, it is estimated that approximately 60 percent will spend at least a year of their childhood in a single-parent home (Norton and Glick 1986:16). Ninety-eight percent of all single-parent families are headed by the mother. A disproportionate number of single-parent families are black, as approximately 50 percent of all black children under eighteen live only with their mother, compared with 15 percent of all white children. In just thirteen years (between 1970 and 1983) the proportion of black families headed by females rose from 31 to 48 percent.

The greatest difficulty experienced by single-parent families is a lack of economic resources. One study reports that two-thirds of single-parent families live below the poverty level (Smith 1980:78). There is also evidence that new laws, such as no-fault divorce, have had disastrous results. A study of the effects of no-fault divorce in California concludes that in ten years divorced women and their children have suffered a 73 percent drop in their standard of living. Ex-husbands are actually better off; their standard of living increases 42 percent in the first year after divorce (Weitzman 1986:338).

There is evidence not only that the mothers in single-parent homes form a new poverty class, but that their difficult status is also psychologically detrimental. "A review of admission data from mental health facilities found the single most depressed group of mental health service clients to be young, single-parent mothers with young children and low incomes" (Macklin 1987:328).

The second greatest problem encountered by single parents is the lack of time to juggle work, parenting, household tasks, and a personal life. Being deprived of a mate to help share in the parenting responsibilities, the single parent feels both lonely and overwhelmed. Given less attention than they require, the children upon growing up will find that they are deprived educationally, occupationally, and economically (Hetherington, Camara, and Feathermore 1983).

In spite of the extreme difficulty resulting from the lack of economic resources and time, many single-parent families function quite effectively. This is especially true when the other parent continues to take an active interest in the children. An extensive summary of the literature on single-parent families (Gongla and Thompson 1987:397–418) offers the following conclusions:

1. The environment in a single-parent family may be less detrimental than the environment preceding the marital disruption.
2. The event producing the single-parent family, namely the divorce itself, may have a more disruptive impact on children than does the single-parent family structure itself.
3. There is no proven cause-and-effect relationship between upbringing by a single parent and specific problems observed in children.

Single parenting is difficult because one person cannot do what God intended for two people to do together in order to create healthy family life. In light of evidence that single-parent families actually receive less community support than do two-parent families (Wallerstein and Kelly

1980), the Christian church has a golden opportunity to witness by enfolding single-parent families within its supportive network. Married couples in the church need to restructure some of their social activities to include the single parent. Children from one-parent families should also be intentionally included in social and recreational activities. The Christian family needs to be inclusive rather than exclusive in its service.

Remarriage

Eighty percent of persons who get divorced eventually remarry. In general, the younger a person is at the time of divorce, the greater the likelihood of remarrying. Since reaching a peak in 1965, the proportion of persons who remarry has been declining, as singlehood has become a more socially acceptable option.

Contrary to public opinion, the more children a divorced woman has, the greater is the likelihood that she will remarry, and that she will do so quickly. A divorced woman with children usually does not have the luxury of carefully choosing before marrying again. Unless she has a good income, economic necessity demands that she find a husband to assist in providing financial support. This is especially true in cases where the ex-husband is not paying child support or where the court has allocated inadequate child-support payments.

There is a marked difference in the way education affects a woman's and a man's likelihood of remarrying. For women, the likelihood of remarrying is highest among the poorly educated and decreases with the amount of education achieved. Among divorced men, the reverse is true. The remarriage rate is lowest among the least educated and highest among the best educated. Related to the likelihood of remarrying is one's income, which is related in turn to educational level. Better-educated males can afford to remarry. Poorly educated females find it necessary to remarry, while better-educated females can afford not to remarry and may choose to support themselves instead.

Since highly educated men make desirable marriage partners and tend to marry women younger than themselves, the older, better-educated divorced woman may have difficulty finding an educated unmarried man of comparable age to marry. Consequently, some highly educated divorced women are choosing to marry younger men or men of a lower economic status. These women may be interested in finding men who are nurturing, tender, and emotionally expressive.

The Problems of Reconstituted Families

A reconstituted family can be defined as "any remarriage which includes at least one child residing in the household" (Price-Bonham and

Balswick 1980:966). The terms *blended families* and *step families* are also used in the literature to refer to homes in which children from a previous marriage reside. Such families encounter problems in three areas: ambiguity of status, children, and finances.

Ambiguity of Status

The boundaries of reconstituted families are less structured and more permeable because many of the shared experiences, symbols, and rituals that helped maintain the boundaries of the first family are missing. The fact that parental authority and economic responsibilities are shared by two households can also create divided loyalties and affection.

Members of reconstituted families can have difficulty determining the proper relationship between themselves and their newly acquired kin because of the lack of clearly defined norms and rules in regard to financial, sexual, and social matters. Children can become confused living with a stepmother or stepfather while their biological mother or father lives elsewhere. Moreover, a former wife and her current husband (or a former husband and his current wife) may come to be looked on as extended kin. There is also ambiguity in the relationship with former in-laws (the children's grandparents), with whom close ties may have developed.

Although members of reconstituted families may yearn for the elimination of ambiguity, it is a condition that they will need to accept and learn to live with. Children will continue to experience divided loyalties between their natural parents and stepparents. Stepparents who no longer live with the children from their first marriage will also experience divided loyalties. They may be moved by guilt to be a better parent with the new family and, in the process, introduce an intensity that is detrimental to the relationship with their stepchildren (McGoldrick and Carter 1980:270).

Children

According to research, girls make a better adjustment after divorce if they are cared for by their mothers, and boys make a better adjustment if they are cared for by their fathers. Girls in the custody of their fathers and boys in the custody of their mothers profit from remarriage, as the social development of girls improves with the arrival of a stepmother, and the social development of boys improves with the arrival of a stepfather (Santrock, Warshak, and Elliott 1982). Furthermore, given the centrality of the mother in family life, the children of a husband's prior marriage receive less attention than do the children of a wife's prior marriage (Hobart 1987:274).

In the vast majority of cases it is the mother who brings children into

I UNDERSTAND THAT BOTH SUE AND GARY BROUGHT THEIR CHILDREN WITH THEM WHEN THEY REMARRIED, BUT WHY IS IT CALLED A <u>BLENDED</u> FAMILY?

the reconstituted family. Thus the most problematic relationship is usually between the stepfather and the stepchildren. Stepfathers tend to be either very much involved with or disengaged from their stepchildren (Hetherington, Cox, and Cox 1982). One study found that children who live with stepfathers are as happy and successful as are children who live with their biological fathers (Bohannan and Yahraes 1979); another found children who live with stepfathers to be better off than fatherless children (Oshman and Manosevitz 1976).

One source of difficulty in stepchildren/stepparent relationships is an unrealistic expectation on the part of the stepparent, such as, "We will all love each other and share equally in each other's lives." Another source of difficulty is that stepchildren are often more tolerant of the mistakes of their natural parents than of the mistakes of stepparents. Society may condition children to trust only their own parents; as a result, they enter a reconstituted family with feelings of suspicion, overcautiousness, and resentfulness. Even children's literature, with its theme of the wicked stepmother, adds to the problem. Stepparents may try hard to be loving and caring to their stepchildren, but usually retreat to a less active role when they are rebuffed. Stepparents need to be patient and to resist the temptation of trying to replace the natural parent. They need to realize that they may be competing with an ideal who, in the eyes of the child, is perfect. It is less important that stepchildren and stepparents instantly love each other than that they get along.

Finances

Previous marriages can often be a source of financial problems for reconstituted families. Child support is the chief issue. Resentments can arise when promised child support does not come, or when money earned by the stepfather goes to support his biological children. A potential partner's secrecy about money, securities, and financial obligation should cause a person to hesitate before committing to remarriage (Messinger 1976).

A Christian Approach to Broken Families

Divorce and remarriage have never been considered part of normal family life. However, they are becoming more and more common in modern society. For this reason, it is very important that we have a clear idea as to what constitutes a Christian response to divorce and remarriage, both as societal phenomena and in specific individual cases.

Throughout this book we have emphasized that marriage and family relationships should be based on a mutual covenant. When two people marry, God intends for the relationship between them to be a two-way unconditional commitment. This is only the beginning of what God desires. It is God's desire that covenant commitment lead to a relationship in which grace abounds. Both partners will seek to forgive and to be forgiven when human frailty prevents them from being the whole persons they ought to be. Within this atmosphere of grace, they will strive to love each other in action. We have described this as mutual empowering—

each partner uses her or his talents, strengths, and resources to build up and serve the other. Out of mutual empowering comes true intimacy, where each partner knows and is known by the other in a way which compels them to care for each other as they care for themselves.

This ideal for Christian marriage is an honorable aspiration which can by God's grace be achieved in part. However, we would be remiss if we didn't address the fact that there are no perfect people who realize this ideal. All marriages are composed of two imperfect people who will fail and disappoint each other to one degree or another. All couples will struggle with their relationship. Some will find enough grace to overcome human brokenness. Counseling is a means of helping a couple through a healing process which preserves their marriage. But for others, brokenness is heaped upon brokenness, and before the hurt is addressed, it is too late to heal the marriage relationship. Rather than building from covenant to grace to empowering to intimacy to a deeper level of covenant, these marriages are spinning in reverse—from conditional love to emotional distance to possessive power to an atmosphere of law to love which is even more conditional, and so on. For many complex reasons, the estrangement and severing of the relationship occur.

The ultimate reason for all failures in relationships is sin, and divorce can at one level be described as a spiritual problem. Christians, however, must resist the temptation to treat all marital difficulties as problems which can be fixed merely by addressing the spiritual condition. This approach is too simplistic; it ignores the fact that human beings are complex social and psychological creatures. There is a web of complicated factors that affect how two people come to choose each other as well as how their marriage relationship develops (or fails to develop).

God desires permanence in marriage, and married Christians need to do all that they can to honor God in this. However, a combination of social, psychological, and spiritual factors prevents some couples from reaching this ideal. In fact, they find that their marital struggle is destroying not only what is left of their relationship, but their own personhood as well. They see no alternative but divorce. In their own eyes—and in the eyes of the Christian community as well—they have failed at marriage. The question now is, How do we as Christians apply our theology of relationships to these couples and families who walk through the pain of divorce?

To begin with, we must acknowledge that we live in a sinful and broken world in which we all fail in many aspects of our lives. Dwight Small (1977:8) has noted, "We give people the right to fail in business, in school, in careers, but not always in marriage. We reserve a particular stigma for that. The redemptive side of failure is not applied as readily as it ought to be."

Our reaction to a broken marriage needs to be like that of Jesus. Jesus did not condemn the woman at the well for her five broken marriages, but instead offered redemption and a new beginning (John 4). To attempt to restore a broken marriage through legalism and not offer forgiveness, love, and compassion is unacceptable. Ray Anderson and Dennis Guernsey (1985:101) write:

> Jesus presented the basis of marriage from the perspective of the command of God: "What therefore God has joined together, let no one put asunder" (Matthew 19:6). In saying this, Jesus removed both marriage and divorce from the status of being under a law, and reminded his listeners that all people are accountable to God in thought, word, and deed, not least of all in the "one flesh" relation of marriage. Viewed from this perspective, it is clear that there can be no "rules" by which marriage can be dissolved, any more than there are marriages which can be sanctified before God by observing certain legalities.

Wherever in the Bible Jesus talks about divorce (Matt. 5:31–32; 19:3–9; Mark 10:2–12; Luke 16:18), the clear thrust is that marriage is of the Lord and is not to be broken. Christ is calling couples to fidelity in marriage as a lifelong commitment; he does not have in view, however, a marriage of legalism and law which involves a commitment only to the institution itself and not to the relationship.

We agree with the sentiments expressed by John Patton and Brian Childs (1988:184): "We see marriage as a . . . human structure designed to facilitate human care for the earth and all that is in it, not something to be primarily a focus of care itself." It is unfortunate when Christians attempt to develop a theology of marriage which "focuses more on preserving the structure of marriage than on affirming the relationship of the persons involved in it."

This perspective that the well-being of the people involved is more important than the structure of marriage has shaped our view of single parenthood and remarriage. The Christian message is that out of brokenness can come forgiveness and restoration. Some divorced persons with children will choose to remain single and shoulder the responsibility of being the head of a one-parent family. We must not deny them or their families the encouragement and support that are necessary for them to thrive. These members of the church body are to be accepted and welcomed into our midst as legitimate parts of God's family.

Other divorced persons will find restoration through remarriage. We must resist the temptation to develop a legalistic rationale which would deny them the opportunity to find wholeness and hope through remarriage. As Diana and David Garland (1986:171) have stated:

If it is the case that marriage was made for the blessing of humankind, and not humankind for marriage, it would seem that one who has failed in marriage might have another opportunity to remarry. Any moral superiority that the nondivorced person might feel toward the divorced who remarry is undermined by Jesus' claim that everyone who lusts after another is guilty of adultery (Matthew 5:28). Every spouse has broken commitments to the partner, and every relationship experiences alienation from unresolved differences.

Remarried persons who live in reconstituted families have much to offer to our community in Christ. When our theology of relationships is practiced, the restoration and renewal of the remarried will be a blessing and strength to the whole community of believers.

PART 7

Family Life
in Modern Society

Introduction

Any meaningful understanding of the family must integrate analyses of the family at both micro and macro levels. We have focused mainly on microfamily issues—looking inside the family for an understanding of its dynamics. We turn now to an analysis of macrofamily issues—looking outside the family to explore the relationship between the family and the wider social context. Through this exploration we will see that many microfamily issues are, in reality, a reflection of macrofamily issues.

We begin this section by examining the modern social context. The contemporary family lives in a world of urbanization, bureaucracy, and technology. Chapter 16 introduces several major aspects of modernization and their profound negative influence on contemporary family life. In chapter 17, we present a biblical response to modernity. We believe that through radical change a social environment which nurtures the family can be developed, and thus the family can come to terms with the adverse effects of modernity.

16

The Family and Issues of Modernity

I t was the best of times, it was the worst of times." Charles Dickens's description of revolutionary change in eighteenth-century France aptly characterizes the family in the United States today. It truly is the best of times and the worst of times. The contemporary family is an institution of contrasts and contradictions. While the current divorce rate in our nation is almost as high as it has ever been, married couples in greater percentages than in the past report that they are getting satisfaction out of their relationship. Another contrast is that at the very time that millions of children are living in broken families, there is an unprecedented emphasis on love and intimacy in family relationships. And just as some are celebrating the freedom and openness brought about by new family forms, others are horrified at the decline of the American family.

For the family it is indeed the best of times and the worst of times, a contradiction which results from modernity. Our society has traditionally espoused a very optimistic view of the future, based largely upon a faith in progress. Today, however, this very same modernity, which has been heralded as the path to a utopian future, is being blamed for the decline of the family and the quality of much of human life in contemporary society.

Modernity Defined

Any concept as inclusive and encompassing as modernity is very difficult to define. One line of thought considers modernity to be closely tied to technological development. According to Marion Levy (1966:190), "the greater the ratio of inanimate power sources and the greater the extent to which human efforts are multiplied by the use of tools, the more modernized is the society." Peter Berger likewise conceives of modernity as closely linked to technology. His view has been summarized by James Hunter (1983:6): "Modernization is to be understood . . . as a process of institutional change proceeding from and related to a technologically engendered economic growth. . . . Modernity is the evitable period in the history of a particular society that is characterized by the institutional and cultural concomitant of a technologically induced economic growth."

Other theorists understand modernization as social change in various spheres. Neil Smelser (1973:748), for example, sees modernization as occurring

> (1) in the *political* sphere, as simple tribal or village authority systems give way to systems of suffrage, political parties, representation, and civil service bureaucracies; (2) in the *educational* sphere, as the society strives to reduce illiteracy, and increase economically productive skills; (3) in the *religious* sphere, as secularized belief systems begin to replace traditionalist religions; (4) in the *familial* sphere, as extended kinship units lose their pervasiveness; (5) in the *stratificational* sphere, as geographical and social mobility tends to loosen fixed, ascriptive hierarchical systems.

The sociological concept of modernization reflects both evolutionary theory and structural functionalism. Evolutionary theory assumes that a society advances from a simple to a complex state. This process is usually described as "development," underdeveloped societies being traditional agrarian communities with minimal technological innovation. Modernization, then, is conceived as occurring in stages. Walt Rostow (1961), for instance, speaks of a five-stage progression: agrarian society, preconditioning for takeoff, takeoff, drive to maturity, and high mass-consumption.

Structural functionalism assumes that as economic development takes place, new social and cultural forms will need to emerge. It is argued that new institutional forms are desirable and necessary in view of the changes in economic life. Some Christians, who see God-given ideals behind traditional social institutions, experience modernity as a threat. While the threat is real, modernity also affords the opportunity to examine existing social structures and re-create them in light of the biblical ideal.

The Crisis and Challenge of Modernity

A primary feature of modernity is the disintegration of traditional forms. Nathan Glazer has said that being modern involves "a sense of the breaking of the seamless mold in which *values, behavior,* and *expectations* were once cast into interlocking forms" (cited in Seeman 1957:411). With this breakdown of traditional forms comes the responsibility to create new institutional structures. And with this opportunity come threats of social, moral, and intellectual chaos, making the creative task of reconstructing institutions rather overwhelming. We live in the tension created by the dual realities of choice and a series of modern deterministic factors which Jacques Ellul (1976:27) characterizes as "a collection of mechanisms of indescribable complexity—technics, propaganda, state, administrative planning, ideology, urbanization, social technology." This tension leads us to see only the threats of modernization. Rather than facing up to modernity, as Peter Berger has advised, we too often retreat or try to avoid the issues.

The origins and moving forces of modernization continue to be debated by social scientists. While some theorists believe that modernization is fueled primarily by economic and technological forces, others point out that ideological changes have made modernization possible. We believe that modernization unfolds in a dialectical manner, fed by both material and ideological aspects of life. No part of society and culture is autonomous; no social entity develops purely in terms of its own internal organization. This is true of every one of the major structural units of contemporary society—the church, the family, the economy, education, and politics.

While there is interaction between all of the major dimensions of life, the economic and technological are dominant in present-day Western society. The other dimensions of life have been cast into a responsive rather than a leading role. On the other hand, the various internal crises of modernization may lead to changes in the current balance of power. For example, the issue of moral legitimation in modern society may lead to a new role for religious and moral institutions. Many question whether a society built on moral pluralism and its attendant, moral uncertainty, can maintain itself. As Berger (1983) has suggested, the crisis of secularization may lead to an awareness of the need for a new moral, if not religious, consensus in modern society.

In developing a framework to analyze the modern situation, we will consider four dimensions of sociocultural life: consciousness, communication, community, and commodities (see figure 22, where the solid arrows represent logical priority, and the broken arrows feedback between the various dimensions). Modernization is rooted largely in economic reality (commodities); changes at this level are reflected at the other levels of sociocultural life. In addition, each level sends feedback to the others. The dialectical model we are suggesting is similar to a general model of social structure in which each part is conceived as influencing and being influenced by each other part. We hasten to add that these dimensions should be considered as analytical constructs only. They should not be reified and considered separate components of reality.

In facing up to the challenge of being modern we must address all areas of life. We have chosen these four dimensions because they are the settings in which major crises are occurring today. We will first explore the general dilemma being posed in each of these layers of sociocultural life, and then turn our attention to the specific negative effects on the family.

Consciousness

Consciousness refers to the individual's subjective experiences, including thoughts, beliefs, images, and emotions. Crises in this area can occur both within and between individuals—both subjectively and inter-subjectively.

Within the individual, consciousness is fragmented between different spheres of life. The individual must negotiate between the impersonal competition of the marketplace and the intimacy of friendship and family, between rationality in the school and faith in the pew, between the fast-paced solutions of television and the routine open-endedness of daily life. Even the best of minds and the most stable of personalities can quickly lose a sense of centeredness, a clear grasp of meaning and reality.

This fragmentation of thought has resulted in a disjunction between faith and life. We ask the questions, How do our beliefs and values affect the structure of our lives? Do competing values and beliefs shape different areas of our lives? Do our commitments and beliefs as Christians distinguish us from other people?

In *Ideology and Social Psychology* Michael Billings (1982) suggests that people today live in a state of cognitive dissonance. We have adapted to apparently inconsistent beliefs and lack of congruency between values

FIGURE 22 **The Four Dimensions of Sociocultural Life**

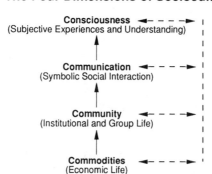

and behavior. For example, interpersonal commitments and intimacy are highly valued, but relationships are unstable. Many Christians speak about having compassion for the poor, but avoid those in need. To paraphrase the apostle Paul, we are trapped in a sociological "body of death," doing not the good we want, but the evil we do not want—and we do not understand our actions (Rom. 7:15–25).

A diversity of world-views is available to us. The more modern we become, the more we are aware of this diversity and the more relative our own views appear. Peter Berger (1967) refers to this as the pluralization of consciousness. For some, this opens the door for a challenging dialogue with others to help in the construction of one's personal value system. This can be an awesome and lonely task. Others will try to mold a new consensus either by creating a new synthesis through dialogue or by cutting the dialogue short and imposing their own beliefs on the other participants. Another possible way of proceeding is subjectivization. As Hunter (1982:40) puts it:

> When the institutional routines and ideologies are rendered implausible, modes of conduct and thought, *morality included*, are deliberated. If institutions no longer provide consistent and reliable answers to such questions as "What do I do with my life?", "How do I raise my children?", "Is it acceptable to live with a member of the opposite gender outside of marriage?", etc., the individual must necessarily *turn inward* to the subjective to reflect, ponder and probe for answers. The process of "turning inward" is the process of subjectivization.

As Hunter further suggests, the process of subjectivization is not negative—it is simply a structural feature of modern society. It can, however, foster "an incessant fixation upon the self . . . [an] abiding absorption with the 'complexities' of individuality."

Communication

Communication in modern society both shapes and reflects the fragmentation, pluralization, and subjectivization of modern consciousness. Significant symbols—terms which everyone understands in precisely the same way—are the basis of communication. But in modern society we cannot assume that everyone will understand a term in precisely the same way. Even the words *family* and *church* have a variety of meanings which can arouse emotional debate. The denotative or referential meanings of words vary considerably—consider the multitude of meanings of the word *love*. The connotative or associative meanings are even more diverse. Lack of consensus on meanings creates a dilemma. On the one hand, our diverse backgrounds and uniqueness as individuals make communication more necessary than ever. On the other hand, our lack of significant symbols makes communication more problematic than ever.

A variety of questions arise in the context of our attempts to communicate: How can we communicate if we cannot assume that others will understand our words as we understand them? How is dialogue possible if there is no shared basis of interpreting language? Are our vocabularies authentic? How free are we to create new vocabularies and to give new meanings to words? What is the relationship between experience and language? Can we trust the very process of communication? Will language become, like advertising, one more technique to mystify and control others?

The difficulties of communicating are compounded today by the proliferation of technical and professional languages which mystify the common person. We also see attempts to transcend the traditional means of symbolic communication through various forms of nonverbal communication. In general there is an impoverishment of everyday language and conversation because of the impossibility of capturing complex and confusing realities in simple words.

Community

The breakdown of traditional (homogeneous and geographically based) communities has been lamented by many as the major crisis of the modern era. Without such communities we have no means of social control and are thus vulnerable to ourselves (to our own moral laxity) and to strangers around us. What Peter Berger and others have called the homeless mind (1973) is in search of a new home or community in which to find meaning and purpose. What is often forgotten when we lament the loss of traditional communities, however, is the provincialism and lack of autonomy which are characteristic of them. Isolated villages and tribal groups are noted for their ethnocentrism.

Concurrent with the disintegration of community life is the centralization of economic and political functions in corporate and governmental bureaucracies. The picture that emerges is of the isolated individual and nuclear family confronted with the faceless image of mass society. The community which once mediated between the individual and larger institutions is no longer there. Judicial and political institutions are called upon to settle more and more family, church, and community disputes. Government encroachment into areas previously considered private or sacred has become a serious social question to which there are no apparent answers.

Some social scientists have suggested that networks are the modern substitute for traditional communities. Friends, co-workers, social, educational, cultural, and religious groups—together these networks can satisfy all or almost all of the individual's needs. However, networks tend to be unstable and specialized and thus lack the virtues associated with community—unconditional commitment and a sense of belonging which embraces the whole of a person's life.

There is a wide range of responses to the disintegration of traditional communities. At one extreme we see the trend toward a self-contained individualism which denies dependence on others and makes no commitment to them. At the other extreme we see people experimenting with various forms of communities focused around some common value such

IS THIS WHAT PAUL MEANT BY CHRISTIAN COMMUNITY, DAD?

as economic sharing, family life, or religious devotion. In between these extremes we see many people searching for a sense of community in institutional contexts such as the church, where the community metaphor is familiar, and in homogeneous neighborhoods such as suburban housing developments, where names like Homewood, Pleasantdale, and Community Heights imply commonality and identity.

Commodities

In advanced capitalism the economic sphere has been largely secularized. Economic life develops unguided by any particular religious ideology. This differentiation of economic life is characteristic of modern institutions. The fragmentation of consciousness, complexity of communication, and disintegration of community make an integration of life around economics seem viable. Richard Fenn (1974:41–42) argues that religion has not served to integrate modern society and that uniformity or consensus will most likely be limited to political and economic issues. Remaining unanswered is the question whether a society based solely on economic and political consensus can maintain itself.

Economic principles do dominate modern social life. Jacques Ellul notes in *The Technological Society* (1964) that the principle of technique or rational efficiency has moved from the economic realm to all other areas of life, including the political, educational, and interpersonal. As the principles and values associated with economic life enter other areas, we can see a pattern of the "commodification" of social life developing (Wexler 1983).

Karl Marx maintained that the capitalist emphasis on commodities results in the alienation of the worker. The intrinsic meaning of work is lost. Work becomes only a means to the end of making money. Consequently, workers define themselves and others in terms of their ability to make money. Money has become a spiritual force in society as well as a moral criterion for judging people and their activities (Ellul 1984). Social interaction and the creative process are subservient to the goals of efficiency and production. The twin phenomena of careerism and consumerism, two evidences of these trends, are found at the center of economic, church, and family life.

The Impact of Modernity on the Family

With this basic understanding of modernity, we can now examine the dilemmas it poses for the family, as well as the false hopes it has generated (see table 9).

The Fragmentation of Consciousness

The problem. The fragmentation of consciousness has produced a crisis in the areas of morality and authority within the family. Each family must

TABLE 9

The Impact of Modernity upon the Family: Dilemmas and False Hopes

Dilemmas of Modernity	Dilemmas for the Family	False Hopes
Fragmentation of Consciousness		
Fragmentation of thought	Crisis in morality and authority	Traditionalism: restoring the family of the past
Religious and moral pluralism	Dichotomy between private and public	Cult of the expert
Disjunction between faith and life	life	Privatization
Subjectivization		
Complexity of Communication		
Decline of significant symbols	Diverse backgrounds and linguistic styles	Overreliance on techniques of communication
Mystifying technical language	Generation gap	Isolation of communication from regular
Impoverished conversation		activities
Disintegration of Community		
Disintegration of traditional community	Isolated nuclear family	The family as a self-contained unit
life	Lack of community support and control	Extrafamilial care of children, the elderly, and
Lack of social control	Increased family dependence on mass	handicapped
Individuals confronted by bureaucracy	institutions	Alternative family forms
and mass society	Development of a youth culture	
Government encroachment into private	Little parental stake in children's	
matters	marriages	
	Lack of ties between extended families	
	Diminished parental authority	
	Equalization of power within the family	
Dominance of Commodities		
Integration of society around economic	The family as the unit of consumption	Assessment of the fair market value of
values	instead of production	housework
Separation of economic from church life	Separation of work and family life	Community through consumption
"Commodification" of social life	Individual and family worth determined	The family as the center of cottage industry
Dominance of technical means	by economics	Full employment for both husband and wife
		(careerism)

construct its own value system, usually without the support of the extended family. Difficulties are especially likely to arise when children reach their teenage years and begin to compare their family's system of morality with that of their friends. Parents are put in the position of having to defend their view of morality against the view of their children's peers. The crisis in authority brought about by the fragmentation of consciousness also includes questions of the authority of the extended family over the nuclear family, and of the husband over the wife. The current redefinition of sex roles comes into play here.

The fragmentation of consciousness has led as well to a dichotomy between public and private life. In traditional societies there tends to be little separation between the two; the primary social unit in both work and private life is one and the same—the family, clan, or tribe. By contrast, the recent separation of work and private life has led to two levels of social functioning. While working, individuals experience others as relatively impersonal beings and themselves as anonymous functionaries (Berger et al. 1973:34). This anonymity precludes any involvement on a plane higher than what might be described as pseudointimacy. People attempt to find genuine intimacy, meaning, and fulfilment in their private lives. But we suspect that modernity may have so weakened the private institution of the family that even here intimacy and fulfilment are not possible.

False hopes. As the Christian community has felt the crisis created by the fragmentation of consciousness, a major response by conservatives has been traditionalism—an attempt to restore the family to what it was in the past. With the confusion created by modernity many Christians are quick to hold up the nineteenth-century American version of the family as the biblical ideal. We believe that this is a false hope because it is less the biblical perspective on the family in modern society than it is a defense of what the family has been in the past. Christians commonly fall into the trap of assuming that the particular family form existing in their culture is God's ideal. They read their own cultural standards into Scripture and accept all biblical accounts of family life as if they were normative. But some of the accounts of how the family was organized during biblical times were never intended to dictate how it should be organized in all cultures at all times.

A second response to the fragmentation of family consciousness is to rely upon expert opinion, another false hope. Parents often experience a crisis in confidence and are unwilling to trust their common sense out of fear that they may be doing something wrong in rearing their children. Such self-doubt frequently occurs in the Christian community, where many parents hold to a deterministic view of parenting: they wrongly believe that right parenting is a guarantee of God-fearing children. Unfortunately, this view is reinforced by a variety of self-proclaimed experts, who attract large numbers of parents eager to be relieved of the agonizingly difficult task of parenting in modern society.

Another false hope is the privatization of family life, an offshoot of the dichotomy between private and public life. In the words of J. A. Walter (1979:49–50):

> In modern society, marriage and the family enable me to construct a home world in which I am known as the self I would like to be and in which I, in turn, confirm the self of my spouse. Or at least this is the hope. Marriage and the family provide a whole universe of meanings which is for the family members real reality as opposed to the artificial reality of the public world out there. Marriage provides a do-it-yourself reality kit.

To the extent that the do-it-yourself family creates a consciousness which is out of touch with external reality, it can be described as a false hope. Also, the privatization of family life can easily lead to an amoral familism, where the family is so preoccupied with its own concerns that it fails to serve far needier people. The amoral privatized family dishonors the biblical concept of family life.

Complexity of Communication

The problem. The complexity of communication in modern society saps vitality from family life. That there is no exact universal understanding of words like "family," "love," "parenting," "intimacy," and "sharing," complicates communication and relations. To the extent that a husband and wife come from diverse backgrounds, or experience differing patterns of growth, they will encounter difficulty in communication. It may very well be that the seemingly unending search for intimacy in contemporary society is an attempt to fill a void resulting from a lack of shared experiences.

Parents with teenage children are quick to realize that a good part of what is referred to as the generation gap is in large measure a gap in communication. With the emergence of the adolescent subculture come not only new meanings for old words (cool, hot, tight, bad, square), but also new words (punk, new wave, mod, rad, oye). To appreciate the complexity of communication among adolescents, one must realize that there is no monolithic adolescent subculture, but rather adolescent subcultures (Preppies, Mods, Stoners, Rockers, New Wavers, Surfers, and Straights), each developing their own style of communication (much of it nonverbal).

False hopes. Overreliance on the techniques of communication is a common response to the complexity of communication in the family. One need only glance at the many how-to books written on marital and family communication to realize the heavy emphasis which is placed on technique. But a focus on technique can actually reduce communication. Spouses may find themselves talking about talking rather than engaging in genuine dialogue. (The overreliance on technique has spread even into the area of sexual communication; manuals promise a couple complete sexual fulfilment if they will only follow the suggested step-by-step procedure.)

Another response to the complexity of communication is to isolate communication from our customary activities. Many parents, realizing the need to explain to their children the reasons for family rules and values, set aside time for discussion rather than having such conversations as a natural part of life together. Essentially, then, family communication is removed from the normal course of activity and becomes one more task for the modern family. It is better to explain family rules and values whenever a suitable occasion presents itself. Communication will be greatly improved if it is embedded in the common experiences of developing family relationships.

Disintegration of Community

The problem. The extended family has been replaced by the nuclear family in most modern societies. With the uprooting of the nuclear family from its extended family, clan, or tribal base comes the loss of community support and control of family life. The isolated nuclear family in modern society is a very fragile system. Gone is the day-to-day support provided by the extended family. The young married couple must go it alone. With no one else to share in the task of child care, the absence of either husband or wife (or of both) from the home can be severely disruptive.

It has been argued that the isolated nuclear family is the most functional social unit for modern industrial society. At a time when others were announcing the decline of the American family, Talcott Parsons and Robert Bales (1955:9) made the optimistic assessment that the family is not in a state of decline, but rather is becoming more specialized:

> The family has become *a more specialized agency than before,* probably more specialized than it has been in any previously known society. This represents a decline of *certain* features which traditionally have been associated with families, but whether it represents a "decline of the family" in a more general sense is another matter; we think not. We think the trend of the evidence points to the beginning of the relative stabilization of a new type of family structure, in a new relation to a general social structure, one in which the family is more specialized than before, but not in any general sense less important, because the society is dependent *more* exclusively on it for the performance of its vital functions.

Parsons and Bales envisioned small community-based organizations like churches, neighborhood schools, clubs, and voluntary associations taking over the traditional family functions. The family in modern society, however, has become increasingly dependent upon mass economic and governmental institutions. Gone are the smaller community-based mediating structures between the nuclear family and the impersonal, centralized, bureaucratic structures of modern mass society.

The lack of community moorings has freed family members to become part of social networks over which the family has very little control. As mentioned previously, teenage youths have become part of adolescent subcultures. The trend in society is for family members to participate as individuals in a variety of specialized interest groups. Although most groups are not likely to foster intimate relationships, those that do will further disintegrate the family as a community.

In his book *World Revolution and Family Patterns,* William Goode (1963) identifies three components of the modern ideology which set the individual above the traditional community: (1) the primacy of industrial growth over tradition and custom; (2) equality between the sexes; and (3) the primacy of the conjugal relationship over extended-family relationships. Goode sees the emergence of these emphases as serving to free the individual from the domination of the extended family and from the bonds of traditional ways of doing things.

One of the major strengths of Goode's work is the historical and cross-cultural support he garnered for his thesis. On the basis of this evidence Goode concludes that modern societies are moving toward a family system which centers on the conjugal relationship. Among the characteristics of this system are: (1) a bilateral method of reckoning kinship ties, that is, since husband and wife come from different families, they will recognize a somewhat different set of kindred; (2) little parental stake in children's marriages; (3) mate selection on the basis of romantic love; (4) absence of customs like the dowry and bride price, which traditionally served to unite extended families; (5) the diminishing of parents' authority over children and husbands' authority over wives; and (6) the equalization of power within the family and the emergence of negotiation as a means of decision making (Goode 1963:7–10). Goode is right in his observation that these changes have served to free the individual from the dominance of the extended family. However, modern ultraindividualism with its lack of accountability to the community causes us to wonder if too large a price is being paid for this freedom.

False hopes. At least three responses to the disintegration of community prove to be false hopes. First, some families become self-contained units. They attempt to meet their every need internally. They develop their own ideology, strive for economic self-sufficiency, and become deeply enmeshed. The self-contained family is an unrealistic ideal which is doomed to fail in modern society. It is also inconsistent with Jesus' definition of family (Mark 3:31–35).

Out of necessity other families in modern society are turning to extra-familial institutions for the care of dependent members. Many of these families are fractured units which do not have the resources needed to provide adequate care for children, the elderly, or the handicapped. In other instances the stress on individualism and personal self-fulfilment prevents family members from actively assuming caretaking responsibilities. They ignore the fact that the quality of care which large institutions are able to give needy persons rarely measures up to the New Testament standard of *koinōnia* (fellowship, community).

The third response has been alternative family forms. Now it is true that family forms must change in response to modernity; to think otherwise is to accept the traditional American family as the biblical ideal, instead of merely one among several equally justifiable cultural alternatives. Christians must be aware, however, that, as a result of modernity's secularizing influence, among the alternatives which are currently being suggested are homosexual marriage, group marriage, planned single parenthood, and nonmarital cohabitation. That is to say, there currently exists a relativistic predisposition to re-create the family in any form which might suit the demands of individual self-fulfilment and modern society. Adoption of such an alternative ignores not only scriptural authority, but also the possibility that it might well be that the demands of the individual and of modern society should be changed for the sake of the family rather than the other way around.

Dominance of Commodities

The problem. A major effect of the dominance of commodities has been to change the family from the basic unit of production to the basic unit of consumption. It is rare to find family members together for the purpose of producing; it is equally rare to find family members together for any purpose other than consuming. The world of work and family life are separated; this is, as we have seen, one of the symptoms of the fragmentation of consciousness.

Another effect of the dominance of commodities is that the ability to acquire them is the chief determinant of the worth of individuals and families. Others gauge us by our success in the marketplace, and we gauge ourselves by how much money we earn relative to others. In many instances a raise is needed more for the purpose of building up self-esteem than for meeting financial obligations.

False hopes. There have been various attempts to respond to the dominance of commodities in modern society. Certain feminists have argued that the only way true equality will be achieved by housewives is for the state to pay them a wage for the work done. A less radical suggestion is to assess the market value of their housework in terms of the money earned by their husbands. Home economists estimate that the work of the average American housewife would have a fair market value of $32,000 per year. Armed with these figures, housewives would be in a strong position to bargain for more power in the marriage relationship. While not negating marital equality as a biblical ideal, we believe that even this less radical suggestion is a compromise with the view that marriage is based on social exchange, both partners seeking to gain more from the relationship than they give up. We do not deny that this is the basis for many modern marriages; we believe, however, that it flies in the face of the biblical ideal of mutual submissiveness.

Some families wrongly believe that they can create a sense of community solely through consumption, for example, by watching television or going to a movie together. We do not deny that some activities of this nature can play a small role in producing a sense of community; we do deny, however, the naive assumption that the family that consumes together blooms together.

In *The Third Wave* (1979) Alvin Toffler sees a bright future for the family in the technological society. He predicts that large segments of the work now being done outside the home will revert to the home. In view of the computer revolution which is currently in progress, it is only a matter of time before homes will be turned into electronic cottage industries. Reminded of the medieval guild, Toffler regards the home as a place where work will be done, where children will learn what work entails, and where apprentices will acquire a trade. While this delightful image may prove to be a reality for some families, given the multitude of unsolved social problems engendered by modernity, it must be viewed as only a false hope at this time.

A final false hope is the phenomenon of careerism. Over fifty percent of all married women in the United States work outside of the home. It is unfortunate that some Christians take issue with the wife's working outside the home. We believe that the chief concern ought not to be her working, but the adequacy of parental (both paternal and maternal) nurturing of and bonding with dependent children. We believe that a structural change is needed: economic institutions should make provisions for child care and be receptive to adjustable working schedules for employees who have young families.

The phenomenon of careerism needs to be addressed, not as a feminist issue, but as an identity problem for all adults. Careerism, whether only one or both spouses are involved, promotes the false equation of individual worth with career success. Careers, like money, take on spiritual significance and detract from the establishment and maintenance of intimate relationships within the family and society as a whole.

We have in this chapter presented a fairly dismal picture of modern society. The present age seems to be the worst of times—consciousness is fragmented, communication is overly complex, the traditional community has broken down, and there is an obsession with commodities. The family is in a wretched predicament, and whatever attempts are made to ameliorate the situation have proven to be false hopes. What is called for is radical change built on biblical principles.

17

Creating a Positive Environment for Family Life

In the previous chapter we looked at the social environment of the contemporary family. By examining the effect of modernity upon the family, we gained an understanding of why it is difficult to live according to biblical ideals. What is needed is a positive environment which strengthens family life.

In this chapter we propose some ideas on how to create a healthy environment for family life. Fundamental changes must be made in two general areas: (1) families must make a radical response to modernity; and (2) community and societal structures must incorporate the biblical ideals of *koinōnia* and *shalom*.

Toward a Radical Response to Modernity

The family has been greatly challenged and changed by modernity. The challenges—fragmentation of consciousness, complexity of communication, disintegration of community, and dominance of commodities—make it imperative that we come up with fresh insights as to how to create a positive environment in which the family can give glory to God and through their relationships show evidence of the salvation and freedom offered in Christ Jesus. This redemption, which enables us to meet

293

the challenges of modernity, was purchased at a great cost and demands of us in turn a radical response.

It is important to keep in mind that redemption is an unfolding creative work of God in the lives of individuals, families, and societies. We need release from our bondage to commodities, which in turn will make reconstruction of community possible, which will provide an arena for revitalization of communication, which will eventually lead to reintegration of consciousness.

In contemplating restoration of the family, we must have a general acquaintance with previous attempts which have proven to be false hopes. One general category consists of reactionary endeavors to return the family to an idealized past. These efforts are based on twin fallacies: (1) that the nineteenth century was a golden age of family life; and (2) that the traditional patriarchal family represents the biblical ideal for society today. This approach ignores the complexity of the issues. Its attempts to reconstitute the past overlook the dominance of commodities, disintegration of community, complexity of communication, and fragmentation of consciousness.

A second category of efforts which have failed to restore the family consists of attempts to simply adapt to the march of progress, to adjust the family lifestyle in accordance with whatever innovations are introduced into society. Some of these responses to modernity are based on naturalistic and relativistic assumptions about the family. While avoiding the pitfall of idealizing a particular cultural and temporal form of the family, proponents of this approach fail to acknowledge any norms or absolutes for the family. Our thesis is that the family must recognize the forces of modernity and respond in a creative, nonreactionary, and nonadaptive manner.

Release from Bondage to Commodities

The first step toward a healthy environment is to free ourselves from the dominance of commodities (see table 10). One need not be a Marxist to acknowledge that capitalism dominates all of modern life. We are a people for whom the term *productivity* automatically connotes commodities. Clearly, the restoration of family life cannot be accomplished without liberation from the pervasive influence of our economic system.

Without a revolution to free us from our bondage to commodities we will inevitably be pulled toward conformity to the system that promotes it. Techniques, money, careers, and material growth have become spiritual forces in society. We cannot count on society to change by adopting our Christian values; rather, we must be willing to sacrifice and risk appearing foolish in resisting the power of worldly values.

Christian employers can take the lead. They can, for example, establish

TABLE 10

Creating a Positive Family Environment

Challenges of Modernity	Christian Responses
Dominance of Commodities	Release from Bondage to Commodities
	Employment programs which give priority to relationships
	Family sacrifice of socioeconomic goals
	Church support
	Mutual empowerment (rather than social exchange) as the basis of family relations
Disintegration of Community	Reconstruction of Community
	Effective boundaries around the family
	Emphasis on the inclusiveness of the family
Complexity of Communication	Revitalization of Communication
	Family communication during shared activities
	Development of family rituals
Fragmentation of Consciousness	Reintegrating of Consciousness
	Dependence on the beliefs and values provided by the church
	Openness to people who are different
	Service and witness to Christ

policies which provide ways for their employees to give priority to family relationships. One option is to offer flexible schedules for both mothers and fathers who desire to be with young children. A strategy which reverses the two-hundred-year-old trend of giving economic institutions priority over parenting would make a significant contribution. Such a program could involve concessions for difficult pregnancies, maternity/paternity leave, and child care on the premises. It would inevitably cost the company in monetary profits, but gains would be realized in the strengthening of family relationships, in the employees' personal well-being, and in their loyalty to the company. These employees would benefit from the commitment, care, and empowering provided by their employers.

Similarly, Christian employers could make advancement opportunities available to employees who elect not to move their families to a new community. The average young American family moves every three years. It is inconceivable that the community support systems which families need, especially during periods of stress and crisis, can develop within such a mobile society.

There also need to be commitments from employers to the welfare of their employees, as well as commitments from the employees to produce high-quality work. The present economic system, which makes the profit motive the major consideration, works directly against the development of any sense of loyalty or pride in the quality of work performed. Christian employers must provide, in addition to salary, a context in which the employee is given incentives and rewards for creative service and pride in production.

Within the family itself, consumerism and careerism must be replaced by a focus on relationships and a sharing of resources with others. This would require, in addition to an attitude of mutual submissiveness, empowering, and servanthood, a willingness to forgo the socioeconomic status and security which we have been conditioned to achieve for ourselves and our families. A basic assumption of middle-class American society is that we are obligated to hand down to our children a certain social status and economic security. Family life is oriented around this goal. A decision to sacrifice socioeconomic status in order to live according to biblical principles will be perceived as a threat to the existing order. The children involved, other family members, and friends may criticize someone who takes a low-paying job in order to spend more time with the family or to serve the community.

It is not an easy task to buck the system and make personal relationships and the serving of others a more important priority than the making of money. Our society respects persons with high-paying jobs, but very seldom prizes those who choose relationships as their supreme goals. A typical case in point is parents who choose to stay home with their children out of dedication to the parenting role. These parents often are judged for not being employed outside the home. A single parent who makes such a decision has the additional stigma of living at the poverty level. Our friend Lloyd, a father who was very proud of the fact that he stayed at home to raise his three young children, constantly faced disdain by others, who made such comments as, "Is that all you do?" and "Why don't you work?" The insinuation was that something had to be radically wrong with him for making such a choice. Needless to say, his rewards for committing himself to family goals had to come from his inner strength rather than from the reactions of the community.

The church must offer its blessing to any individual willing to make sacrifices. Such support and backing will minimize the impact of these sacrifices and protect the individual from the brute economic forces of modern society. Churches can offer sustenance to families that commit themselves to relational goals. They can also provide quality day-care centers for parents who need to be employed outside the home. Further, the church should be sensitive to the special needs of families that have added emotional or financial burdens. The resources provided by a caring community can be of enormous benefit to families coping with handicapped members, major illnesses, or death.

Release from the bondage of commodities can also be achieved by refusing to think of marriage and family relationships in terms of social exchange. Unfortunately, what began as a theory to explain family power has become reified and is now reflected in daily life. Family members maneuver to ensure they gain more from a relationship than they give to it. Indeed, educational materials now advocate that family members consciously engage in a process of self-centered bargaining with one another. This model of family life with its emphasis on commodities needs to be replaced by the biblical model of mutual empowering and servanthood.

Reconstruction of Community

The typical nuclear family in the United States is a partial community at best. It is plundered on one side by demands and intrusions of mass society and on the other by an individualism which has become increasingly narcissistic. What is needed most is a recapturing of the biblical perspective of what it means to be a family. In this regard, two points which may appear to be paradoxical at first reading need to be made.

First, the reconstruction of family life will need to take place in a secure environment with effective boundaries. The family needs protection from the intrusion of a multitude of forces which are currently encroaching upon it and sapping its vitality. We have already mentioned the necessity of protecting the family from economic institutions. A similar appeal could be made regarding governmental, educational, and even religious institutions. In trying to meet all the demands with which they are bombarded by these institutions, the family is fractured. Family members need a central place where they can gather together and be nurtured in an environment of acceptance, intimacy, and mutual concern.

In the intimacy of the family community, we have a place where we can be naked and not ashamed (Gen. 2:25), a place where we can be who we are, free from all the demanding requirements of the outside world. Here is a place where family members can relax and be comfortable in a supportive and encouraging atmosphere. Here they do not have to hide, but can be honest and real before the others in the family.

Family life which is based on contract, law, and conditional love will not provide the refuge that is needed by weary individuals who have been out battling in the competitive world. However, family life which is based on covenant, grace, empowering, and intimacy does provide a haven and place of refreshment. It embodies the New Testament concept of *koinōnia*. Indeed, any family grounded in the principle of mutual servanthood exemplifies the spirit of Christian community.

Second, the reconstruction of community can take place only when the concept of family is regarded as inclusive rather than exclusive. Whereas servanthood and commitment are meant to begin in the family, the Bible presents a moral imperative which will not permit us to be content with any form of amoral familism. There is much in the teaching of Jesus to suggest that loyalty is misplaced if it resides in the family only. In fact, on occasion Jesus speaks of leaving, dividing, and even hating one's family.

A case could be made that Jesus actually undermined the family. First, he chose the single life instead of marriage, and second, he taught a radical discipleship which sets persons at odds with their family: "For from now on, five members of a family will be divided, three against two and two against three; father against son and son against father, mother against daughter and daughter against mother, mother against son's wife and son's wife against her mother-in-law" (Luke 12:52–53 NEB).

In the wider context of Jesus' teaching it would, of course, be a mistake to think that Jesus was against strong family life. The point which contemporary Christians should heed is that loyalty must transcend family and extend to the Christian community as a whole. While Jesus did not dissolve the natural order of the family, he did desire that we expand our circle of caring relationships beyond the family. His redefinition of the family bears repeating. While he was speaking to a crowd, a message came that his mother and brothers had arrived. Jesus replied, "Who is my mother? Who are my brothers?" Then looking at those who were sitting in the circle about him, Jesus said, "Here are my mother and my brothers. Whoever does the will of God is my brother, my sister, my mother" (Mark 3:31–35 NEB). Membership in the body of Christ binds all believers to one another as family.

Inclusiveness and strong family boundaries are paradoxical only in appearance. For only an internally strong family can adequately empower the Christian community, and it is in ministry to the Christian community that the family fulfils its mission. Likewise, only an internally strong church can empower the wider community of which it is a part, and it is in ministry to the wider community that the Christian community fulfils its mission.

Revitalization of Communication

Communication is vital in reconstructing our community life and re-integrating our consciousness. It should reflect both our individual unique-

ARE YOU SURE THIS IS THE BEST WAY FOR US TO
RECONSTRUCT A SENSE OF COMMUNITY, ALBERT?

ness and our shared values and activities. Family communication must
be liberated from overreliance on techniques and obsession with words.
We suggest two ways in which this can be accomplished. First, communication must be contextualized rather than being a separate activity
unto itself. Family members liberated from commodities and living in
community will engage in many activities together. These activities provide
a natural context in which to share and compare experiences and learn
of each other's uniqueness.

Second, families can develop other ways of communicating. Creating or rediscovering family rituals for special occasions is an excellent way of breaking down barriers between people and symbolizing family values. At Christmastime, for example, it is important that the family de-emphasize commodities. Celebrating through symbolic acts, art, plays, song, and dance can create a solidarity in which all members participate. This intimate time of togetherness is also an opportunity for each family member to express personal uniqueness.

Reintegration of Consciousness

Individuals are able to integrate their experiences only if a plausible system of beliefs and values is available to them. The isolated nuclear family is incapable of developing and maintaining such a system. The church can help here by providing a coherent structure of beliefs and values so that the family can achieve a reintegration of consciousness.

Another means of achieving reintegration is for the church and the family to be open rather than closed systems. They should have an expanded awareness of and concern for others who might be different in a variety of ways. The nuclear family can develop fictive kin—persons who, though they are not blood relatives, are taken in as extended-family members. Church members should seize the opportunity to become world Christians rather than focusing only on the plight of their own group. The church should learn about Christians around the world and respond to them as brothers and sisters in Christ. Wherever there are poor and oppressed people, the Christian community should reach out with acts of compassion as well as with monetary and political support.

The family and church must strive together to manifest a love which is patient, kind, hopeful, and enduring. Only as witnesses to and exemplars of God's love can church and family enable their members to resist the alternatives presented by the world. The beliefs and value systems of the world are firmly entrenched, ready at all times to oppose the Word of God. This has always been the case; the modern situation is unique only in its specific challenges and temptations.

Through service and witness to Christ we have a great hope of re-integrating our lives. We must keep in mind, however, that the disintegrating effects of modernity will be overcome only in part in the present world. Perfection will come in the future. "For we know in part, and we prophesy in part. But when that which is perfect is come, then that which is in part shall be done away. . . . For now we see through a glass, darkly; but then face to face: now I know in part; but then shall I know even as also I am known" (1 Cor. 13:9–12 KJV).

The fact that change will be only partial and imperfect in our human social systems is no excuse for retreat from giving a radical response to modernity. It is essential that Christians neither deny nor be paralyzed by the serious disruptive effects of modernity. They must be both realistic and optimistic. Contemporary society is currently staggering from the blows of modernity. Within this context the people of God must call for, and serve as salt and light effecting, the transformation of American culture. Nothing short of such a radical response to modernity will do!

Support Structures

Our focus in this chapter so far has been on how a biblical family structure can be created in the face of modern society. But more is needed, for the family does not exist in a vacuum. It is vitally connected, for better or for worse, with community and society. The family, community, and society are interrelated support structures (see figure 23). We have suggested that covenant, grace, empowering, and intimacy are biblical themes upon which family life might be patterned. We suggest that the corresponding biblical ideals for community and society are *koinōnia* and *shalom*. (For a fuller discussion of these concepts and an analysis of how they might be applied, see Jack Balswick and J. Kenneth Morland, *Social Problems: A Christian Perspective* [Grand Rapids: Baker, 1990].)

FIGURE 23 · **Support Structures**

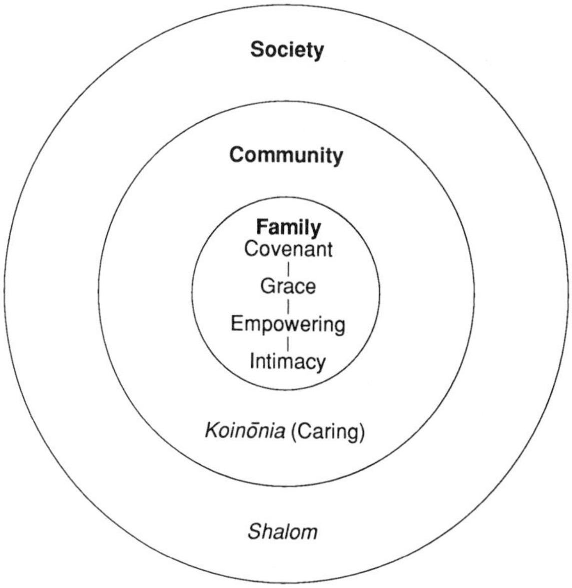

Society

Community

Family
Covenant
|
Grace
|
Empowering
|
Intimacy

Koinōnia (Caring)

Shalom

Extended Families

Families need caring communities within which they can find a sense
of identity and social support. Wherever the extended family is the basic
social unit, nuclear families have a built-in supportive community. The
basic social unit is in large measure determined by the level of societal
complexity (see figure 24). In hunting and gathering societies, where the
level of societal complexity is very low, the basic unit is the nuclear family.
The nomadic lifestyle with its subsistence economy simply cannot support social units larger than nuclear families. With the domestication of
plants and animals, people began to settle in specific locations. Agricul-
ture-based societies can support larger concentrations of people. In addition, ownership of land, tools, and animals fosters the development of
larger family units. The extended family is the dominant social unit in
virtually all agricultural economies.

The Industrial Revolution, which began in the eighteenth century, required that people concentrate in large cities. The high social and geographical mobility which was involved caused a decline in the extended-
family system. The dominant social unit in highly industrial economies
is the isolated nuclear family.

What about the future of family life in postindustrial societies? There

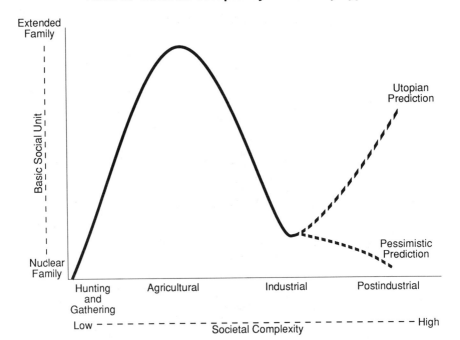

FIGURE 24 **Societal Complexity and Family Type**

are two lines of thought. The pessimistic view is that the fragile isolated-nuclear-family system found in industrial societies will become even weaker. Those who make this prediction suggest alternatives such as nonmarital cohabitation and temporary marriages, which would provide the flexibility needed in postindustrial society. The utopian view is that the emerging electronic revolution will serve to reunite work and family life. We have already noted Alvin Toffler's prediction of the emergence of cottage industries: parents will work at home on computers and teach their children and apprentices their trade. The results will include closer relationships between parents and their children and the emergence of nonrelated extended families as others (the apprentices) come to live within the home for a while. Only a minority of families will benefit, however.

Koinōnia in Communities

There is today a great emphasis on community. There is little evidence, however, that most of what we call community is providing the care and support which members of isolated nuclear families require. We believe that the New Testament concept of *koinōnia* is an ideal solution. *Koinōnia* refers to a community in which Christians are united in identity and purpose. In the New Testament prototype, members of the church voluntarily shared all of their possessions. They joined together in both *politeia* (civic life) and *oikonomia* (family life). *Koinōnia* came to represent a new type of community between the all-inclusive, impersonal state and the exclusive, blood-based household.

In his book *Paul's Idea of Community*, Robert Banks (1980:42) argues that since the first Christian churches met in the houses of believers, the size of any one fellowship was limited to about twenty or thirty persons. It is significant that recent social-science research has found that a typical individual is able to maintain intimate relationships with a maximum of twenty-five to thirty persons. Those attempting to develop a larger network of intimate friendships find that they lack the time, capacity, and energy to keep each relationship growing and vital (Pattison 1984).

We believe that families need the support of *koinōnia*. Traditional societies are more successful in fostering communities of this type. Mass societies, which are characterized by impersonalization, urbanization, industrialization, rationalization, dehumanization, bureaucratization, and secularization, make *koinōnia* difficult. Churches which practice *koinōnia* emphasize small groups and the relational themes of covenant, grace, empowering, and intimacy. The members of these groups take time to know one another and care for one another in a variety of ways. They also reach out to the greater community and general society.

The Church

The primary locus of *koinōnia* is the church. In form the church should resemble a family; its members after all are described as the children of God and brothers and sisters in Christ. Paul writes, "I will accept you, says the Lord, the Ruler of all being; I will be a father to you, and you shall be my sons and daughters" (2 Cor. 6:18 NEB); and "You are no longer strangers and sojourners, but you are fellow citizens with the saints and members of the household of God" (Eph. 2:19 RSV).

The church, then, is to be a family to families, and a source of identity and support for isolated nuclear families. The church needs to become a community of faith or, in the words of Peter Berger (1967), "a plausibility structure for faith." In seeking to become a community of faith the church must avoid the pitfall of exclusivity and the tendency to accept only certain types of people. It must welcome the widowed, the orphaned, the handicapped, the poor, the single person, and broken families.

The church can become a family of families if it follows several principles: (1) The church must be a place of diversity, including people of various social classes, races, ages, backgrounds, and religious experiences. It must avoid a unity based on similar images or subjective experiences, for true unity is based only in Jesus Christ. (2) The church needs to be a place where persons can get to know one another intimately. There needs to be provision for small groups where members can share their burdens and joys. (3) The church must create (or re-create) roles for all of its members.

What can the church do to ensure that everyone feels at home? Single persons need to be integrated into the body, so they can be nurtured as they, in turn, give of their talents to serve the church community. Women must be encouraged to freely exercise their gifts in the church. The gap between clergy and laity must be minimized so that the pastorate is not viewed as just another career. This means that clergy need to be willing to share the ministry, and that parishioners need to accept responsibility and opportunities for ministry. In short, the empowering process must be practiced in the church. Participatory Bible studies and sermons can focus on communal church life and ways in which to love, forgive, serve, and know one another. Further, individuals should be given the freedom to express their faith creatively. The decline in traditional symbols and language is an opportunity to explore and experiment with our worship expressions. We must be liberated from our fixation on words, which has impoverished communication, and be more open to other ways of communicating God's love. As an inclusive family of families, the church should welcome, for example, the contributions of artists, poets, dramatists, and dancers.

Shalom in Society

Society is larger, more abstract, and more distant from the family than is community. It encompasses political, economic, educational, and religious institutions, each of which entails a complex hierarchy and roles regulated by an integrated set of norms. While it might be easy to picture how communities can be vital sources of support for family life, it is more difficult to imagine ways in which mass society and its institutions can be sources of support.

We saw in the previous chapter that modern society has had a severe impact on family life. There is, then, a desperate need to build a society whose institutions promote the well-being of the family. The Old Testament concept of *shalom* characterizes such a society. *Shalom* is usually translated "peace." However, peace is not seen as merely absence of conflict, but rather as the promotion of human welfare in both material and spiritual ways. *Shalom* denotes a culture characterized by justice and righteousness as well as peace. Such a society is poignantly described in Isaiah 11:6–8:

> The wolf also shall dwell with the lamb, and the leopard shall lie down with the kid; and the calf and the young lion and the fatling together; and a little child shall lead them. And the cow and the bear shall feed; their young ones shall lie down together: and the lion shall eat straw like the ox. And the sucking child shall play on the hole of the asp, and the weaned child shall put his hand on the cockatrice' den. [KJV]

Shalom is present when there are both peace and justice. Thus, chronic unemployment and oppression of the poor must be eliminated before *shalom* is present. One way to deal with poverty is to provide the poor with food, shelter, and clothing. While this is all well and good, if the underlying conditions which cause poverty are not dealt with, *shalom* is still not achieved. For *shalom* entails giving the poor a means of helping themselves. A society characterized by *shalom* does not treat people unjustly, nor does it disempower or patronize them.

We shall know that *shalom* is present when social structures empower the family. When economic institutions demand time at the expense of one's family, *shalom* is not present. When corporations demand that their junior executives move every two years, making it impossible for the family to establish roots in a community, *shalom* is not present. When the unemployed are simply maintained and not afforded the opportunity to earn a living, *shalom* is not present. Where oppression and discrimination prevent minority persons from gaining access to jobs, *shalom* is not present. When churches plan activities for every evening of the week, leaving no time for the family to be together, *shalom* is not present. Where the elderly are denied sufficient resources and health benefits, *shalom* is not present. When divorced women and their children live at poverty levels, while the standard of living of divorced men increases, *shalom* is not present. Where laws make it difficult for divorced fathers to maintain close relationships with their children, *shalom* is not present. Where a single mother must leave her children unattended while she works outside of the home, *shalom* is not present. In these and a multitude of other ways, societal structures are damaging family life.

Hope for the Family and Society

Stable and strong family life can be achieved by recapturing and practicing the biblical concept of the family, which entails covenant love and manifestation of that love through grace, empowering, and intimacy. Although God intends for covenant love to be supremely experienced and exemplified in the context of the family, he also intends for it to be the basis for moral authority in society.

Moral authority is considered effective to the extent that a society is controlled by internal rather than external means. Our own society has of necessity come to depend increasingly upon coercive political and economic means of control. The truth of this statement is to be seen in the fact that social relationships are characterized more by contract than covenant, more by law than grace, coercion than empowering, and alienation than intimacy.

In this regard, it has been pointed out that the family is the cornerstone of the moral order of society. Therefore, any crisis we are currently experiencing in the moral order of society may well be due to the breakdown of the family. It is hardly an overstatement, then, to argue that the hope of society must begin with a recapturing of the biblical concept of family life. Covenant love, which is the basis of family life and manifests itself in sacrificial acts for others, is also necessary for the proper ordering of society. In fact, Jesus himself taught that we must be prepared to extend covenant love to our neighbor (Luke 10:25–37).

As we strive for covenant love first in our families and then in society, we would do well to keep in mind a powerful incident in the life of our Lord: "Jesus saw his mother, with the disciple whom he loved standing beside her. He said to her, 'Mother, there is your son'; and to the disciple, 'There is your mother'; and from that moment the disciple took her into his home" (John 19:26–27 NEB). Our goal in relationships should be to so forgive, empower, and intimately know one another that Jesus would want to send his mother to be a part of our family (Anderson 1985b:23).

Bibliography

Anderson, R. 1982. *On being human: Essays in theological anthropology.* Grand Rapids: Eerdmans.

Anderson, R. 1985a. Theology of the family. Seminar at Fuller Theological Seminary.

Anderson, R. 1985b. The gospel of the family. Fuller Theological Seminary. Unpublished manuscript.

Anderson, R., and D. Guernsey. 1985. *On being family: Essays on a social theology of the family.* Grand Rapids: Eerdmans.

Bach, G., and P. Wyden. 1968. *The intimate enemy: How to fight fair in love and marriage.* New York: Morrow.

Balswick, J. O. 1975. The function of the dowry system in a rapidly modernizing society: The case of Cyprus. *International Journal of Sociology of the Family* 5:158–67.

Balswick, J. O. 1988. *The inexpressive male.* Lexington, Mass.: Lexington.

Balswick, J. O., and J. K. Balswick. 1987. A theological basis for family relationships. *Journal of Psychology and Christianity* 6.3:37–49.

Balswick, J. O., and C. Macrides. 1975. Parental stimulus for adolescent rebellion. *Adolescence* 10:253–66.

Balswick, J. O., and K. Morland. 1990. *Social problems: A Christian perspective.* Grand Rapids: Baker.

307

Balswick, J. O., and D. Ward. 1984. The church, the family, and issues of modernity. Consultation on a theology of the family. Seminar at Fuller Theological Seminary.

Bandura, A. 1977. *Social learning theory.* Englewood Cliffs, N.J.: Prentice-Hall.

Bandura, A., and R. Walters. 1959. *Adolescent aggression.* New York: Ronald.

Banks, R. 1980. *Paul's idea of community.* Grand Rapids: Eerdmans.

Barclay, A., and D. Cusumano. 1967. Father absence, cross-sex identity, and field-dependent behavior in male adolescents. *Child Development* 38:243–50.

Bartchy, S. 1978. Power, submission, and sexual identity among the early Christians. In *Essays on New Testament Christianity,* ed. C. Wetzel, 50–80. Cincinnati: Standard.

Bartchy, S. 1984. Issues of power and a theology of the family. Paper presented at seminar, Consultation on a Theology of the Family, Fuller Theological Seminary.

Baumrind, D. 1972. Socialization and instrumental competence in young children. In *Research on young children,* ed. W. Hartup, 202–24. Washington: National Association for the Education of Young Children.

Baumrind, D. 1978. Parental disciplinary patterns and social competence in children. *Youth and Society* 9:239–76.

Baumrind, D., and A. Black. 1967. Socialization practices associated with dimensions of competence in preschool boys and girls. *Child Development* 38:291–327.

Bell, A., M. Weinberg, and S. Hammersmith. 1981. *Sexual preference: Its development in men and women.* Bloomington: Indiana University Press.

Bellah, R., et al. 1985. *Habits of the heart: Individualism and commitment in American life.* Berkeley: University of California Press.

Belsky, J., B. Gilstrap, and M. Rovine. 1984. The Pennsylvania infant and family development project, I. Stability and change in mother-infant and father-infant interaction in a family setting at one, three, and nine months. *Child Development* 55:692–705.

Belsky, J., R. Lerner, and G. Spanier. 1984. *The child in the family.* Reading, Mass.: Addison-Wesley.

Berger, B. 1967. Hippy morality—more old than new. *Transaction* 5:19–26.

Berger, B., and P. Berger. 1983. *The war over the family.* Garden City, N.Y.: Doubleday.

Berger, P. 1967. *The sacred canopy.* Garden City, N.Y.: Doubleday.

Berger, P. 1983. From the crisis of religion to the crisis of secularity. In *Religion and America: Spiritual life in a secular age,* ed. M. Douglas and S. Tipton, 14–24. Boston: Beacon.

Berger, P., B. Berger, and H. Kellner. 1973. *The homeless mind: Modernization and consciousness.* New York: Random.

Berger, P., and H. Kellner. 1964. Marriage and the construction of reality. *Diogenes* 46:1–23.

Billings, M. 1982. *Ideology and social psychology: Extremism, moderation and contradiction.* London: Blackwell.

Bohannan, P. 1971. *Divorce and after.* Garden City, N.Y.: Doubleday.

Bohannan, P., and H. Yahraes. 1979. Stepfathers as parents. In E. Corfman, ed., *Families today: A research sample on families and children.* NIMH science monograph. Washington, D.C.: U.S. Government Printing Office.

Booth, A., and J. Edwards. 1985. Age at marriage and marital instability. *Journal of Marriage and the Family* 47:67–74.

Borland, D. 1975. An alternative model of the wheel theory. *The Family Coordinator* 24:289–92.

Boss, P. 1987. Family stress. In *Handbook of marriage and the family,* ed. M. Sussman and S. Steinmetz, 695–723. New York: Plenum.

Broderick, C., and J. Smith. 1979. The general systems approach to the family. In *Contemporary theories about the family,* ed. W. Burr et al., 2:112–29. New York: Free.

Caplow, T. 1971. *Elementary sociology.* Englewood Cliffs, N.J.: Prentice-Hall.

Chalfant, H., R. Beckley, and C. Palmer. 1987. *Religion in contemporary society.* Palo Alto: Mayfield.

Chartier, M. 1978. Parenting: A theological model. *Journal of Psychology and Theology* 6:54–61.

Chodorow, N. 1978. *The reproduction of mothering: Psychoanalysis and the sociology of gender.* Berkeley: University of California Press.

Cowan, J. *Science of a new life.* 1870. New York: Cowan and Cowan.

Cox, H. 1984. *Religion in the secular city: Toward a postmodern theology.* New York: Simon and Schuster.

Crano, W., and J. Aronoff. 1978. A cross-cultural study of expressive and instrumental role complementarity in the family. *American Sociological Review* 43:463–71.

Curran, D. 1983. *Traits of a healthy family.* Minneapolis: Winston.

Dinnerstein, D. 1977. *The mermaid and the minotaur: Sexual arrangements and human malaise.* New York: Harper and Row.

Douglas, M. 1970. *Natural symbols: Explorations in cosmology.* New York: Pantheon.

Dreikurs, R., and V. Soltz. 1964. *Children: The challenge.* Des Moines: Meredith.

Ellul, J. 1964. *The technological society.* New York: Random.

Ellul, J. 1976. *The ethics of freedom.* Grand Rapids: Eerdmans.

Ellul, J. 1984. *Money and power.* Downers Grove, Ill.: Inter-Varsity.

Ellul, J. 1985. *The humiliation of the word.* Grand Rapids: Eerdmans.

Erikson, E. 1963. *Childhood and society.* New York: Norton.

Fenn, R. 1974. Toward a new sociology of religion. In *Religion American style,* ed. P. McNamara, 41–52. New York: Harper and Row.

Ferguson, A. 1984. On conceiving motherhood and sexuality: A feminist materialist approach. In *Mothering: Essays in feminist theory,* ed. J. Treblicot. Totowa, N.J.: Rowman and Allanheld.

Figley, C., and H. McCubbin. 1983. *Stress and the family.* Vol. 2, *Coping with catastrophe.* New York: Brunner/Mazel.

Filley, A. 1975. *Interpersonal conflict resolution.* Glenview, Ill.: Scott, Foresman.

Flavell, J. 1963. *The developmental psychology of Jean Piaget.* Princeton, N.J.: Van Nostrand.

Flavell, J. 1985. *Cognitive development.* 2d ed. Englewood Cliffs, N.J.: Prentice-Hall.

Forward, S., and J. Torres. 1986. *Men who hate women and the women who love them.* New York: Bantam.

Fowler, J. 1981. *Stages of faith.* New York: Harper and Row.

Freud, S. 1949. *An outline of psychoanalysis.* New York: Norton.

Freud, S. 1954. *The origins of psychoanalysis: Sigmund Freud's letters.* New York: Basic.

Fromm, E. 1956. *The art of loving.* New York: Harper and Row.

Galvin, K., and B. Brommel. 1986. *Family communication: Cohesion and change.* 2d ed. Glenview, Ill.: Scott, Foresman.

Gangel, K. 1977. Toward a biblical theology of marriage and family. *Journal of Psychology and Theology* 5:55–69, 150–62, 247–59, 318–31.

Garfinkel, P. 1985. *In a man's world: Father, son, brother, friend and other roles men play.* New York: Norton.

Garland, D. S. Richmond, and D. E. Garland. 1986. *Beyond companionship: Christians in marriage.* Philadelphia: Westminster.

Gilligan, C. 1982. *In a different voice: Psychological theory and women's development.* Cambridge, Mass.: Harvard University Press.

Gjerde, P. 1986. The interpersonal structure of family interaction settings: Parent-adolescent relations in dyads and triads. *Developmental Psychology* 22:297–304.

Glenn, N., and K. Kramer. 1987. The marriages and divorces of the children of divorce. *Journal of Marriage and the Family* 49:811–25.

Glueck, S., and E. Glueck. 1950. *Unraveling juvenile delinquency.* Cambridge, Mass.: Harvard University Press.

Gongla, P., and E. Thompson. 1987. Single-parent families. In *Handbook of marriage and the family,* ed. M. Sussman and S. Steinmetz, 397–418. New York: Plenum.

Goode, W. 1963. *World revolution and family patterns.* New York: Free.

Guidubaldi, J., H. Cleminshaw, J. Perry, B. Nastasi, and J. Lightel. 1986. The role of selected family-environment factors in children's post-divorce adjustment. *Family Relations* 35:141–51.

Guinness, O. 1983. *The gravedigger file: Papers on the subversion of the modern church*. Downers Grove, Ill.: Inter-Varsity.

Guttentag, M. 1977. Women, men and mental health services. National Institute of Mental Health report MH–26523.

Hadden, J., and C. Swann. 1981. *Prime time preachers: The rising power of televangelism*. Reading, Mass.: Addison-Wesley.

Hansen, D., and V. Johnson. 1979. Rethinking family stress theory: Definitional aspects. In *Contemporary theories about the family*, ed. W. Burr et al., 1:582–603. New York: Free.

Hauerwas, S. 1981. *A community of character: Toward a constructive Christian social ethic*. Notre Dame, Ind.: University of Notre Dame Press.

Hersey, P., and K. Blanchard. 1988. *Management of organizational behavior*. 4th ed. Englewood Cliffs, N.J.: Prentice-Hall.

Hetherington, E. 1972. Effects of father absence on personality development in adolescent daughters. *Developmental Psychology* 7:313–26.

Hetherington, E., K. Camara, and D. Feathermore. 1983. Achievement and intellectual functioning of children in one-parent households. In *Achievement and achievement motives*, ed. J. Spence, 205–84. San Francisco: Freeman.

Hetherington, E., M. Cox, and R. Cox. 1982. Effects of divorce on parents and children. In *Nontraditional families: Parenting and child development*, ed. M. Lamb, 233–88. Hillsdale, N.J.: Erlbaum.

Hill, R. 1949. *Families under stress*. New York: Harper and Row.

Hite, S. 1976. *The Hite report*. New York: Macmillan.

Hobart, C. 1987. Parent-child relations in remarried families. *Journal of Family Issues* 8:259–77.

Hocker, J., and W. Wilmot. 1985. *Interpersonal conflict*. Dubuque, Iowa: William C. Brown.

Holmes, T., and R. Rahe. 1967. The social readjustment rating scale. *Journal of Psychosomatic Research* 2:213–18.

Hunter, J. 1982. Subjectivization and the new evangelical theodicy. *Journal for the Scientific Study of Religion* 21:39–47.

Hunter, J. 1983. *American evangelicalism: Conservative religion and the quandary of modernity*. New Brunswick, N.J.: Rutgers University Press.

Jacobson, D. 1978. The impact of marital separation/divorce on children, II. Interparent hostility and child adjustment. *Journal of Divorce* 2:175–94.

Kerckhoff, A., and K. Davis. 1962. Value consensus and need complementarity in mate selection. *American Sociological Review* 27:295–303.

Kilmann, R., and K. Thomas. 1975. Interpersonal conflict-handling behavior as reflections of Jungian personality dimensions. *Psychological Reports* 37:971–80.

Kinsey, A. 1948. *Sexual behavior in the human male.* Philadelphia: Saunders.

Kinsey, A. 1952. *Sexual behavior in the human female.* Philadelphia: Saunders.

Kohlberg, L. 1963. Moral development and identification. In *Child psychology: Sixty-second yearbook of the National Society for the Study of Education,* ed. H. Stevenson, 277–332. Chicago: University of Chicago Press.

Kübler-Ross, E. 1970. *On death and dying.* New York: Macmillan.

Laing, R. 1969. *The politics of the family.* New York: Vintage.

Lamb, M., A. Frodi, C. Hwang, M. Frodi, and J. Steinberg. 1982. Mother- and father-infant interaction involving play and holding in traditional and nontraditional Swedish families. *Developmental Psychology* 18:215–21.

Lasch, C. 1977. *Haven in a heartless world: The family besieged.* New York: Basic.

Levinson, D. 1978. *The seasons of a man's life.* New York: Knopf.

Levy, M. 1966. *Modernization and the structure of societies.* Princeton, N.J.: Princeton University Press.

Lewis, C. S. 1958. *The allegory of love: A study of medieval tradition.* New York: Oxford University Press.

Lewis, C. S. 1960a. *The four loves.* New York: Harcourt, Brace.

Lewis, C. S. 1960b. *Mere Christianity.* New York: Macmillan.

Lewis, J., W. Beavers, J. Gossett, and V. Phillips. 1976. *No single thread: Psychological health in family systems.* New York: Brunner/Mazel.

Lewis, R. 1972. A developmental framework for the analysis of premarital dyadic formation. *Family Process* 11:17–48.

Lewis R., and G. Spanier. 1979. Theorizing about the quality and stability of marriage. In *Contemporary theories about the family,* ed. W. Burr et al., 1:268–94. New York: Free.

Longfellow, C. 1979. Divorce in context: Its impact on children. In *Divorce and separation: Context, causes and consequences,* ed. G. Levinger and O. Moles, 287–306. New York: Basic.

Maccoby, E. 1980. *Social development: Psychological growth and the parent-child relationship.* New York: Harcourt Brace Jovanovich.

McDonald, G. 1980. Family power: The assessment of a decade of theory and research, 1970–1979. *Journal of Marriage and the Family* 42:841–54.

McGill, M. 1985. *The McGill report on male intimacy.* New York: Harper and Row.

McGoldrick, M., and E. Carter. 1980. Forming a remarried family. In *The family life cycle,* ed. E. Carter and M. McGoldrick, 265–94. New York: Gardner.

MacKay, D. 1974. *The clockwork image.* Downers Grove, Ill.: Inter-Varsity.

Macklin, E. 1987. Nontraditional family forms. In *Handbook of marriage and the family,* ed. M. Sussman and S. Steinmetz, 317–53. New York: Plenum.

McLain, R., and A. Weigert. 1979. Toward a phenomenological sociology of the family: A programmatic essay. In *Contemporary theories about the family,* ed. W. Burr et al., 2:160–205. New York: Free.

McLean, S. 1984. The language of covenant and a theology of the family. Paper presented at seminar, Consultation on a Theology of the Family, Fuller Theological Seminary.

Matson, F. 1966. *The broken image.* New York: Braziller.

May, R. 1969. *Love and will.* New York: Norton.

Mead, G. H. 1934. *Mind, self and society.* Chicago: University of Chicago Press.

Mead, M. 1928. *Coming of age in Samoa.* New York: Mentor.

Mead, M. 1935. *Growing up in New Guinea.* New York: New American Library.

Messinger, L. 1976. Remarriage between divorced people with children from previous marriages: A proposal for preparation for remarriage. *Journal of Marriage and Family Counseling* 2:193–99.

Miller, D., and G. Swanson. 1958. *The changing American parent.* New York: Wiley.

Monahan, T. 1957. Family status and the delinquent child: A reappraisal and some new findings. *Social Forces* 35:250–58.

Munsch, R. 1986. *Love you forever.* Scarborough, Ontario: Firefly.

Murstein, B. 1980. Mate selection in the 1970s. *Journal of Marriage and the Family* 42:777–92.

Norton, A., and P. Glick. 1986. One-parent families: A social and economic profile. *Family Relations* 35:9–17.

Norwood, R. 1985. *Women who love too much.* New York: Simon and Schuster.

Nye, F. 1957. Child adjustment in broken and in unhappy unbroken homes. *Marriage and Family Living* 19:356–61.

Olson, D., D. Sprenkle, and C. Russell. 1979. Circumplex model of marital and family systems: Cohesion and adaptability dimensions, family types, and clinical applications. *Family Process* 18:3–28.

Olthuis, J. 1975. *I pledge you my troth: A Christian view of marriage, family, friendship.* New York: Harper and Row.

Osherson, S. 1986. *Finding our fathers: The unfinished business of manhood.* New York: Free.

Oshman, H., and M. Manosevitz. 1976. Father absence: Effects of stepfathers upon psychosocial development in males. *Developmental Psychology* 12:479–80.

Parsons, T., and R. Bales. 1955. *Family, socialization and interaction process.* Glencoe, Ill.: Free.

Pattison, M. 1984. The church and the healing of families. Consultation on a theology of the family. Seminar at Fuller Theological Seminary.

Patton, J., and B. Childs. 1988. *Christian marriage and family: Caring for our generations.* Nashville: Abingdon.

Peterson, G., and B. Rollins. 1987. Parent-child socialization. In *Handbook of marriage and the family*, ed. M. Sussman and S. Steinmetz, 471–507. New York: Plenum.

Piaget, J. 1932. *The moral judgment of the child*. London: Kegan Paul, Trench, Trubner.

Plaskow, J. 1980. *Sex, sin and grace: Women's experience and the theologies of Reinhold Niebuhr and Paul Tillich*. Lanham, Md.: University Press of America.

Price-Bonham, S., and J. Balswick. 1980. The noninstitutions: Divorce, desertion, and remarriage. *Journal of Marriage and the Family* 42:959–72.

Raschke, H. 1987. Divorce. In *Handbook of marriage and the family*, ed. M. Sussman and S. Steinmetz, 597–624. New York: Plenum.

Reiss, I. 1960. Toward a sociology of the heterosexual love relationship. *Marriage and Family Living* 22:139–45.

Reiss, I. 1980. *Family systems in America*. 3d ed. New York: Holt, Rinehart and Winston.

Reiss, I. 1986a. A sociological journey into sexuality. *Journal of Marriage and the Family* 48:233–42.

Reiss, I. 1986b. *Journey into sexuality: An exploratory voyage*. Englewood Cliffs, N.J.: Prentice-Hall.

Rekers, G. 1986. The family and gender identity disorders. *Journal of Family and Culture* 2.3:8–31.

Riesman, D. 1950. *The lonely crowd*. New Haven: Yale University Press.

Ringer, R. 1979. *Winning through intimidation*. New York: Fawcett.

Rollins, B., and D. Thomas. 1979. Parental support, power, and control techniques in the socialization of children. In *Contemporary theories about the family*, ed. W. Burr et al., 1:317–64. New York: Free.

Rossi, A. 1984. Gender and parenthood. *American Sociological Review* 49:1–19.

Rostow, W. 1961. *The stages of economic growth: A non-communist manifesto*. New York: Cambridge University Press.

Rubin, L. 1983. *Intimate strangers: Men and women together*. New York: Harper and Row.

Safilios-Rothschild, C. 1970. The study of family power structure: A review, 1960–1969. *Journal of Marriage and the Family* 32:539–52.

Salts, C. 1979. Divorce process: Integration of theory. *Journal of Divorce* 2:233–40.

Santrock, J., R. Warshak, and G. Elliott. 1982. Social development and parent-child interaction in father-custody and stepmother families. In *Nontraditional families: Parenting and child development*, ed. M. Lamb, 289–314. Hillsdale, N.J.: Erlbaum.

Satir, V. 1982. *Conjoint family therapy*. 3d rev. ed. Palo Alto: Science and Behavior.

Sattel, J. 1976. The inexpressive male: Tragedy or sexual politics? *Social Problems* 23:469–77.

Scanzoni, J. 1979. Social processes and power in families. In *Contemporary theories about the family,* ed. W. Burr, 1:295–316. New York: Free.

Seeman, M. 1957. On the meaning of alienation. In *Sociological theory,* ed. L. Coser and B. Rosenberg. New York: Macmillan.

Sennett, R. 1970. *The uses of disorder.* New York: Random.

Sennett, R. 1980. *Authority.* New York: Random.

Sheehy, G. 1978. *Passages.* New York: Bantam.

Skinner, B. F. 1953. *Science and human behavior.* New York: Macmillan.

Slater, P. 1961. Parental role differentiation. *American Journal of Sociology* 67:296–311.

Small, D. 1977. *Dwight Small talks about . . . divorce.* Glendale, Calif.: Regal.

Smedes, L. 1976. *Sex for Christians.* Grand Rapids: Eerdmans.

Smelser, N. 1973. Processes of social change. In *Sociology: An introduction,* 2d ed., ed. N. Smelser, 671–728. New York: Wiley.

Smith, M. 1980. The social consequence of single parenthood: A longitudinal perspective. *Family Relations* 29:75–81.

Snow, M., C. Jacklin, and E. Maccoby. 1983. Sex-of-child differences in father-child interaction at one year of age. *Child Development* 54:227–32.

Snyder, H. 1983. *Liberating the church.* Downers Grove, Ill.: Inter-Varsity.

Sparks, J. 1977. *The mindbenders: A look at current cults.* Nashville: Nelson.

Spock, B. 1968. *Baby and child care.* New York: Pocket.

Sternberg, R. 1986. A triangular theory of love. *Psychological Review* 93:119–35.

Szinovacz, M. 1987. Family power. In *Handbook of marriage and the family,* ed. M. Sussman and S. Steinmetz, 651–93. New York: Plenum.

Tallman, I., and L. Gray. 1987. A theory of problem solving applied to families. Paper presented at seminar, Theory-Methodology Workshop, National Council on Family Relations, Atlanta.

Tiger, L. 1969. *Men in groups.* New York: Random.

Tiger, L., and R. Fox. 1971. *The imperial animal.* New York: Holt, Rinehart and Winston.

Toffler, A. 1970. *Future shock.* New York: Random.

Toffler, A. 1979. *The third wave.* New York: Morrow.

Torrance, J. 1975. Reformed theology: A critique of the covenant concept. Colloquium at Fuller Theological Seminary.

Trotter, R. 1986. The three faces of love. *Psychology Today* 9:46–54.

Turner, R. 1970. *Family interaction.* New York: Wiley.

U.S. Bureau of the Census. 1984. *Statistical abstract of the U.S.: 1985.* Washington: Government Printing Office.

Viorst, J. 1986. *Necessary losses.* New York: Ballantine.

Wallerstein, J., and J. Kelly. 1980. *Surviving the breakup: How children and parents cope with divorce.* New York: Basic.

Walter, J. 1979. *Sacred cows: Exploring contemporary idolatry.* Grand Rapids: Zondervan.

Weitzman, L. 1986. *The divorce revolution: The unexpected social and economic consequences for women and children in America.* New York: Free.

Wexler, P. 1983. *Critical social psychology.* Boston: Routledge and Kegan Paul.

Zelditch, M. 1955. Role differentiation in the nuclear family: A comparative study. In *The family, socialization and interaction process,* ed. T. Parsons and R. Bales, 307–51. Glencoe, Ill.: Free.

Index

317